EXCEL™
A Business User's Guide

Related titles of interest from Wiley

Advanced Excel for the IBM PC, PS/2 and Compatibles, Ashley and Fernandez
Advanced WordPerfect: A Power User's Guide, Farrell
WordStar Professional Release 5: An Advanced Book, Ashley and Fernandez
R: BASE for DOS: A Business User's Guide, Condliffe
Paradox 3.0: A Business User's Guide, Condliffe
Using dBASE IV: Basics for Business, Brownstein
The PC Upgrader's Manual: How to Build and Extend Your System, Held
IBM PS/2 User's Reference Manual, Held
OS/2: Features, Functions, and Applications, Krantz, Mizell, and Williams
OS/2: A Business Perspective, Conklin
OS/2 Presentation Manager Programming, Cheatham, Reich, and Robinson
Ventura Publisher for the IBM PC: Mastering Desktop Publishing, Jantz
Desktop Publishing with WordPerfect 5.0, Tevis
Desktop Publishing with PageMaker 3.0: IBM PC AT, PS/2 and Compatibles, Bove and Rhodes
Desktop Publishing with PageMaker 3.02: Macintosh, Bove and Rhodes
The Power of Quattro: A Business User's Guide, Salkind
Using Lotus Agenda, Goodman and Wolf
Macros, Menus and Miracles for Lotus 1-2-3, Lunsford
Lotus 1-2-3 Release 2.2, Williams
Lotus 1-2-3 Release 3, Williams
Mastering Enable OA: Office Automation Software, Spezzano
Hard Disk Smarts: Everything You Need to Know to Choose and Use Your Hard Disk, Bosshardt

EXCEL™
A Business User's Guide
IBM and Macintosh

Neil J. Salkind

John Wiley & Sons, Inc.
New York • Chichester • Brisbane • Toronto • Singapore

This publication is designed to provide accurate and authoritative information in regard to the subject matter covered. It is sold with the understanding that the publisher is not engaged in rendering legal, accounting, or other professional service. If legal advice or other expert assistance is required, the services of a competent professional person should be sought. FROM A DECLARATION OF PRINCIPLES JOINTLY ADOPTED BY A COMMITTEE OF THE AMERICAN BAR ASSOCIATION AND A COMMITTEE OF PUBLISHERS.

Copyright © 1989 by John Wiley & Sons, Inc.

All rights reserved. Published simultaneously in Canada.

Reproduction or translation of any part of this work beyond that permitted by section 107 or 108 of the 1976 United States Copyright Act without the permission of the copyright owner is unlawful. Requests for permission or further information should be addressed to the Permission Department, John Wiley & Sons, Inc.

Excel is a registered trademark of Microsoft Corporation
The names of some of the products to which reference is made in this book may be protected by Federal, State, or Commonlaw trademark laws.

Library of Congress Cataloging-in-Publication Data

Salkind, Neil J.
    Excel : a business user's guide : IBM and MacIntosh / Neil J. Salkind.
      p.   cm.
    Bibliography: p.
    ISBN 0-471-50878-0
    1. Microsoft Excel (Computer program) 2. IBM Personal Computer--Programming. 3. Macintosh (Computer)—Programming. 4. Business--Data processing. I. Title.
    HF5548.4.M523S25 1989
    650'.028'55369—dc20   89-14718
                                                                                       CIP

Printed in the United States of America

89 90 10 9 8 7 6 5 4 3 2 1

To Michael Greenwald

Acknowledgments

Thanks to Bill Gladstone and my Wiley editors, Teri Zak and Ellen Greenberg, and David Sassian of G&H Soho for his production assistance.

Contents

Introduction	1
Welcome to Excel!	1
Who Should Use This Book?	4
How to Use This Book	5
Some Hints to Keep in Mind (Especially for Beginners!)	5
What You'll Find in *Excel: A Business User's Guide*	6
What You Need to Use Excel	7

Part I • Excel Refreshers

Chapter 1 / Excel Basics	11
Installing Excel	11
Starting Excel	12
The Opening Screen	12
Mouse or Keyboard?	16
Working with Excel Windows	17
Excel Menus	20
Selecting Menu Options	22
Using Excel Help	22
Context Sensitive Help	24
Chapter 2 / Creating a Worksheet	25
Entering Data	25
Entering Numbers	27
Entering Text	27

Contents

Editing Cell Entries	27
Excel Undo	28
Saving a Worksheet	29
Retrieving a Worksheet	30
Using a Password	31
Changing the Format of a Spreadsheet	32
Using Excel Formulas	37
Pointing to Create a Formula	39
Using Excel Functions	40
Using Formulas and Functions in Other Places	41
Previewing a Worksheet	42
Printing a Worksheet	43

Chapter 3 / Managing Data with Excel   44

Files, Records, and Fields	45
Creating a Database	46
Sorting a Database	47
Sorting on More Than One Field	47
Searching Through a Database	49
Creating a Criteria Range	50
Finding and Selecting Records	51
Extracting Records	51
Using a Data Form	52

Chapter 4 / Using Excel Charts   54

Creating a Chart	55
Using the Chart Gallery	57
Working with Chart Elements	57
Adding a Legend	58
Formatting Charts	59
Attaching Text to Charts	60
Attached Text	61
Unattached Text	61
Adding an Arrow	63
Printing an Excel Chart	63
Saving an Excel Chart	64

Chapter 5 / An Introduction to Excel Macros   65

Why Excel Macros?	65
Creating a Command Macro	67

Contents

Macro Sheets	68
Executing a Macro	69
From One Worksheet to Another	70
Building a Macro Library	71

Part II • Excel Business Applications

Chapter 6 / Accounting Worksheets — 75

Accounts Receivable	75
Accounts Payable	79
Balance Sheet and Ratio Analyses	82
Consolidated Income	86
Fixed Assets Management	89
Inventory Count, Location, and Control	93
Net Worth	97
Promissory Note/Loan Application Worksheet	100
Royalty Computation	104
A Simple Invoice	106

Chapter 7 / Forecasting Worksheets — 109

Charting Market Trends as a Moving Average	109
Exponential Smoothing and Sales Prediction	113
Forecasting Sales Using Linear Regression	118
Moving Averages Forecasting Accuracy	123

Chapter 8 / Investment Worksheets — 128

Amortization Schedule	128
Computing the Interest Rate	132
Future Value of an Annuity	136
Internal Rate of Return	139
Stock Portfolio	142

Chapter 9 / Management Worksheets — 146

Analysis of Personnel Referrals	146
Bidding on a Project	150

Contents

	Breakeven Analysis	154
	Hourly Work Sheet	158
	Payroll Ledger	165
	Property Management	170
	Tracking Utility Expenses	174
	Weighted Employee Comparison	177
Chapter 10 / Personal Worksheets		**183**
	Comparing Job Opportunities	183
	Conversion of Foreign Currency/Dollars and Dollars/Foreign Currency	188
	Conversion of Measurement Units	192
	Personal/Family Budget	196
	Personal Asset Inventory	202
	Personal Finances	208
	Starting a Business	213
Chapter 11 / Retail Worksheets		**216**
	Advertisement Analysis	216
	Analysis of Productivity—Products	220
	Analysis of Productivity—Sales	222
	Cash Flow Analysis	226
	Determining a Markup Based on Retail Price	231
	Determining a Retail Price Based on Markup	233
	Estimating Size of Salesforce	235
	Keeping Track of Auto Expenses	238
	Making Seasonal Adjustments	243
	Markup Ratios	246
	Merchandise Budgeting	249
	Multiple Regression	252
	Overhead to Sales Ratio	257
	Salary and Bonus Summary	263
	Salary versus Commission Comparison	267
	Sales Pricing and Discounts	270
	Sales per Square Foot	274
	Salesperson Analysis	277
Chapter 12 / Statistical Worksheets		**280**
	Item Analysis	280
	Pearson Correlation between Two Variables	283

Significance of the Difference between Correlated Proportions	286
Spearman Rank Order Correlation	288
Significance of the Difference between Correlation Coefficients	291
Survey Analysis	292
t-Test for Dependent Means	298
t-Test between Independent Means	300

Part III • The Excel Financial Functions

Depreciation of an Asset (DDB)	304
Future Value of an Investment (FV)	306
The Interest Payment on an Investment (IPMT)	308
Internal Rate of Return (IRR)	310
Modified Internal Rate of Return (MIRR)	312
Number of Payments of Investments (NPER)	314
Net Present Value (NPV)	317
Periodic Payment on an Investment (PMT)	319
Payment on the Principal of an Investment (PPMT)	322
Present Value of an Investment (PV)	324
Rate of Return on an Investment (RATE)	326
Straight-Line Depreciation (SLN)	328
Sum-of-Year Depreciation (SYD)	331

Appendix: List of Worksheets by Area	335
Index	337

Introduction

Welcome to Excel!

True story. Susan and David run a large sporting goods firm as well as a restaurant and a brewery. The one thing that all these businesses have in common is that they have accounts payable and accounts receivable transactions almost on a daily basis. One day, a friend visited and noticed Susan and David doing the books using the time-tested and traditional method of recording row and column values on large sheets of paper and then using quick fingers on a tiny desktop calculator. After some convincing, they invested in some personal computers and Excel. In no time at all, they saw an increase in the accuracy of their work and gained new time that they intend to fill with training new salespeople and pursuing other business opportunities.

Like Susan and David, you're a business person who probably can't find enough time during the day to finish all the tasks that

Introduction

need to be done. Since you can't create more time, the only alternative is to use it more efficiently. That's where Excel and *Excel: A Business User's Guide* come in.

Excel can be your electronic information management tool that allows you to combine the best of three different programs into one:

- a worksheet that organizes and manipulates numbers that are entered in rows and columns
- a database that manages records and selects and organizes them as you specify
- an easy-to-use graphics program that generates informative and persuasive visual images of your worksheet and database information

Here are just some examples of how Excel has helped others and can help you organize and manage the information that you deal with in your everyday business and personal affairs.

- Michael is the financial officer in a large company that manages real estate developments. He needs to keep track of such things as rental income, management fees, security deposits, and so on. He uses Excel to record the operating expenses for each of the developments and has the data current and available at all times.
- Lew just started his pediatrics practice and figures if he can get 1,500 patients within three years he can make a go of it. He'd like to track his patients' ages so that he knows what kinds of literature parents might be interested in reading. He uses an Excel database to search for and select only those children of specific ages. Once he knows this, he prints a mailing label for the parents and sends the materials.
- Sara manages the inventory and parts department of an electronics repair chain and has to know where every part is located. When new parts are delivered, she uses Excel to enter the part number and its description into the database, and in a moment she can search and find the status of any of the 1,200 parts that are in stock, including their retail price and whether she needs to order additional parts to keep the stock current.

Introduction

- Bill leases computer time to several companies that cannot afford to own their own system and bills them on the first of the month. He generates his invoices with Excel and keeps track of who is current and who is 30, 60, or 90 days overdue (when he then sends out another notice).
- Joan certainly will not forget "Meltdown Monday," when stocks dropped in value almost 30%. Using Excel's graphing feature, she tracked the trend the week before and decided that her profits were enough that she should get out! Of all her investments, Excel was clearly the one that paid off the best.
- It was the first time that Darwin's small software company was about to turn a profit. After the orders started coming in, it was time to think about expanding. "What if. . .?" questions about financing, increasing or decreasing the price of the product, hiring another programmer, and others were answered with Excel's tools for predicting outcomes and determining the breakeven price for products.

All these people illustrated the results of their Excel activities using Excel's charting capabilities.

These examples show how versatile Excel is for helping you organize and manage your business affairs. In fact, how you apply Excel is limited only by your imagination. While there are other worksheet programs that are popular, such as Lotus 1-2-3, Quattro, and Filemaker, Excel offers several features that set it apart from the others:

- You can navigate your way through Excel using either keyboard commands or a mouse and the many menus and menu options that are available. You can even customize the menus and rewrite or reorganize them to fit your specific work needs.
- If you get into trouble, just ask for Help. The Excel Help system is structured so that you can move from topic to topic by selecting special Glossary and Jump terms within the Help window.
- You can import files from other database and worksheet programs such as Lotus, Quattro, dBase, and Paradox. The **Import** command automatically converts them into the ap-

Introduction

propriate format when you retrieve them. You can save them into alternative formats as well.

- Excel macros allow you to program Excel to accomplish simple and complex tasks with the touch of a few keys. No longer will you need to do repetitious tasks again and again. In addition, you can copy these macros for use on more than one worksheet.
- Predefined calculations are a breeze with Excel's more than 130 functions, such as **FV** (future value of an investment) and **AVG** (average a set of numbers), which allow you to perform predefined operations. Excel also offers 13 individual financial functions, which provide the basis for quick and convenient calculations in business-related worksheets.
- **Sort** allows you to sort data in your worksheet (or database) in numerical or alphabetical order, saving you time and trouble. You can also sort by more than one characteristic, for example sorting first by the number of an inventory part and then by its retail price.
- Finally, use the **Search** command to scan from 10 to 1,000 records to find a specific cell entry and then replace it with another entry. You can even instruct Excel to search using a set of multiple criteria, such as searching for all the records in the northeastern portion of the United States that showed a profit in the last quarter, and then tell Excel to print them in ascending order.

Who Should Use This Book?

Excel: A Business User's Guide is for anyone who wants to learn how to use Excel in specific business applications, such as generating payroll ledgers, computing the future value of an investment, and completing a cash flow analysis. The book is designed so that both the experienced and the inexperienced worksheet user can use the examples and be up and running in no time.

Introduction

It assumes that you are familiar with basic Macintosh and DOS commands and the use of your computer. If not, see your owner's manuals.

How to Use This Book

If you have never used a spreadsheet program before, begin with Part I and read through all the chapters carefully. They are full of basic information about worksheets in general and Excel in particular. Part I is a brief but fairly comprehensive tutorial that will provide you with the basics (and even some of the advanced concepts) that you need to understand and use Excel.

Even if you are an experienced spreadsheet user, it may be a good idea to review this material. While Excel offers all the features of the leading spreadsheets, it has its own way of doing things that you need to know about before you begin working with the actual worksheets in Part II.

If you are an experienced spreadsheet user, feel free to go right to Part II.

Some Hints to Keep in Mind (Especially for Beginners!)

Wherever you decide to begin reading, keep the following things in mind:

If you start with Chapter 1, put the dog out, get a sitter for the kids (or wait until they're in bed), get yourself a nice cup of whatever, and find a comfortable chair to sit in and browse through the book. Look at how the book is organized so you get some idea about the order of the chapters and how the material is presented. It's always a good idea to briefly review the material that you'll be working with before you actually begin. Here's your chance to see the big picture and to put things in perspective.

Second, follow the examples in the book and do what is suggested. When you get to a part that asks you to enter data or create your own worksheet, do it! Doing is the best way to learn. All

Introduction

of the actual worksheets and hands-on instructions have been used by both beginners and advanced worksheet users, and they have been refined so they are clear and straightforward.

Third, don't try to do too much in one sitting. Read and work for as long as you feel comfortable without getting tired and pushing yourself too hard. When this happens, you begin to make mistakes, and the pleasure that Excel should bring you turns instead into frustration.

Next, if you have trouble with a certain section, stop for a few minutes and then go back to a point where you understood the material. Start from there, and carefully begin working again.

Fifth, if you now use another worksheet on a regular basis and are changing over to Excel, use only Excel from now on! It is hard enough to retrain our brains and fingers to do different things, and the faster that you get started with new instructions and menus, the faster Excel will become second nature. Even though this might mean going "cold turkey," the sooner you solo on Excel, the faster you'll learn it and the more at ease you'll find yourself. Besides, Excel can read most other worksheet files so you don't even have to rekey much, if any, data.

Finally, explore Excel, take some chances, and have fun! Personal computers and programs such as Excel should provide you with hours of enjoyment in learning new ways to accomplish old and often tiresome tasks. Using a book like this one is a learning experience, and you should not be afraid to take chances and ask yourself such questions as, "I wonder what would happen if I . . . ?" The worst that can happen is that you will have to start this or that chapter or worksheet over again. Excel doesn't let you make fatal mistakes very easily, so let loose, open your mind, and begin!

What You'll Find in Excel: A Business User's Guide

This book is intended for people who are familiar with worksheets and Excel in general and want to learn how to use Excel in everyday business applications. It is organized into three parts.

Part I, "Excel Refreshers," contains five chapters and all the information you need to get going with Excel. This is a review of the most important things you need to know to create, edit, and use a worksheet and to work with Excel functions and formulas, the database, and the graphics components. It also covers the purpose and design of macros.

Part II, "Excel Business Applications," offers you a set of 75 completed worksheets that you can enter and begin using right away in your own business. Each worksheet is accompanied by an explanation of what it does and how it works, as well as an illustration of every single cell entry that makes up the worksheet. You'll read more about each of these descriptions at the beginning of Part II.

Part III provides an example of each of the 13 financial functions that Excel offers the business community. Some of these are similar in format to the worksheets located in Part II, but all contain new material. Here, unlike in Part II, the emphasis is on the use of the function and not the content.

In order to use the worksheets in Part II, you must enter all of the cell information. If you choose, you can use the coupon at the back of the book to purchase a disk that contains the exact cell contents of each of these worksheets.

What You Need to Use Excel

Here's a list of the hardware and software you need to use to make Excel behave.

For IBM users, you need the following:

- An IBM AT or an IBM AT compatible computer with a hard or a fixed drive. In order to install Excel you must have at least 5 megabytes of space free on that disk. Sorry, but Excel just will not work with floppies—not enough room.
- A minimum of 640K bytes of system memory, or RAM (which is the room inside of your computer for working).
- A disk-operating system (such as MS-DOS) that is version 3.0 or higher.

Introduction

A graphics card that is IBM EGA or VGA compatible or a Hercules card. Other cards that are compatible with Microsoft Windows will also work just fine.

There are also some options that you might want to add on.

A color monitor will allow you to see the wonderful-looking worksheets and graphics you produce.

A mouse is an option since Excel will run just fine without one, but it sure can make your life easier by taking advantage of Excel's graphic interface. A mouse is not very expensive—you can get one for as little as $75, and it will pay for itself in no time at all.

Mac users need the following:

A Macintosh Plus, SE, SE/30 II, or IIX that has at least 1 megabyte of RAM.

Two double-sided floppy drives or a hard disk.

A version of the System and the Finder that corresponds to your Macintosh model as follows.

Model	System Version #	Finder Version #
Plus	3.2	5.3
SE	4.0	5.4
II	4.1	5.5

Let's get on with the basics of Excel and finding those solutions to your business challenges. Good luck, and have fun!

Part I
Excel Refreshers

1 / Excel Basics

Installing Excel

If you are using the Macintosh version of Excel, no installation procedure is necessary.

If you are using the IBM version, before you can even begin using the program, you have to install it onto your system's hard disk. Installing Excel is a simple procedure that requires inserting the Set Up disk that came with the Excel package. Once the disk is inserted in drive A (remember that the active drive is C), enter the following command:

A:setup

Excel will take it from there and lead you through the installation process. This should take about 20 minutes. If you run into trouble, you can always leave the installation of Excel and start over. Just follow the instructions on the screen.

Starting Excel

Once the IBM version of Excel is installed, starting the program requires you to enter the word *excel* at the prompt as follows:

C > **excel**

The next thing you know, you'll see the Microsoft announcement (a little title window with a copyright notice) and then the Excel opening screen.

To start the Macintosh version of Excel, just click on the **Excel** icon.

The Opening Screen

The opening screens for the two versions of Excel are virtually identical, except for the small Apple menu located in the upper left hand corner of the Apple screen. This is a Macintosh menu and not an Excel menu.

The Excel worksheet is organized into rows and columns. What you see in Figures 1.1 and 1.2 is a small portion of the maximum 256 columns and 16,384 rows that are the entire available work space; the whole work space simply cannot fit on your screen. You could conceivably create a worksheet with more than 4 million filled cells (4,194,304 to be exact). Now that's a lot of information, and you would need a ton of memory in your computer system to do that. Excel was designed with computers of the future in mind that may very well allow us to store and work with that much information.

Every Excel worksheet contains many different areas and tools that you will use to enter and work with your data.

What follows is a description of the different parts of the opening screen. Later in this chapter we'll talk about windows and their function within Excel.

The first thing you probably notice is the menu bar (File, Edit, etc.) across the top of the window, providing you with a variety

Excel Basics

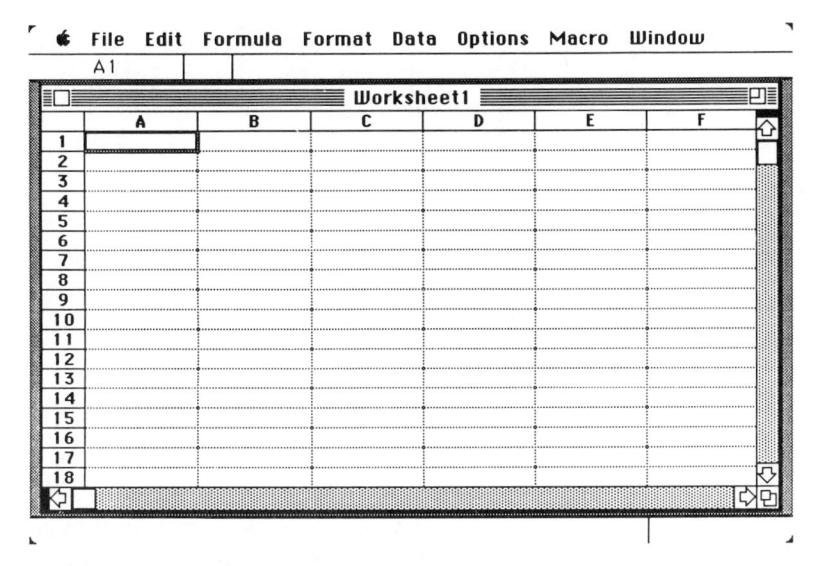

1.1 The Mac Excel opening screen

of choices. Each of these individual menus has a set of options associated with it. You'll learn more about menus and these options later in this chapter.

Right below the menu bar is the title bar of the worksheet. This is the name of the file that was assigned to this specific

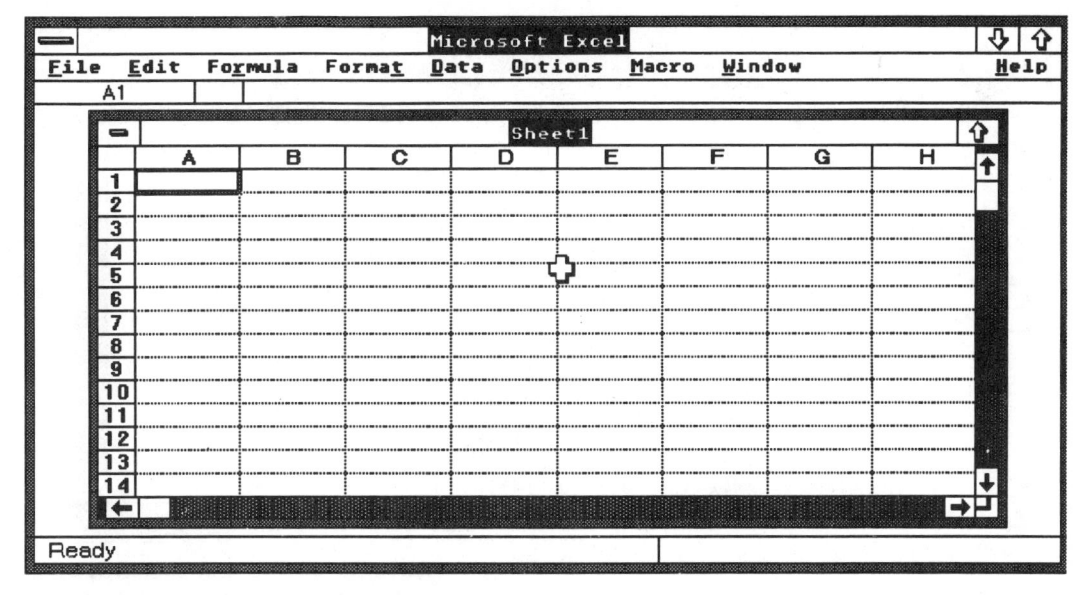

1.2 The IBM Excel opening screen

Excel Refreshers

worksheet when it was saved. If you are using the IBM version, Excel automatically titles the first new worksheet (in a work session) Sheet1, the second, Sheet2, and so forth. If you are using the Macintosh version, your worksheets are labeled Worksheet1, Worksheet2, and so forth.

There are row headings (numbers such as 1, 2, 3, etc.) and column headings (letters such as A, B, C, etc.) that appear at top of columns and to the left of rows in the worksheet itself. In Figure 1.3 you can see that the Payment Number (1, 2, 3, etc.) is used as a row heading and Principal Due, Interest Due, Total Payment, and Remaining Balance are used for column headings. The spreadsheet in Figure 1.4 consists of 35 rows (1 through 35) and has 5 columns (A through E) as its workspace.

A cell is where a row and a column intersect. Cells have addresses (as in where they reside) that consist of a column letter and a row number. In Figure 1.3, cell D7 contains the value $537.30. Figure 1.3 also shows how the formula in cell E12 computes the Remaining Balance column in the worksheet.

The active cell is the one that is highlighted (in this case E12).

Immediately above the worksheet is a formula bar that starts with a cell address (whichever one is active at the time). This

1.3 A sample spreadsheet

Excel Basics

	A	B	C	D	E
1	AMORTIZATION SCHEDULE				
2					
3	Principal			$50,000.00	
4	Annual Interest			10.00%	
5	Length of Loan (Years)			15	
6					
7	PAYMENT			$537.30	
8					
9	Payment	Principal	Interest	Total	Remaining
10	Number	Due	Due	Payment	Balance
11					
12	1	$120.64	$416.67	$537.30	$49,462.70
13	2	$125.11	$412.19	$537.30	$48,925.39
14	3	$129.59	$407.71	$537.30	$48,388.09
15	4	$134.07	$403.23	$537.30	$47,850.79
16	5	$138.55	$398.76	$537.30	$47,313.49
17	6	$143.02	$394.28	$537.30	$46,776.18
18	7	$147.50	$389.80	$537.30	$46,238.88
19	8	$151.98	$385.32	$537.30	$45,701.58
20	9	$156.46	$380.85	$537.30	$45,164.28
21	10	$160.93	$376.37	$537.30	$44,626.97
22	11	$165.41	$371.89	$537.30	$44,089.67
23	12	$169.89	$367.41	$537.30	$43,552.37
24	13	$174.37	$362.94	$537.30	$43,015.07
25	14	$178.84	$358.46	$537.30	$42,477.76
26	15	$183.32	$353.98	$537.30	$41,940.46
27	16	$187.80	$349.50	$537.30	$41,403.16
28	17	$192.28	$345.03	$537.30	$40,865.86
29	18	$196.75	$340.55	$537.30	$40,328.55
30	19	$201.23	$336.07	$537.30	$39,791.25
31	20	$205.71	$331.59	$537.30	$39,253.95
32	21	$210.19	$327.12	$537.30	$38,716.65
33	22	$214.66	$322.64	$537.30	$38,179.34
34	23	$219.14	$318.16	$537.30	$37,642.04
35	24	$223.62	$313.68	$537.30	$37,104.74

1.4 The printed spreadsheet from Figure 1.3

formula bar is where the entries you make into a worksheet appear as they are being typed in. It is also in this area that you can edit entries once they have already been entered.

In the formula bar, an X represents the cancel box and a "check" represents the enter box. The cancel box is used in conjunction with the mouse to cancel an entry that is in the formula bar before it becomes part of the worksheet (when it's "locked in"). The enter box is what you click with the mouse when an entry in the formula bar is satisfactory.

To the right of the information entered in the worksheet is a gray-shaded scroll bar used in conjunction with the mouse to move around the worksheet. The scroll box and the scroll arrow are also used to move from one part of the worksheet to another.

In the lower right hand corner of the worksheet you will find the size box. This box is used in conjunction with the mouse to change the size of the worksheet. You may want to resize a worksheet when you need to open another one and have them both on the screen simultaneously.

Finally, in the lower left hand corner of the screen is the status bar, which indicates Excel's current activity. For example, when you are entering information into a cell, the message displayed (as in Figure 1.3) is **Ready**.

The only other thing on the opening screen you need to know about (for now!) is the mouse pointer, shaped like a two-dimensional cross when it is located over a cell. When the mouse is moved, this pointer moves a corresponding amount.

Mouse or Keyboard?

Excel offers you the luxury of using a mouse alone or sets of key combinations such as **Alt+F,N** for the IBM version or ⌘+**N** for the Macintosh version to open a new file. You can use either a mouse or key commands to perform any Excel operation. (Throughout this book, a "+" between keys means that you depress the first while you press the second. When a comma separates two keys, it means you press them in sequence. For example, the key combination **Alt+F,N** means "while holding down the **Alt** key, press the **F** key, release them both, and then press the **N** key.")

If you are using a mouse, you should be familiar with the standard mouse operations, such as clicking and dragging. If you will be using the keyboard, you will find an explanation of each key combination you need to use to perform Excel commands in the reference manual that came with your software.

There are advantages to both the keyboard and the mouse. Here are some for the keyboard, especially for IBM users who may not have a mouse. Many of these are not issues for the Macintosh user.

Excel Basics

- Most obvious, you might not have a mouse and not want to invest the money to purchase one, or you might simply not want to work with a mouse regardless of the advantages. After all, the keyboard comes with the system.
- Using the keyboard might be your preference if you are a fast typist and you don't want to take your hands off the keyboard to perform any mouse functions.
- The mouse may take up space inside (if you need a card) or outside (another port) your machine, which means that you might need to give up something else.

Here are some votes for the mouse:

- You might use a mouse on a regular basis and want to continue doing such. This is especially true for Excel Macintosh users who would like to switch over to a DOS-based system or for Macintosh Excel users.
- No doubt about it, a mouse is fast. You can get from one point on the screen to another very quickly.
- Finally, there are some things that the mouse can do better than keyboard commands. For example, scrolling through a large spreadsheet can be very easy if you use the mouse and drag the scroll box.

Actually, the mouse and the keyboard can be used together very effectively. For example, you can use the keyboard to quickly select items from menus, especially those that are frequently done (such as opening a new worksheet window). But using the mouse to move the location of a window is faster and easier than using keyboard commands.

The answer? Just choose what works best for you. If you have a mouse you may, indeed, find that some things are more efficient to do with the mouse than the keyboard, and vice versa.

Working with Excel Windows

A window is Excel's way of allowing you to interact in an easy and convenient fashion with the data. Windows are a tool for

Excel Refreshers

presenting Excel features in a simple and straightforward manner. As you will see, each worksheet appears in its own window.

Windows can be used in a number of ways.

To select a window with a mouse, just click anywhere inside of the window. If you have several windows open at the same time, it's easy to tell which one is active—the title bar is darker than in the ones that are not opened. If you are using the keyboard, you'll soon learn how to select the Window menu (see Figure 1.5) to reveal a numerical listing of all opened documents. Now select the number of the document you want.

To change the size of the window, drag the size box (in the lower right hand corner) vertically, horizontally, or diagonally to produce the size of window you want. If you are using the IBM version of Excel and the keyboard, use the **Alt+Hyphen,S** key combination. Once you do this, the cursor will change its shape and you will see a shadow border that you can resize using the up, down, right, and left cursor arrow keys after using them to select the two sides you want to change. Once the window is the size that you want, press the **Enter** key and the window will be redrawn.

If you are using the Macintosh version of Excel, just drag the

1.5 Selecting the Window menu

Excel Basics

size box in the lower left hand corner of the screen until the size of the screen is set.

To move a window in either the IBM or the Macintosh version, place the mouse pointer on the title bar and drag the window to another location, as you can see in Figure 1.6. If you are using the IBM version and the keyboard, use the **Alt+Hyphen,M** key combination. Once you do this, you will see a shadow border. Use the cursor arrow keys to move the shadow border to the position you want the window relocated and press **Enter**. The window will then be redrawn in its new location.

Finally, you need to know about scrolling through a window using the scroll bar located on the right hand side of the worksheet. Scrolling becomes important when all the information in the spreadsheet cannot fit in one screen. If you are using a mouse, you can

- drag the scroll box down the scroll bar to move from one part of the worksheet to another
- click below (or above) the scroll bar to move one screen's worth up or down, and click on a scroll arrow to move either up one row or down one row

1.6 Moving a window to a new location

Excel Refreshers

The horizontal scroll bar will accomplish corresponding screen and column changes.

If you are using the keyboard to scroll, use the following key combinations:

- To move up or down one row, use the up or down cursor arrow.
- To move up or down one window, use the **PgUp** and **PgDn** keys.
- To move to the left or right one window, use the **Ctrl** and the **PgUp** (for left) and **PgDn** (for right) for the IBM version and the ⌘+**PgUp** and ⌘+**PgDn** key combination for the Macintosh version.

Windows are what you use to look deep into Excel's many features. Learn to work with them so these skills become second nature.

Excel Menus

One of the buzz words about computers these days is "user-friendly," and everyone tries to attach that label to their product. Software is user-friendly when it doesn't take hours to get to first base and it's as easy to learn as it is easy to use.

One reason why Excel fits this description is because it is menu driven, whether you use a mouse or the keyboard commands to make your selections. In other words, Excel presents you with a menu of choices from which you choose the required command. To take advantage of any Excel feature, you access it by selecting the menu you want from the menu bar at the top of the worksheet. By using Excel menus in this interactive fashion, you become an active participant, not just an observer.

All menus provide you with options from which to choose. On the Main menu, these options (or commands) lead you deeper into Excel's powerful options through submenus. For example, on the Format menu you see in Figure 1.7, you can select different options to change the format of numbers (such as $130.00 or 130 or $130), the alignment of cell contents (such as centered or left), or the font that you use (Times Roman in this example).

Excel Basics

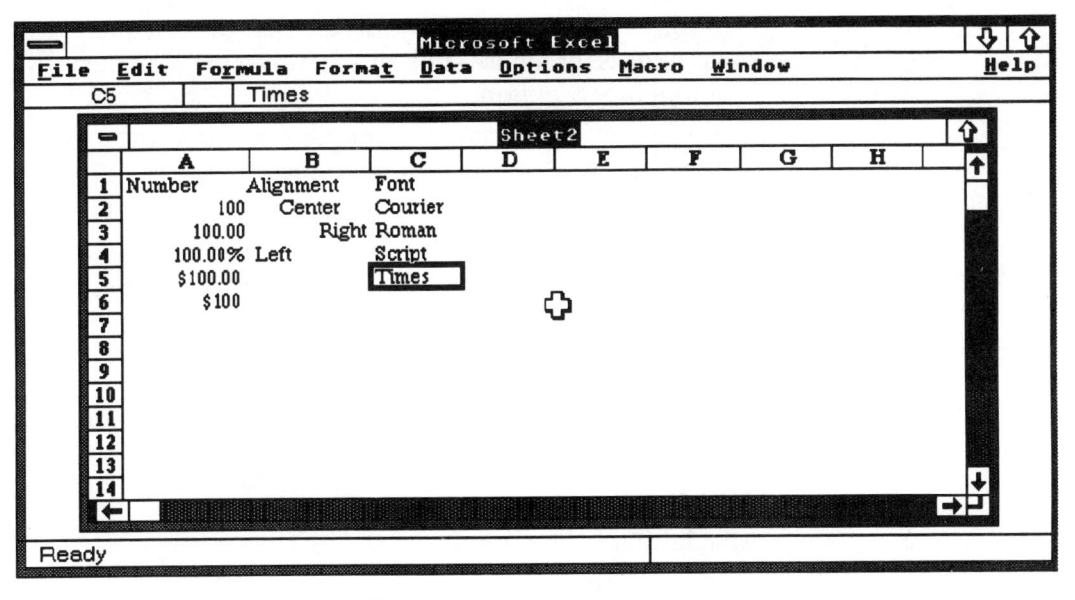

1.7 Changing the format of a cell

Here's a brief overview of what options are located within each of the menus.

The File menu allows you to create new files, open existing ones, and control the saving and printing of worksheets.

The Edit menu lets you make changes within and between worksheets including cutting, copying and pasting, and deleting and inserting rows and columns.

The Formula menu allows you to access, modify, and use formulas and functions, the tools that make Excel so easy to work with.

The Format menu allows you to change the appearance of the worksheet.

The Data menu is what you use to create a database and then manipulate the information within it.

The Options menu provides alternatives for displaying different parts of the worksheet, protecting documents for security reasons, and determining when pages will break when printed.

The Macro menu opens up the world of macros, or recorded keystrokes, which can save you time and effort. Using the

Excel Refreshers

options on this menu you can record a sequence of keystrokes (or mouse strokes) and replay the sequence with a touch of a button.

The Window menu makes it possible to show any or all of the open worksheets or to rearrange them.

The Help feature appears as a menu all by itself for IBM users and as a part of the Window menu for Macintosh users.

Selecting Menu Options

If you are using a mouse, you can select a menu option with three simple steps:

1. Select the menu you want.
2. Highlight the option.
3. Release the mouse.

Just move to the menu that you want to use and select the option you need.

If you are using keyboard commands, selecting a menu option consists of using key combinations and the underlined letter in the menu and menu option. For example, to select the New option from the File menu in the IBM version, use the following key combination:

Alt+F,N

In the Macintosh version, the key combination is

⌘+N

That's all there is to selecting any menu option from either the IBM or Macintosh versions.

Using Excel Help

As you have already learned, you can select Excel Help by using either the **Alt+H** key combination or the mouse on the IBM version or by calling up the screen from the Window menu on

Excel Basics

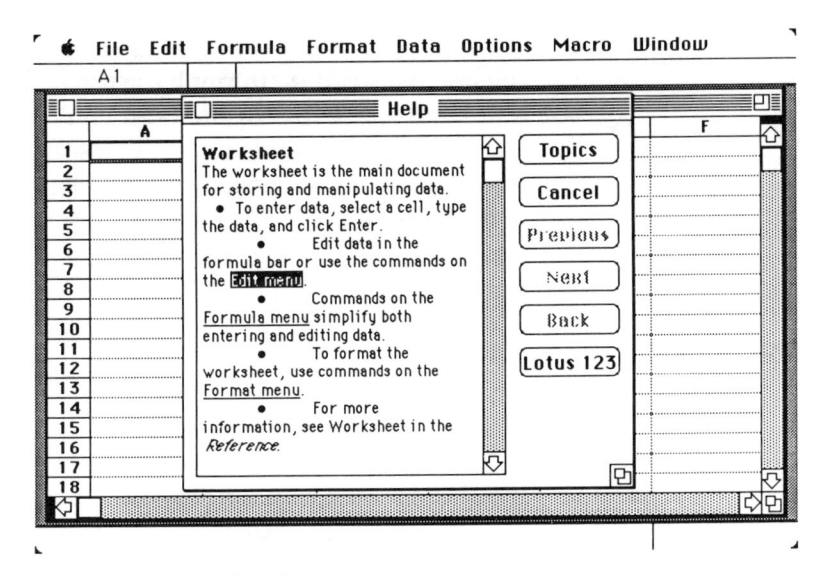

1.8 The Mac Excel Index

the Macintosh version. Once you are in Help, you can then select one of the commands displayed in the window.

The most important of these is the **Index** command, which provides you with a listing of the important terms you can find out more about, as shown in Figures 1.8 and 1.9 (for both ver-

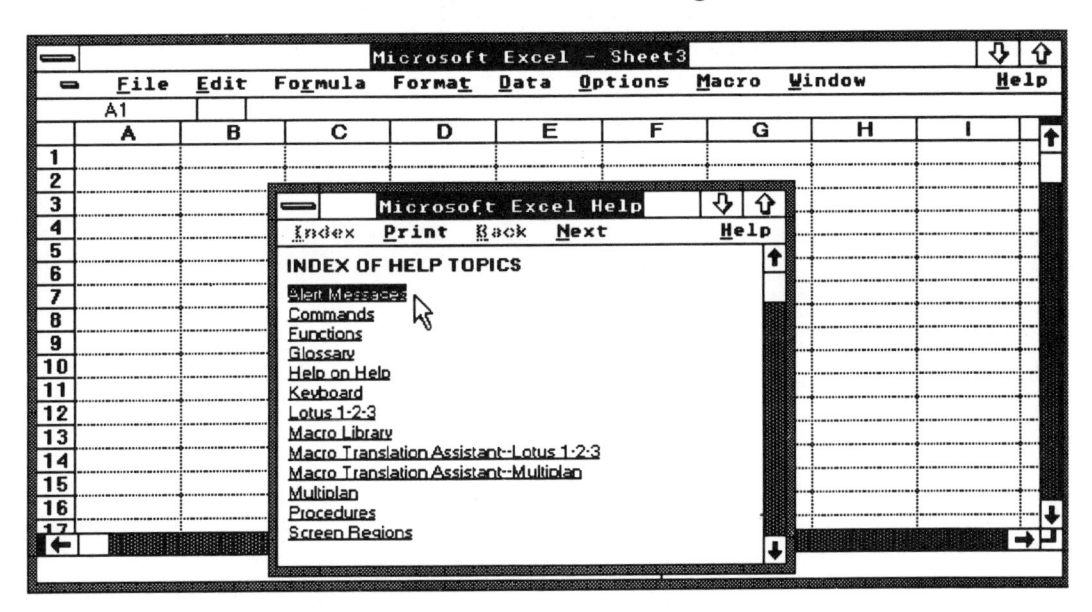

1.9 The IBM Excel Index

23

sions of Excel). Once you have located the particular topic that you are interested in (through the use of the mouse or the direction keys), select the option and you'll find detailed help. As you can see, you can learn about the most simple or the most complex features of Excel. Since you can have this window open while other Excel windows are open, Help can always be available.

Context Sensitive Help

There's another way to get help. Excel knows where you are in any of its many menus. For example, if you want to know more about the Save option on the File menu, press the **F1** function key when Save is active. Help will come in a moment and about that specific topic! What could be easier?

Another way to get help is through the use of the **Shift+F1** key combination. When you select this, the mouse pointer or cell pointer changes to a question mark. Using regular selection procedures, any option that is selected will then produce help on that topic.

There you have it—some Excel basics that should get you on your way. By the time you finish the next chapter you'll have created and printed a new worksheet.

2
Creating a Worksheet

In this chapter you'll use Excel to create a worksheet and practice many of Excel's most basic and important operations, such as entering data, saving a worksheet, and using formulas and functions.

Entering Data

Entering data into a worksheet is no more complex than entering text using a word processor or any other computer application. The only difference is that you have to learn Excel's system for entering, editing, and changing the appearance or the layout of the information that you enter.

Many experienced spreadsheet program users first plan out their worksheets using pencil and paper before actually enter-

Excel Refreshers

ing any data using Excel. It's much easier to plan ahead and not have to change things after the fact. This way you can be relatively sure of what row and column headings should be, what cells you'll be using, how big the worksheet needs to be, and so on.

With a blank Excel worksheet on your screen, enter the labels (the row and column headings) and the values (the cell entries) that you see in Figure 2.1, a simple worksheet that lists employee identification, age in years, store affiliate, and years of service. These are the basic steps for entering data into an Excel worksheet:

- Highlight the cell where you want the data entered.
- Enter the data.
- Press the **Enter** key.

Use the mouse or the direction keys to move the cell indicator from one place in the worksheet to another, and notice that before you press the **Enter** key to actually enter the label or value in the cell, it first appears on the formula bar at the top of the worksheet window.

Keep in mind that wherever the cell indicator (or the

	A	B	C	D
1	Employee Information			
2				
3	Name	Age	Store	Years of Service
4				
5	BJ	37	2	15
6	PM	43	4	12
7	ME	44	3	21
8	MO	45	1	14
9	LS	38	1	19

2.1 A simple worksheet

highlighted block) is located, that's where the entry showing on the formula bar will appear after the **Enter** key is pressed and the entry is "locked in."

Entering Numbers

Excel recognizes a numerical entry as any entry that contains only numerical values, such as 37 in cell B5 in Figure 2.1. If a value contains text (such as 1235 Tennessee Street), it is not treated as a number.

In addition to numbers, you can use any of the following characters within an entry:

$$E\ e\ \$\ .\ +\ -\ (\ )$$

The use of these characters probably does not come as any surprise to you since they are often parts of formulas and other mathematical expressions.

Entering Text

Text is entered into a cell and locked in. The length of any text entry is restricted to 255 characters.

There's nothing much you have to remember about entering text into a cell unless you want to enter a text that consists of numbers and not have Excel read it as a number. For example, if you want to have column headings for years, you can use the column heading 1988 and have Excel treat it as text if you precede it with an equals sign, as shown here:

=1988

The equals sign tells Excel this is a formula; we'll discuss formulas later in this chapter.

Editing Cell Entries

As you enter data, it appears in the formula bar, and the insertion point moves to the right as each new character is entered.

Excel Refreshers

This insertion point acts as your guide for making corrections to entries before they are locked in.

If you make an error while entering a label or value, you can simply use the backspace key. Just backspace until you have deleted that part of the entry you no longer want. Then re-enter the correct information. Once you press the **Enter** key, the information becomes locked into the active cell.

If you are using a mouse, then you can drag over the incorrect part of the entry and use the **Del** key to delete it. If you are using the keyboard and the IBM version of Excel, you have to enter the Edit mode with the **F2** key and then backspace and enter characters as needed. You can also click on the cancel box to delete the entire entry.

If you accidentally press **Enter** and the wrong or incomplete information is placed in the cell, you can do one of three things. First, you can select the cell that contains the incorrect information and then use the backspace and **Del** keys to edit what needs to be changed. The second editing method is to select the cell and then simply retype the contents and press the **Enter** key. The new contents will replace the old and you're on your way! Finally, you can select the cell, then use the **Edit+Clear** key combination.

Excel Undo

If there's any Excel feature that has saved the day for thousands of users, it's the **Undo** command located on the Edit menu.

This command does exactly what its name says: it undoes an Excel command. For example, you might have just entered the value $35.78 in a cell to replace the value $35.87 and locked it in. If you select the **Undo** option on the Edit menu, you will see **Undo Entry** listed. If you select that option, Excel will return you to the cell's contents ($35.87) before the change was made. Be careful with this command, however, for it will not undo deleting a file or deleting data from a database.

Saving a Worksheet

Whether your worksheet is small or large, you probably want to save it as soon as possible, and certainly as you work if a good deal of data entry is required. This way, should you have a power failure, kick out your plug, or do one of heaven knows countless other things, you'll only lose as much as you entered from the last save.

Saving the employee information worksheet shown in Figure 2.1 will be your first chance at using Excel menus and dialog boxes. To save any worksheet, follow these steps.

1. Select the **Save** option from the File menu. Once you do this, you'll see the dialog box shown in Figure 2.2. A dialog box is Excel's way of asking you for more information.
2. Enter the name you want to use for the worksheet and press **Enter** or click the **OK** button with your mouse. The file will be saved under that name.

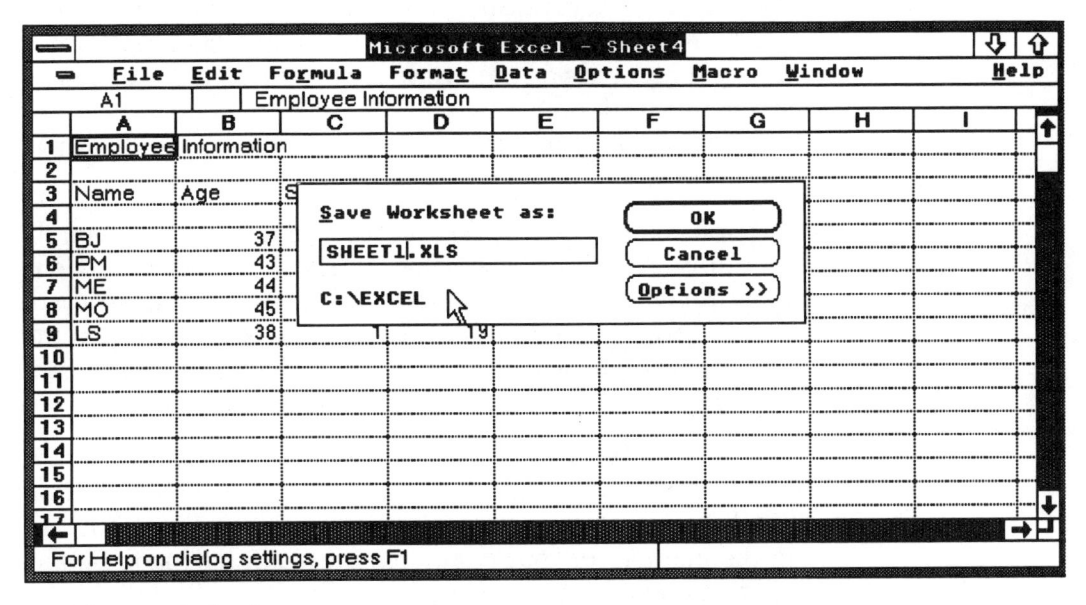

2.2 The save dialog box

Excel Refreshers

While it might seem obvious what you should name a worksheet, there are some things you need to keep in mind. The first is that you should use names that are descriptive of the file's contents. For example, auto_exp (for the IBM version) or Auto Expenses (for the Macintosh version) is descriptive of a worksheet that computes auto expenses; sheet1 or worksheet1 is not.

Second, IBM version users are limited to eight characters in the name of any file. For example, **autoexpenses** is not legal, so IBM Excel will only record the first eight characters, or auto-expe. In naming any Excel file, you need to follow the same conventions for naming any DOS file. Mac users are virtually unlimited in the number of characters they can use.

Finally, the IBM version of Excel will automatically attach the extension .XLS to any worksheet. No extension is added in the Macintosh version.

Retrieving a Worksheet

You may not always finish working with any one worksheet during one session at the computer. Excel wouldn't be of much value unless it allowed you to retrieve a worksheet after it had been saved and work on it again.

To retrieve a worksheet that has already been saved, follow these steps:

1. Select the **Open** option on the File menu. When you do this, you will see the dialog box shown in Figure 2.3. Here, the employee information worksheet is being retrieved.
2. Using the mouse or the cursor arrow keys, highlight the name of the worksheet that you want to retrieve or open. Then click **OK** or press the **Enter** key.

The saved file will shortly appear on your screen in a new window with the name of the opened file located in the title bar. You can retrieve as many windows as Excel has room for in the memory of your computer, although having too many open at once can be unwieldy.

Creating a Worksheet

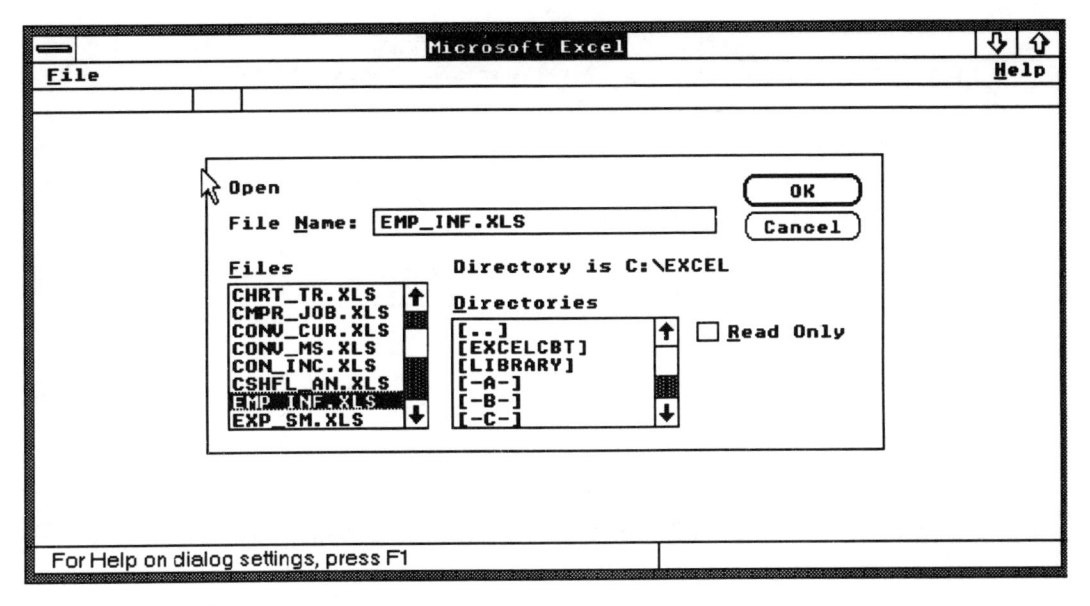

2.3 Opening a file

Using a Password

James Bond. Inspector Gadget. Inspector Clouseau and Sherlock Holmes. All detectives of a sort who used clues to solve mysteries.

While using Excel doesn't automatically place you in their league, there may be times when you need to make your worksheets secure so that others cannot access them without the use of a password.

To assign a password to any worksheet, follow these steps.

1. Select the **Save As** option from the File menu.
2. Enter the name of the file.
3. Select the **Options** button and you will see the dialog box shown in Figure 2.4 with the option for supplying a password.
4. Enter the password you want to use.

The next time you go to open the worksheet that was saved using a password, you will be greeted with a dialog box from

Excel Refreshers

2.4 Using a password

Excel asking you for the exact password. We hope you can remember it, because if you can't, there's no way to open that worksheet. The moral of this story is use passwords that you can remember, but not ones that other people can guess. Don't use your initials or your phone number or your age, for example. But things such as the last two digits of your driver's license or your favorite color are usually safe.

Changing the Format of a Spreadsheet

Excel allows you to customize the look of your cell contents through the use of the Format menu.

The basic steps in changing the format of a cell entry are as follows:

1. Select the cell or group of cells you want to work with.
2. Select the **Format** option from the Format menu.

Selecting Cells and Cell Ranges. The first step in many Excel operations is the selection of cells or a group of cells. A selection is the highlighted part of a worksheet.

To select a single cell, just click on it with the mouse. If you are using the keyboard, move to the cell you want to select using the cursor arrow keys and press the **Enter** key.

A range of cells is a contiguous set of cells (that is, they all touch). To select a range of cells using the mouse, just click and drag the pointer icon across the range you want to select. If you are using a keyboard, select the first cell, then hold down the **Shift** key and use the cursor arrow keys to move in the direction you want to select additional cells, as you see in Figure 2.5.

You can select multiple ranges (more than one range as you see in Figure 2.6) by holding down the **Ctrl** key (for IBM users) or the ⌘ key (for Macintosh users) and using the mouse as you make the selections.

If you are using the IBM version and the keyboard, select the first cell, and then press the **F8** function key (Extend). Now use the cursor arrow keys to select the range, and when you are finished, press the **Shift+F8** key combination to keep that range intact. Now move on and do the same thing again for any other ranges you might want to select.

2.5 Selecting a range of cells

Excel Refreshers

2.6 Selecting more than one range of cells

Working with Numbers. When you select the **Numbers** option from the Format menu, you will see the dialog box shown in Figure 2.7. Select the format that you want to use and press **Enter** or the **OK** button. Keep in mind that the dialog box has so many different choices you have to use the scroll bars to see them all.

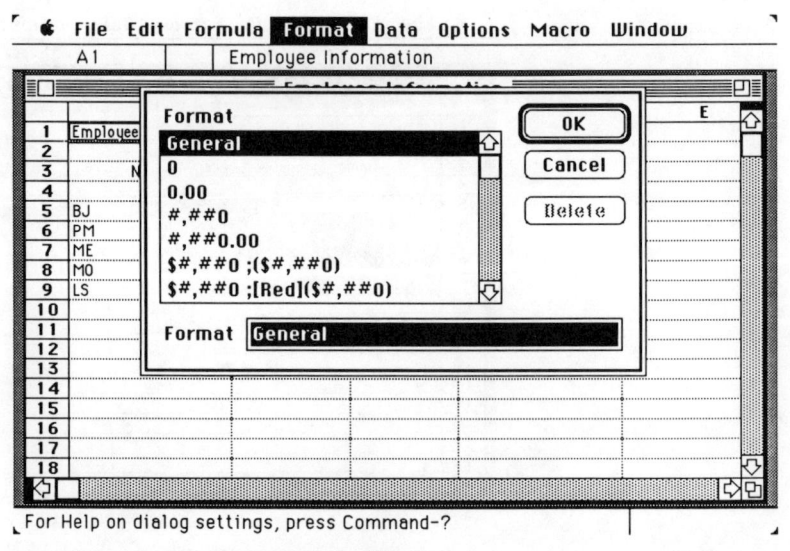

2.7 Changing the format of numbers

Creating a Worksheet

Here's an example of what the format is and what it looks like when applied to the contents of a cell or a range of cells.

General	80.4 (general format)
Ø	81 (integer format)
0.00	81.40 (decimal format)
#,##0	81
#,##0.00	81.40
$#,##0;($#,##0)$	81 (currency format)
$#,##0;[RED]($#,##0)$	81 (currency format)
$#,##0.00;($#,##0.00)$	81.40 (currency format)
$#,##0.00;[RED]($#,##0.00)$	81.40 (currency format)
0%	81.4% (percent format)
0.00%	81.40% (percent format)
0.00E+00	81.014+E3 (exponential format)
m/d/yy	5/10/84
d-mmm-yy	10-May-84
d-mmm	10-May
mmm-yy	May-84
h:mm AM/PM	11:05 PM
h:mm:ss AM/PM	11:05:32 PM
h:mm	23:05
h:mm:ss	23:05:32
m/d/yy h:mm	3/29/44 20:50

Working with Alignment. When you select the **Alignment** option from the Format menu, you will see the dialog box shown in Figure 2.8. Select the format that you want to use and press the **Enter** key or the **OK** button. Figure 2.9 shows you an example of the five different alignments that are available.

Working with Fonts. A font is a particular type style, and Excel provides you with a host of choices to use in the creation of your worksheets.

When you select the **Font** option from the Format menu, you will see the dialog box shown in Figure 2.10. Select the font and the style (bold, underlined, etc.) that you want to use, as well as the size. When you press **Enter** or click the **OK** button, the highlighted cells will be changed. Figure 2.11 shows you some of the varieties of font and style combinations you can use.

Excel Refreshers

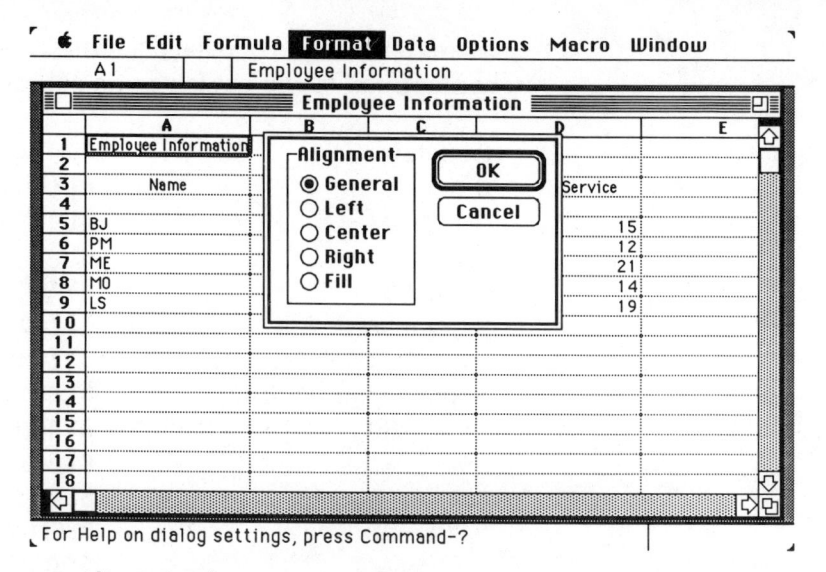

2.8 Aligning information in cells

Just a word of warning here. Some people think that these choices of fonts and styles are akin to being 12 years old and in a candy store on the way home from school. Be selective. The more fonts, styles, and sizes that you use, the less impact any one has.

2.9 Different alignment options

Creating a Worksheet

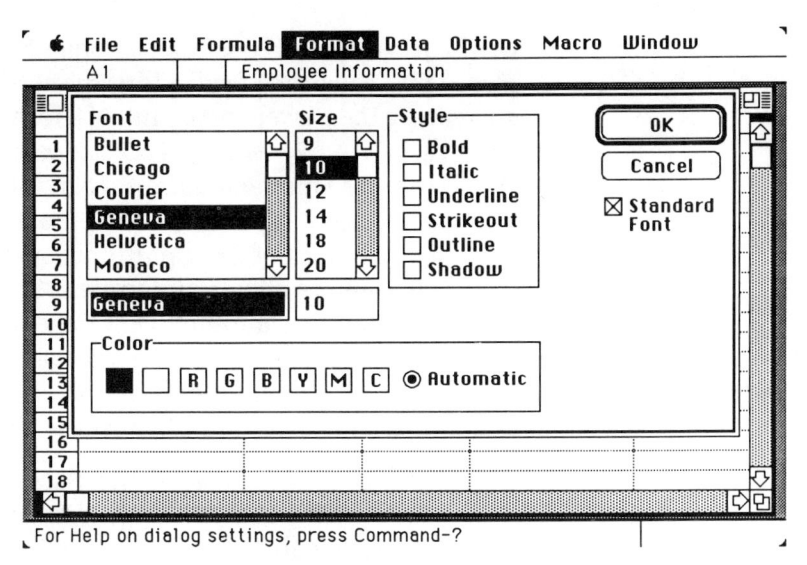

2.10 Formatting the font

Using Excel Formulas

Worksheets like Excel would not be of much use if all you could do was record numbers. The use of formulas is your first illustration of how powerful the information manipulation capability of worksheets can actually be.

A formula contains directions that Excel executes and involves both values, such as 1, 234, 5/5, and 67890, and operators, such as + (add), – (subtract), / (divide), • (multiply), > (greater than), and ~ (to the power of). Formulas always begin with an equals (=) sign to let Excel know what's coming.

An example of a formula that involves values and operators

	Bold	Underlined	Italic
Courier 12 point	**Courier 12 point**	Courier 12 point	*Courier 12 point*
Helvetica 10 point	**Helvetica 10 point**	Helvetica 10 point	*Helvetica 10 point*
Venice 14 point	***Venice 14 point***	*Venice 14 point*	*Venice 14 point*

2.11 Font and style combinations

37

Excel Refreshers

could be **=12+6+7+34**. You can enter actual values, but Excel also allows you to enter cell addresses, which represent numbers increasing the power and utility of a formula. For example, the formula **=A1+A2+A3+A4+A5** can be used to sum five values in column A. This same formula can then be applied to other columns of cells, since Excel remembers the relative position of cells regardless of their particular value.

In the example shown in Figure 2.12, you'll enter a simple formula that will compute the average number of years of service per employee by adding the values in column D and dividing by 5, the number of employees.

To enter and use a simple formula, follow these steps:

1. Move the cell indicator to the place in the worksheet where you want the computed value to appear. In this example, it will be cell D11.

2. Enter the formula on the input line so that the worksheet looks like the one shown in Figure 2.12. The formula is **(D5+D6+D7+D8+D9)/5**.

3. Press the **Enter** key and presto, the sum of the cells divided by 5 appears in cell D11.

	A	B	C	D
1	Employee Information			
2				
3	Name	Age	Store	Years of Service
4				
5	BJ	37	2	15
6	PM	43	4	12
7	ME	44	3	21
8	MO	45	1	14
9	LS	38	1	19
10				
11			Average	16.2

D11 =(D5+D6+D7+D8+D9)/5

2.12 Using a simple formula

Creating a Worksheet

You've just written and used a formula. For those of you who are already thinking ahead, yes, Excel offers a powerful set of specially designed formulas called functions, one of which, **=AVERAGE**, would have accomplished the same thing as the formula shown above. We'll get to those next.

Remember that the contents of a cell will not always be the same as the way the cell itself will appear in a worksheet. The formula that computes the average number of years in service is the cell entry, but what actually appears in the cell is the result of that formula. You can see this in Figure 2.12, where the value in cell D11 (16.2) is different from the contents of the cell (the formula used to compute the sum).

Pointing to Create a Formula

Another way to construct a formula is most useful when you may not be able to remember the exact address of all the cells that you want to include in the formula. This happens when you have a particularly large worksheet and would have to move around it to find the location of each of the cells you need.

Pointing lets you literally point to the cell that you want to include in the formula. Here are the steps to use in writing the formula that will compute the average age placed in cell C11. The formula is

$$=(C5+C6+C7+C8+C9)/5$$

which is simply the sum of all the numbers divided by the number of occurrences (which is 5).

1. Move the cell pointer to the location where you want the formula to appear (which is C11).
2. Enter = (an equals sign) as the first step in creating the formula. Now enter a left parenthesis.
3. Select the first cell you want to include in the formula, which in this case is C5. You will see the cell address (not the value in the cell) appear in the formula line.
4. Continue to do this with each of the operators and cell addresses in the formula until you are finished. Now enter a right parenthesis.

Excel Refreshers

5. Press the **Enter** key and the formula is entered and the value computed.

If you click on the cell that contains the results of the formulas, what do you think you see in the formula bar? The value that is in cell? No, you see the actual formula that you created.

Using Excel Functions

An Excel function is a special kind of formula; it is predefined, and Excel has over 130 in 13 categories from which you can choose. All functions consist of two parts: the name of the function and the function's argument. This *name + argument* combination is the syntax of the function and always remains the same. For example, here's the function that averages a range of cells from cell A1 through cell A5.

$$=AVERAGE(A1:A5)$$

The argument defines the area of the worksheet that Excel will use when it executes the function.

To use a function, follow these steps.

1. Select the **Paste Function** option from the Formula menu. When you do this, you see the dialog box shown in Figure 2.13 listing all of Excel's functions.
2. Select the function you want to use. When you do this by either double clicking with the mouse or using the cursor arrow keys and the **Enter** key, the selected function will be entered into the formula line.
3. Enter the argument and press the **Enter** key. You can use the mouse to point to the cell addresses to enter them as well. You can see in Figure 2.14 the function with the argument already completed as well as the value that it returned into cell D11.

Excel functions can be quite simple or complex. They are cell entries like any other Excel entry and can be edited as such. Remember that Excel knows the function by its name, so if you change that, you can't expect Excel to perform the function's task.

Creating a Worksheet

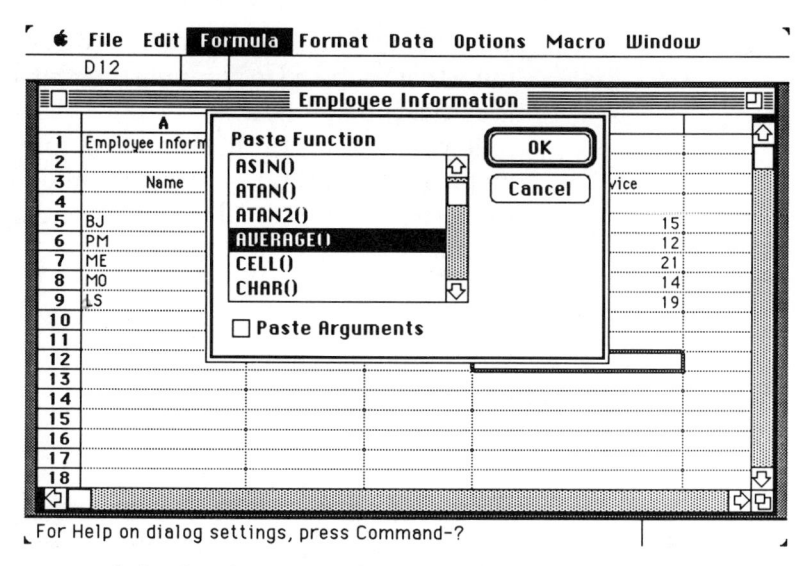

2.13 A dialog box listing Excel functions

Using Formulas and Functions in Other Places

Excel has many wonderful features, but one of the best is that you can move a formula to another cell in the worksheet and it will perform the same operation relative to the position of the cells it first used in the formula. For example, to average the

2.14 Using a formula to average a range of cells

Excel Refreshers

column called age in Figure 2.1, you could copy the same formula that was used to compute the average years in service that is located in cell D11.

If you added an additional column (column E) to the employee information worksheet called Bonus, you could find the average bonus for all the employees by copying the formula from cell D11 to cell E11.

Previewing a Worksheet

We're ready to start talking about printing a worksheet and producing a hard copy you can send to someone else or put in your file cabinet.

Before we do, Excel offers a feature that lets you check to see if your worksheet looks the way you want it to: the **Preview** feature. To preview a spreadsheet, you first need to select the **Print** option from the File menu, select the **Page Preview** option from the dialog box you see in Figure 2.15, then select **OK**. When you do this, you will see a reduced version of the full

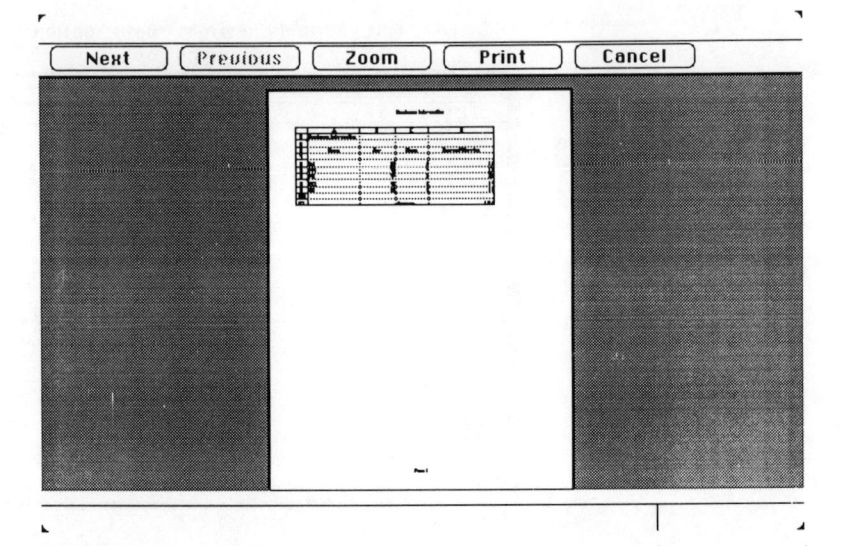

2.15 Previewing a worksheet

worksheet as shown in Figure 2.1 and the cell pointer in the shape of a magnifying glass.

When you want to inspect a certain portion of the worksheet, just go to that portion with your mouse pointer and click once. If you want to zoom with the keyboard, move the cell pointer to the position and press the **Enter** key.

As you can also see on the **Preview Page** screen, you can move from one page to the next by using the **Previous** and **Next** commands. You can print directly from this screen as well.

Printing a Worksheet

At last, a hard copy of the worksheet! Excel allows you to print out what you see on your screen.

To print a worksheet, simply select the **Print** command from the File menu. Excel will tell you when it is printing and will shortly produce that hard copy you have been waiting for. While you cannot adjust Excel to reduce or expand the size of a worksheet, you can print a "smaller" worksheet by reformatting using a smaller font. In this way you can fit more onto one sheet.

You've done it: created a worksheet from a blank Excel screen, edited some of the data, used a formula or two, and printed it. The next chapter in this "Excel Refresher" is an introduction to using Excel as a database, where you'll learn about sorting and selecting information.

3 / Managing Data with Excel

You already know that worksheets are organized by rows and columns and that the values in cells can be manipulated. Besides the techniques you've already learned, Excel can also be used to create and work with a database, a collection of information that is organized according to some predefined structure.

All worksheets are organized by rows and columns. While a simple worksheet is used mostly for manipulation and computation of values, databases are used for manipulating records.

Before we get into the basic terminology of databases, look at the one created in Figure 3.1, a set of records containing last name, first name, service level, and representative responsible for servicing the area in which the client lives.

Planning is especially important in creating and using a database. For example, if you are entering a client's name, you shouldn't consider both the first and last name as one entry since this would prevent sorting or searching on a singular part of a name, such as the last name. Keep the pieces of information

Managing Data with Excel

3.1 A set of database records

that you consider to be important to the database as separate entries.

Many database users take some time to plan out how the database will be set up using graph paper, before they even begin entering any data.

Files, Records, and Fields

All databases consist of fields (the columns in Figure 3.1), which when read across for any one case or individual make up a record (the rows in Figure 3.1). The entire set of records is saved as a file. The file in Figure 3.1 was created and named Service since it represents service records.

In sum, a database is a file that contains several different records, and each of these records contains one or more fields. You do not need to have a complete set of fields for each record, but you do need to have all the fields available for each record.

Using Excel's features, you will learn how to do such things as sort (alphabetically or numerically) and select certain records based on criteria that you specify.

Excel Refreshers

A database is created in exactly the same way as a spreadsheet, with identical editing procedures and cell indicator commands.

Creating a Database

Creating a database is as simple as telling Excel what part of the worksheet will make up the database. You first enter the information you want to become part of the database and then you define it. In most cases, the material within the entire worksheet will become the database.

To create a database, follow these steps:

1. Enter the names of the fields that you want to use as column headings in adjacent columns.

2. Enter records as rows in adjacent rows.

3. Select the range of cells you want to use as the database as you see in Figure 3.2. Now define the database by selecting the **Set Database** option from the Data menu. That's it, the database is now defined.

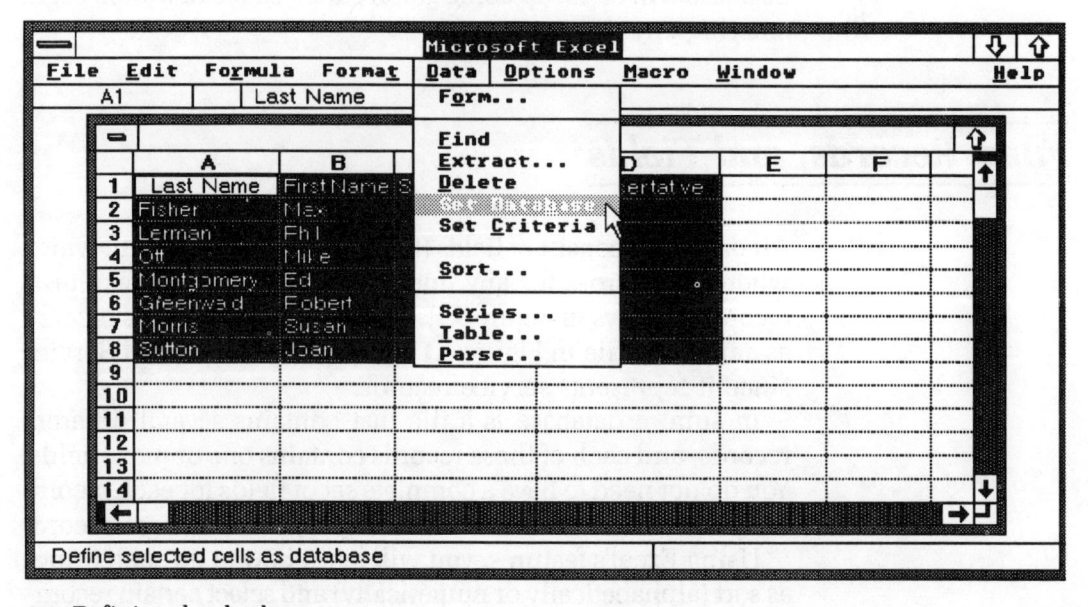

3.2 Defining the database

When you select the area of the worksheet that you want to define as the database, you should select a few extra rows (or blank records). This will allow you to add records at the end of the database without having to redefine it each time. You can now add or delete records at any place in the database. As long as these records are added (or deleted) within the boundaries of the originally defined database, you don't have to worry about redefining it.

Sorting a Database

One of the most often used functions of a database is sorting on one or more field. The most simple example is using the database to alphabetize. For example, in the database shown in Figure 3.1, you might want to sort the client list alphabetically by last name or sort on the area representative (rep code).

The general strategy for sorting records, whether on one or several fields, is as follows:

1. Define the database as we discussed above.
2. Select the set of records that you want to sort. Do not select the field titles because you do not want to sort those!
3. Select the **Sort** option from the Data menu and you will see the sort dialog box as shown in Figure 3.3. Excel assumes that you want to sort in ascending order (A, B, C, D, etc., or 1, 2, 3, 4, etc.) by rows.
4. Click **OK** and you'll see the database sorted as shown in Figure 3.4.

If you make an error (such as sorting on the wrong field), just use the **Undo** option on the Edit menu, which will return you to the worksheet before it was sorted.

Sorting on More Than One Field

You might want to sort on more than one field. If you do, then you need to specify in the sort dialog box the keys and their importance in the sort.

Excel Refreshers

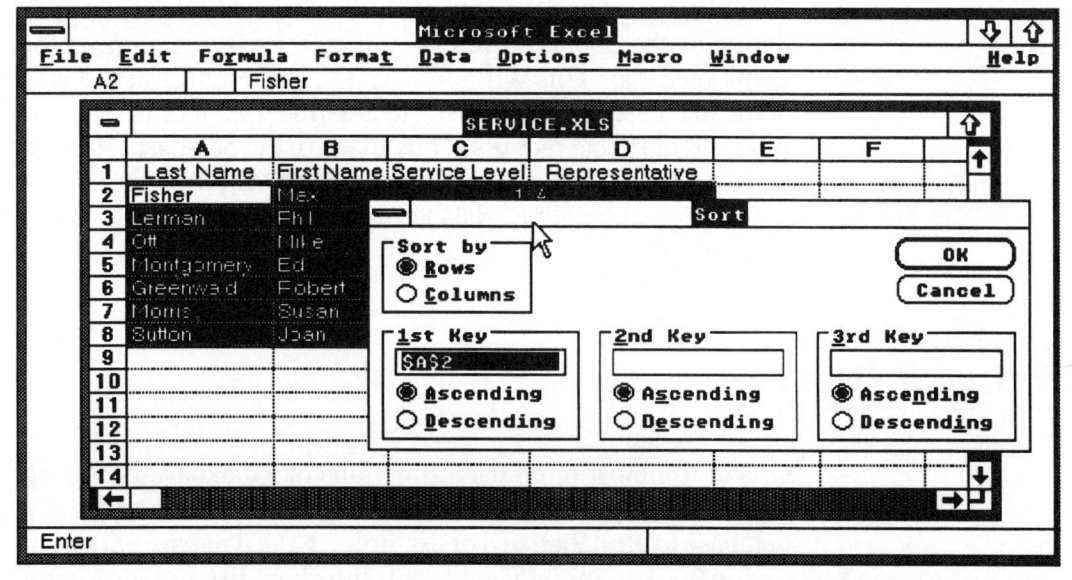

3.3 The sort dialog box

Say, for example, that you wanted to alphabetize the names of clients within a representative's regions. You would define the first key for sorting on cell D2 and the second key on cell A2. You can see how the first and second keys are defined in

3.4 The results of the sort

Managing Data with Excel

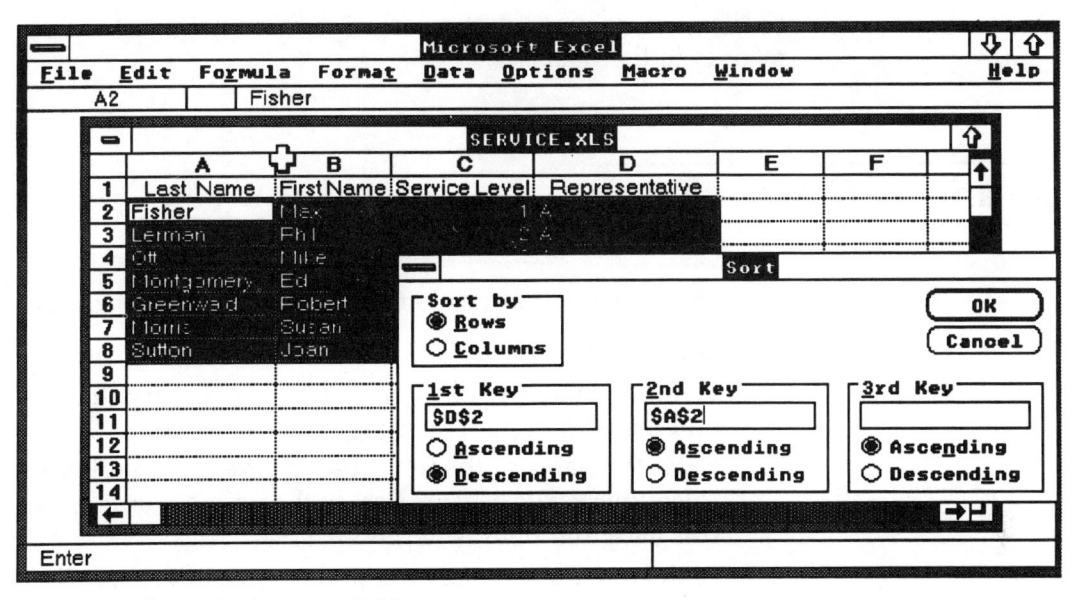

3.5 Sorting by more than one field

the sort dialog box. When you sort, you'll see the database reorganized as shown in Figure 3.5, only this time the sort by Representative is in descending order while the sort on the client's last name is in ascending order within each Representative category.

Searching Through a Database

Another frequent use for a database is to search for a particular record or for some information about a particular record. For example, you might want to search through an extended database and select only those clients who are in Rep B's sales area.

When you search through an Excel database, you are requesting information from the database. In any such operation, Excel needs to know where the data is located and what data it is that you want to find. You tell the program where the data is by defining the database, which you already know how to do, and you specify the data you want to find through the use of

49

Excel Refreshers

a criteria range, or a set of criteria that Excel will use to match records in the database.

Creating a Criteria Range

The general steps in the creation of a criteria range are as follows:

1. Define the database.
2. Go to an empty area of the worksheet where you will create and place the criteria range.
3. Enter the name of the field that will be the criterion for selection exactly as it appears in the defined database. In this case, the field is Representative.
4. In the row immediately under the name of the criterion, enter the actual value of the criterion. In this case, it would be **B** as you see in Figure 3.6. When told to, Excel will search for all records that have **B** in the field titled Representative.

3.6 Defining criteria

Managing Data with Excel

The criteria range has just been created and you are ready to move on to finding and extracting records.

Finding and Selecting Records

Once you have defined a criteria range, there are two important operations you can perform. First, you can search through a database and find records. Second, you can extract these records and place them into another part of the worksheet.

For example, let's say we want to find all of the records with **B** in the field titled Representative. To find a record follow these steps:

1. Define the database and the criteria range as discussed above.
2. Select the **Find** option from the Data menu you see in Figure 3.6. Once this option is selected, Excel will find all records that match the information defined in the defined criteria range. Once it finds a match, it will highlight the record as you see in Figure 3.7, and the scroll bar will have strips in it instead of a gray pattern.

To find other records that may fit the match, use the up and down arrow keys.

Extracting Records

To extract information from a database, follow the same general set of instructions. The only difference here is that you need to provide a place for Excel to locate the information once it is extracted from the original database.

To extract information from a database, follow these steps:

1. Define the database and the criteria range as discussed above.
2. Select an area of the worksheet where you can place the extracted records. In this area, you need to place the names of the fields that will be extracting information. Be sure

Excel Refreshers

3.7 Finding records in a database

you select a large enough number of rows to provide sufficient room for the extracted records.

3. Select **Extract** from the Data menu and the records that fit the criteria that you defined will be extracted and placed in the selected range that you defined, as you see in Figure 3.8.

Remember to leave enough room for the records and to copy the field names exactly as they appear in the originally defined database. One way to assure yourself that the names are exactly the same is to copy the names (using the **Copy** command on the Edit menu) and then **Paste** them in.

Using a Data Form

There's a way to add data to a database after it has been created that makes working with the number of records in the database, and editing them, very easy. This is through the use of a data form. A data form is a predefined template that Excel

Managing Data with Excel

	A	B	C	D	E	F	G	H
1	Last Name	First Name	Service Level	Representative				
2	Morris	Susan	1	C				
3	Greenwald	Robert	2	B				
4	Montgomery	Ed	2	B				
5	Fisher	Max	1	A				
6	Lerman	Phil	2	A				
7	Ott	Mike	3	A				
8	Sutton	Joan	2	A				
9								
10	Representative							
11	B							
12								
13	Last Name	First Name	Service Level	Representative				
14	Greenwald	Robert	2	B				
15	Montgomery	Ed	2	B				
16								
17								

3.8 Extracting records

automatically generates once you define a database. A data form lists all of the fields in the database for this specific record.

You can add, delete, and review records in a database using a data form by selecting the appropriate button in the data form dialog box you see in Figure 3.8. For example, if you want to add a new record, just select the **New** button and the template will be blank. Enter the new data and the record when complete will become part of the database as it appears within the original worksheet.

You can also edit any record that you want through the use of the template. Just use the scroll bars to find the record you want to edit and make the necessary changes using the same editing techniques that you have used all along in other Excel operations.

Data forms are great for speeding along the entry of data, but remember, you must define the database before you can use the data form. Otherwise, Excel will give you an error message since it does not know on what you want to base the creation of the data form.

Now it's time to learn how you can illustrate information stored in Excel spreadsheets using the easy and incredibly useful graphics capability.

4 / Using Excel Charts

Excel offers many of the same features as other spreadsheets, but Excel's charting capabilities put this spreadsheet in a class all by itself. Excel gives you a choice of seven different types of charts, with many other combinations possible, and all are easy to generate and customize.

Visual information seems to add a dimension of understanding that sets a spreadsheet apart from the simple rows and columns that it consists of. Excel has a very powerful system for generating and customizing charts so that your complete charts can be done in one of many styles with other options customized. Besides, creating an Excel chart is as easy as 1-2-3!

In this chapter, the sales information shown in Figure 4.1 will be used to generate various graphs.

Using Excel Charts

```
┌─────────────────────────────────────────────────────────────┐
│ ═                        Microsoft Excel              ⇩ ⇧   │
│ File  Edit  Formula  Format  Data  Options  Macro  Window  Help │
│      A1              Sales by Region                        │
│   ┌─────────────────────────SALREG.XLS──────────────────⇧─┐│
│   │     A      B      C       D        E       F       G      H ↑││
│  ↕1 Sales by Region                                          ││
│  ↕2                                                          ││
│   3                        1st Quarter 2nd Quarter 3rd Quarter 4th Quarter ││
│   4              Region #1     12        15        16        14 ││
│   5              Region #2     23        25        21        26 ││
│   6              Region #3     18        18        18        21 ││
│   7              Region #4      9        12        16        14 ││
│   8                                                          ││
│   9                                                          ││
│  10                                                          ││
│  11                                                          ││
│  12                                                          ││
│  13                                                          ││
│  14                                                        ⇩ ││
│   ⇦                                                       ⇨ ││
│ Ready                                                        │
└─────────────────────────────────────────────────────────────┘
```

4.1 Information used to generate graphs

Creating a Chart

The general steps in creating an Excel chart are the same. Here they are.

1. Select the range of cells that you want to chart.
2. Select the **New** option from the File menu.
3. Select the **Chart** button. You're done. Your first Excel chart should be showing on your screen as you see in Figure 4.2.

Once the first chart is generated, you will see a Chart menu at the top of your screen with several new menus. One of the most important is the Gallery menu, which allows you to choose the type of chart you want to generate.

For example, if you want a pie chart instead of a bar chart (which is the default), just select the **Pie** option on the Gallery menu and you will see a dialog box illustrating the six types

Excel Refreshers

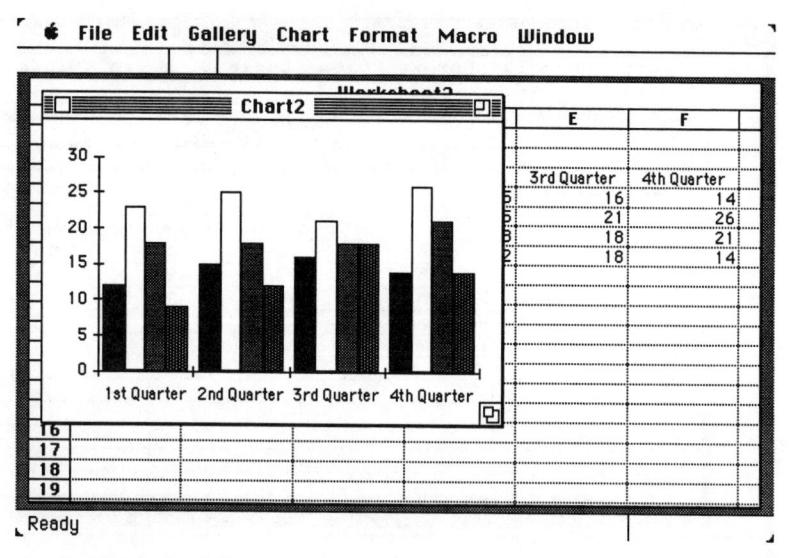

4.2 A simple bar chart

of pie charts you can select. Pie chart style 6 provides labels and percentages for the slices shown in Figure 4.3.

You'll notice that the chart in Figure 4.2 is more or less a vanilla chart with little added on. Let's spruce it up a bit.

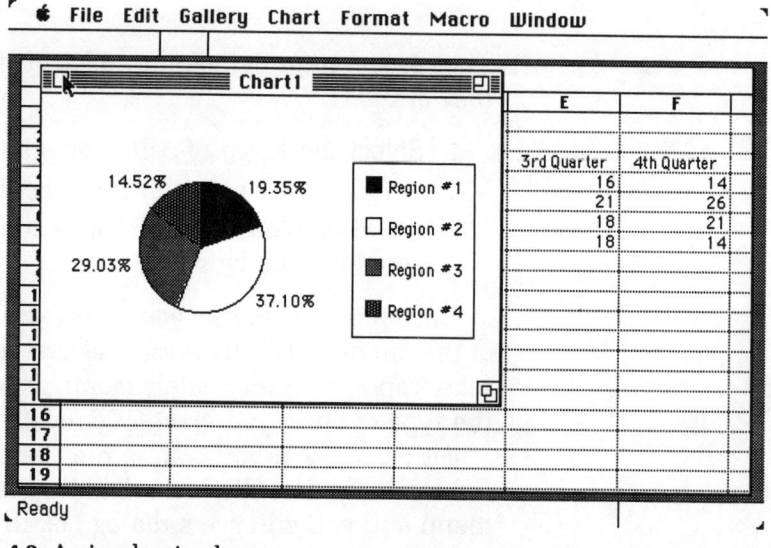

4.3 A simple pie chart

Using Excel Charts

Using the Chart Gallery

First, you can change the type of chart that is being used by simply selecting one of the several available through the Gallery menu. The default bar chart will not always be the one that best illustrates your data.

For example, Figure 4.4 shows a line chart that plots changes over time in sales for each region; a line chart was chosen since it best represents changes over time. As usual, Excel first created a bar chart, but it's simple to select **Line** from the Gallery menu and then choose whatever type of line chart you want. Excel automatically knows to use Region #1 and 1st Quarter as labels in the chart since it assumes that text attached to a range of values is a label for that range.

Working with Chart Elements

The chart that you first create is not the one you have to live with forever! Excel has a set of powerful tools that lets you select

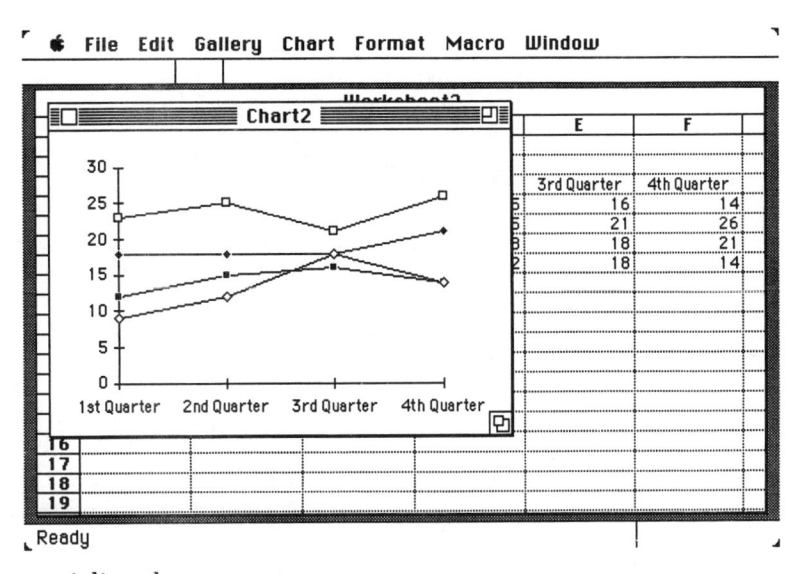

4.4 A line chart

Excel Refreshers

a different part of the chart and enhance its appearance and include additional information.

Adding a Legend

One of the first things that you might want to do is add a legend to your chart. You can do this by selecting the **Add Legend** option from the Format menu. As you can see in Figure 4.5, the legend acts as a code of sorts to allow the reader to identify the different components of the chart.

If you want to change the text within a legend, you will have to go back to the original worksheet from which the chart was created and change the text there. Since the worksheet and its associated chart are linked, any change that you make in the worksheet will show up in the chart that you created.

Using the Chart menu you can also add arrows, work with legends, and work with axes. For example, you will see later in Figure 4.10 how an arrow was added to make the connection

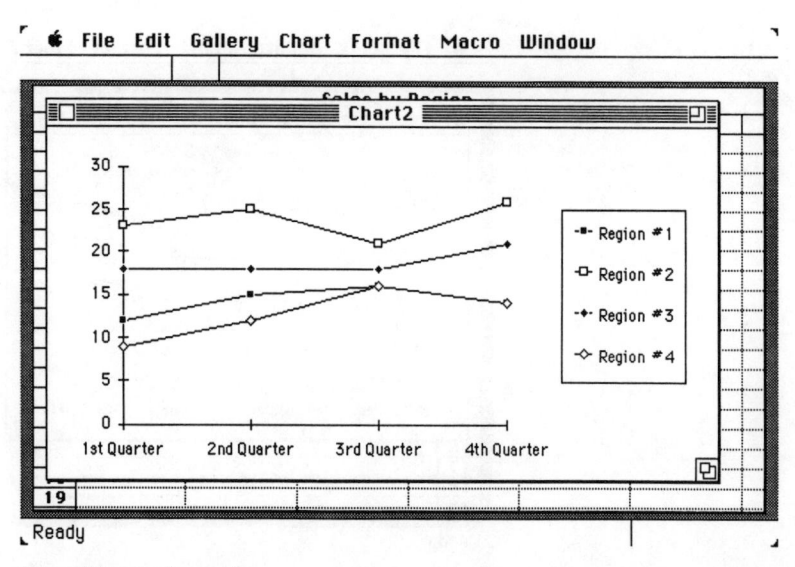

4.5 Adding a legend

Using Excel Charts

between text that was added to the chart and the value in the chart that we wanted to bring to the reader's attention.

Formatting Charts

Charts can also be "dressed up" using the Format menu. For example, you can select an area within the chart window and change the pattern that is used to represent it. Say you want to select one of the series represented in the chart and change its fill pattern so it will appear as shown in Figure 4.6. In this case, the legend was screened using one of the alternatives in the pattern dialog box. To do this, follow these steps.

1. Select the chart area you want to change. When this is done, small square handles appear around the perimeter of the area.
2. Select the pattern from the dialog box (see Figure 4.7) that you want to use and click **OK** or press the **Enter** key. You'll shortly see the selected area change.

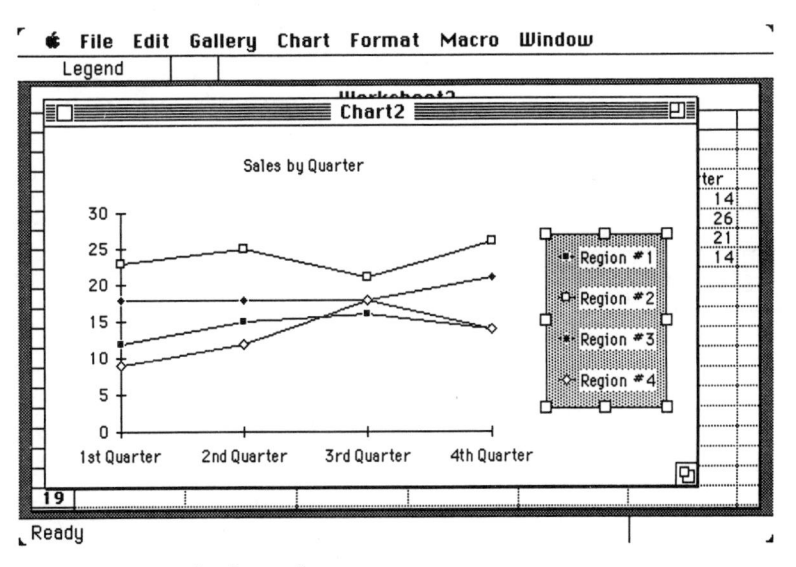

4.6 Formatting the legend area

Excel Refreshers

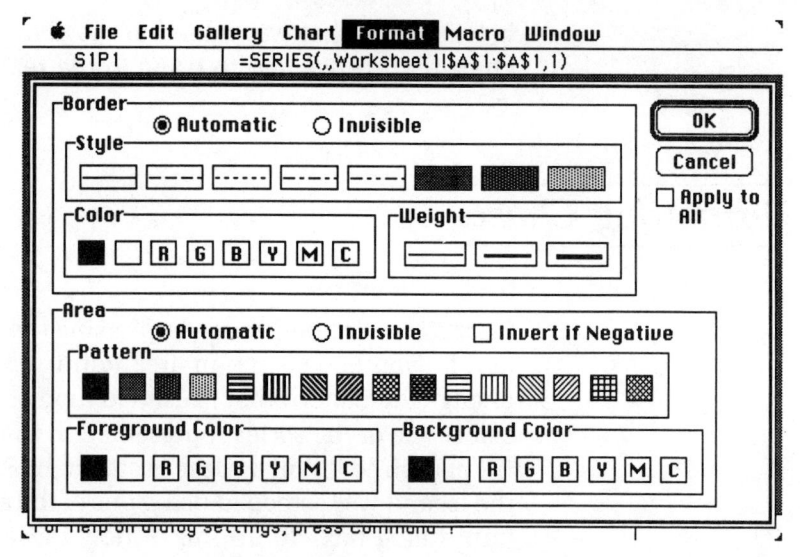

4.7 The pattern dialog box

You can highlight almost any area of a chart, the legend, the entire chart area itself, the individual axes, and then use the format menu to make the types of changes that you want. You can alter line type, color, and even the thickness (weight) of the lines that are used in a chart. No matter what type of changes you make however, be careful of chart junk. That's when every possible option is used to create a meaningless representation of data.

Attaching Text to Charts

There's another Excel feature that allows you to attach text to different parts of the chart. Some of the text is attached in places that Excel defines (this is called attached text) and other types of text can be attached to a chart anywhere you want (this is called unattached text).

Using Excel Charts

Attached Text

To attach text to an Excel chart, select the **Attach Text** option on the Chart menu.

When this is done, you will see the dialog box shown in Figure 4.8.

Using this dialog box you can:

- attach a title,
- attach text to the Y (or value axis),
- attach text to the X (or category axis), or
- attach text to any one of the series points that you identify

Just select the part of the chart you want to attach text to, enter the text, and press the **Enter** key. Figure 4.9 shows you a chart with a title added.

Unattached Text

Besides being able to attach text as a title, you can also attach text anywhere that you would like in a chart. That's how the

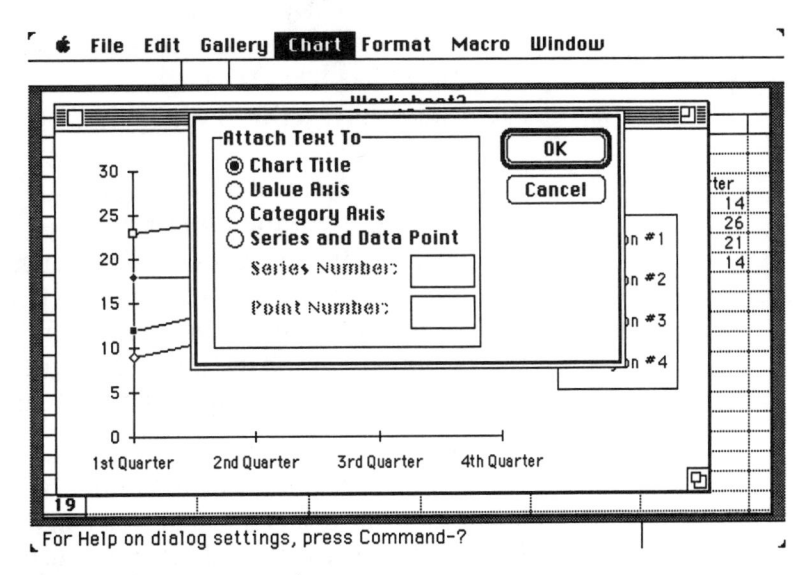

4.8 Attaching text to a chart

Excel Refreshers

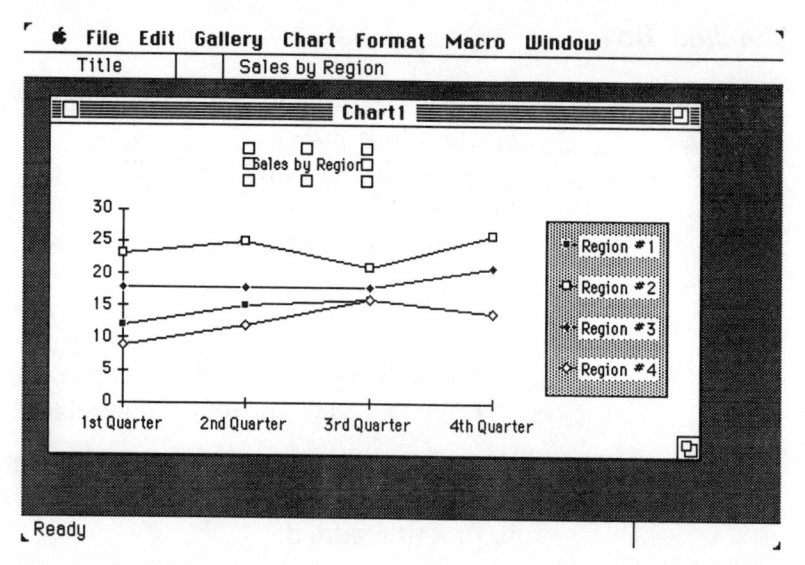

4.9 Attaching a title

text in Figure 4.9, which emphasizes an important point, was done.

To attach text, follow these steps.

1. Be sure that you have no other chart elements selected, that is, there are no other "handles" that indicate something has been selected.
2. Enter the text (Keep your eye. . . .) that you want to attach to the chart (Figure 4.10). As you begin typing, the text will appear in the formula line. When you are finished typing, press the **Enter** key.
3. Now use the mouse or the direction keys to select and move the text to any part of the chart that you would like. In Figure 4.10 the text was created and placed to emphasize a point in the chart. You'll also see an arrow in Figure 4.10. I'll explain how that was added later in the chapter.

You can select attached or unattached text at any time by using the mouse to click within the area or by using the direction keys. Once the area is selected, you can then use the **Text** or the **Font** options on the Format menu to make changes in the chart's appearance, as shown in Figure 4.10 where the attached text was italicized.

Using Excel Charts

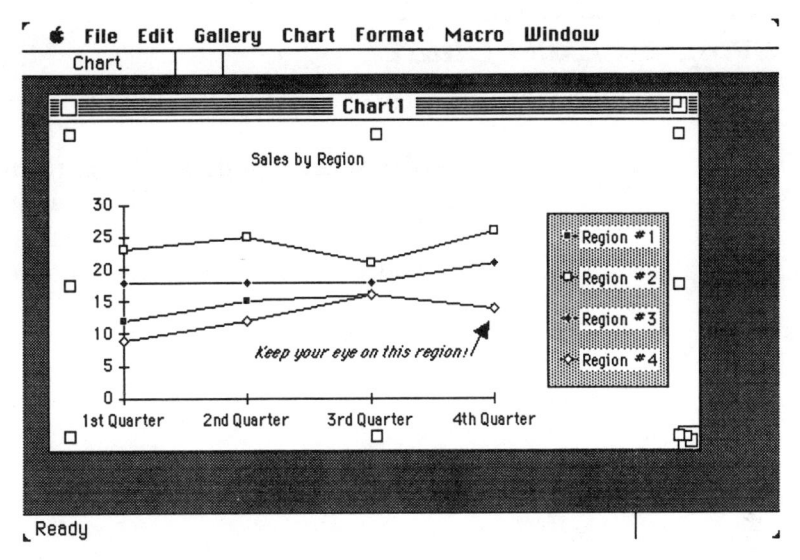

4.10 Attaching unattached text

Adding an Arrow

You may have noticed that you can also add an arrow to a chart through the use of the **Add Arrow** option on the Chart menu. Once an arrow is added you can select it, use the handles to increase or decrease its length, and reposition it as you see in Figure 4.10 by selecting it and dragging it by its shaft.

Printing an Excel Chart

An Excel chart is like any other file, but it is not part of the worksheet that was used to create it. In other words, it needs to be saved all by itself with the extension .XLC (for Excel chart).

63

Excel Refreshers

Saving an Excel Chart

Be sure that when you do save a chart, the file name that you assign is related to the worksheet on which the chart is based. This will help you retrieve the correct chart later on and will prevent you from losing the chart in a listing of others.

5 / An Introduction to Excel Macros

Have you ever had to repeat a tedious spreadsheet task, like saving the file every time you make a change? Welcome to the world of macros—recorded sequences of keystrokes that you invoke at the touch of a button (or two!). While what follows is only an introduction, it will provide you with the information you need to use macros in your most simple or complex spreadsheet applications.

Why Excel Macros?

Creating and using a spreadsheet often requires entering the same information over and over again or repeating the same operation. For example, you might have a spreadsheet that has 100 columns of 80 rows and you want to insert a space between each column and each row. One way you could handle this is to place the cell indicator between columns and use the **Insert** option from the Edit menu. But this would mean doing it some 100 times for the columns and then another 80 for the rows!

An attractive alternative is to design and use a macro that automatically places a space between each column you specify. A macro is a set of stored keystrokes that is executed using the name that you assign. How you use macros is only limited by your imagination. Here are just some of the things you could do with just a few keystrokes.

- design a macro that will draw a general type of graph and will pause when it comes time to enter information such as titles
- use any one of Excel's functions as part of a macro, thereby, for instance, computing the internal rate of return on a column of figures
- place the 12 months of the year across the top of a spreadsheet
- average a list of numbers no matter the length of the list and then take that average and enter it into another part of the spreadsheet
- change the format of a spreadsheet to conform with the standard that is used throughout the office
- create a specific type of graphic that has predefined labels and symbols for markers
- print an entire spreadsheet without worrying about blocking or setting up any other conditions
- go through a spreadsheet and change the format for each cell
- and the time saver: save a spreadsheet

The purpose of this chapter is to familiarize you with some of the basic steps in creating and executing macros. With these tools, you can "program" almost any Excel operation so that it can be completed in much less time and with relatively few keystrokes.

An Introduction to Excel Macros

Creating a Command Macro

Creating an Excel macro consists of going through each of the individual steps that you want that macro to perform when it is invoked. As you go through these strokes, they are recorded using Excel's macro recording function.

For example, let's take the simple but very useful macro that automatically saves a worksheet once changes have been made. Without a macro, you would do this by selecting the **Save** option from the File menu.

The fastest and most efficient way to create a macro is by choosing Excel's **Record** option, located on the Macro menu, and then going through exactly the steps that you would use in saving the file.

Here are the steps for creating a relatively basic macro that saves a file that has already been named and saved once.

1. Select the **Record** option from the Macro menu and you will see the dialog box shown in Figure 5.1.

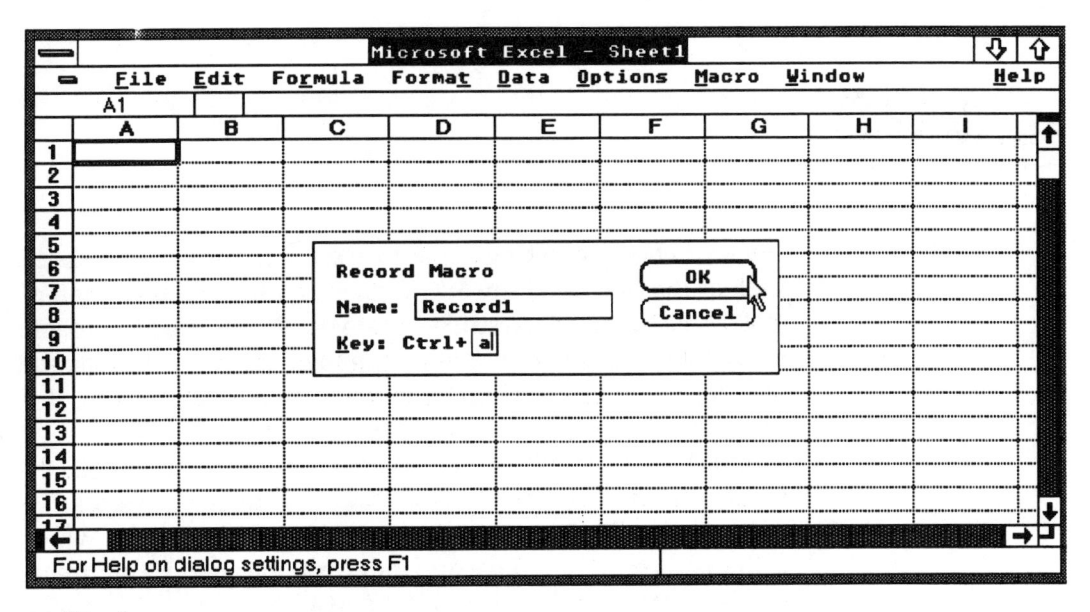

5.1 Naming a macro

2. Enter a name for the macro in the Name: box. Remember to use names that are descriptive of the macro itself. In this case, the macro was named (what else?) save.

   You might notice that Excel offers you the opportunity to assign one letter to the name of the macro that you can use in combination with the **Ctrl** key (for IBM users) or **Options+⌘** (for Mac users), such as in **Ctrl+s** or **Option+⌘+s** for save or **Ctrl+d** or **Option+⌘+d** for delete. Since these are macros that you may use often, one-keystroke names will save you considerable time. Press **Enter** or click **OK**. The macro is now named and the macro recorder is now working.
3. Select the **Save** option from the File menu. As you go through this procedure, Excel is recording each stroke and making it part of the macro. You'll notice that in the status line at the bottom of the worksheet you can see a little message, **Recording**, telling you what Excel is doing.
4. When you have completed the macro, select the **Stop Recording** option from the Macro menu. This will stop the recording of keystrokes, and the creation of the macro is complete.

Macro Sheets

Once you begin creating a macro, Excel creates a macro sheet, such as the one in Figure 5.2. This is an individual worksheet that stores the exact keystrokes that you entered into the macro using Excel's macro command language. Here, it is the second macro sheet created. Each time you create a new macro, it is stored on its own individual macro sheet.

As you can see in the macro sheet shown in Figure 5.2, the set of commands (which always begins with an equals sign) is quite simple. The name of the macro appears in cell A1, which is then followed by a **Save** and a **Return** command. Command macros always end with a **=Return( )**.

If you prefer, you can create the same macro without using the macro recorder by directly entering the same set of macro

An Introduction to Excel Macros

5.2 The macro steps

commands into a macro sheet. To do this, you would have to select the **New** option from the File menu and then select the **Macro Sheet** button. This will provide you with the blank slate on which to enter commands from the macro language. In this way you can customize your macro sheet to the extent necessary.

Executing a Macro

The rule to remember is that a macro must be open (not necessarily active) in order for you to use it. Any macro that is stored on a macro sheet and is not open will not run. The worksheet for which you want the macro to act has to be active and the macro sheet containing the macro has to be open.

There are two ways to execute a macro. One is by pressing the same **Ctrl+key** or **Option+⌘** key combinations that you used to create it. This is by far the quickest and most convenient method. But how many of these combinations can you keep in mind, and how often do you need such a "quickie" macro?

Excel Refreshers

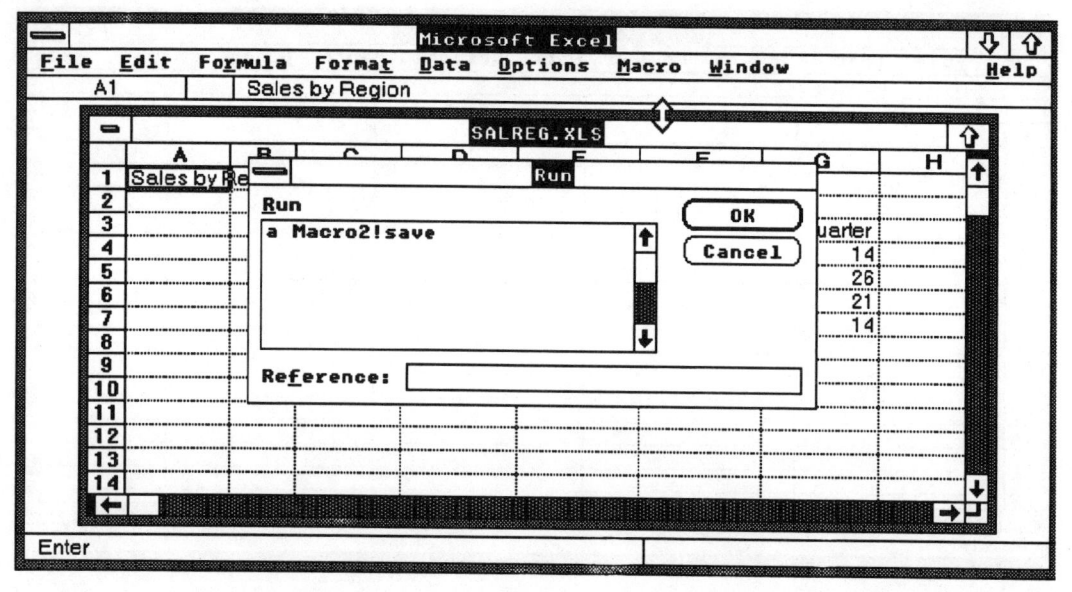

5.3 Running a macro

Perhaps a more practical method is to use the Macro menu. Once you select the **Run** option on this menu, you will see a dialog box (see Figure 5.3) listing all of the macros stored on a specific macro sheet. Just select the macro you want to execute and click **OK** or press **Enter**.

From One Worksheet to Another

At first you might not like the idea that macros are stored as independent of the worksheet for which they were created, but there's a tremendous advantage behind this design. It allows you to easily share macros between other worksheets. You can have any worksheet active and any macro sheet open and use the macro or macros that are available.

In order to share a macro that was created in another worksheet, just have that macro sheet open at the same time that the worksheet is active.

Building a Macro Library

OK, so you've created macros by using either the macro recorder or the macro command language. Does it strike you as somewhat impractical to have only one macro for each macro sheet? I hope so, because it is.

Why not store all the macros that have similar purposes in a macro library? In this way, all you need to do is open this library of macros and then you can access them at any time. For that matter, you can open a series of macro libraries (all on separate macro sheets) and have all your macros ready to go.

Figure 5.4 displays a simple three-macro library titled Align. One macro aligns left, one center, and one right. Once this library is open, any of these macros can be easily invoked. In addition, any of the macros can be moved around on the macro library sheet as long as their name accompanies them.

Macros are a great help for performing not only mundane tasks but also those that take advantage of Excel's more

5.4 Storing macros

Excel Refreshers

sophisticated capabilities. Experiment and use them whenever you can.

That's it for the basics! Now it's time to move on to the actual worksheet examples that will demonstrate how useful Excel can be in a variety of business applications.

Part II
Excel Business Applications

How to Use the Spreadsheets

Each of the spreadsheets in Part II has been selected for its ease of use and application to a business setting.

Each is accompanied by a name, a description of what it does, an explanation of how to work with the spreadsheet, a graph of the data in the spreadsheet (when appropriate), and another worksheet displaying all the cell entries, including functions and formulas. All worksheets are produced by selecting the **Formulas** option from the **Display** option on the **Options** menu.

Keep in mind the following pointers when using the spreadsheets in this part of the book.

First, in the spreadsheet itself you will find values, labels, formulas, and functions. In order for the spreadsheet to work, you must first enter all of the information that is contained in the spreadsheet or, at the least, all of the formulas and the contents of the cells that are addressed in the formula. Otherwise you may get erroneous results. It's best to first enter the data as you see it in the example, and then change it to fit your own needs.

Second, if you want to extend the size of any spreadsheets, be sure that you copy the appropriate formulas or functions down columns or across the rows. To find out where these formulas or functions are, either consult the listing of cell entries or examine the cells directly on the spreadsheet.

Third, you won't have a problem adding additional lines or columns to a spreadsheet as long as you maintain the integrity of the formulas. Be sure that when you do add a row or a column or make format changes, you have not moved a formula that has a relative reference in it or the location of a cell with an absolute address. If you do move such information, make sure you change the reference to its correct cell address.

That's it. Now go enjoy Excel and these spreadsheets. I hope they make you more productive.

6 / Accounting Worksheets

Accounts Receivable

What the Spreadsheet Does

This spreadsheet, very similar in structure to the Accounts Payable spreadsheet that follows, indicates the money that is owed to you, keeps track of invoices that are past due, and uses a criterion table to sum up amounts by number of days past due. The criterion table is based on periods of 0–30 days, 31–60 days, 61–90 days, and over 90 days. The spreadsheet uses the =**NOW**, =**DSUM**, and =**DAVG** formulas to compute the age of the bill and the sum.

The age of the transaction is computed using the =**NOW−H11** formula and then copied down the column.

Excel Business Applications

	A	B	C	D	E
1	ACCOUNTS RECEIVABLE				
2					
3	Invoice	Company	Date Due	Amount	Age
4	31456	Byron's	1/22/89	$245.76	10
5	222	Rusty's	1/8/89	$786.89	24
6	22223	Pickney School	12/22/88	$43.78	41
7	43125	H&H Insurance	12/8/88	$44.23	55
8	3321	Glen's Coins	11/23/88	$123.32	70
9	2311	Mickey's Bikes	11/23/88	$223.56	70
10	13454	Gas	11/23/88	$67.98	70
11	45333	Whel's Lumber	11/23/88	$36.54	70
12	312	A. Smith	10/23/88	$2,112.45	101
13	676	L-Mart	10/23/88	$332.45	101
14					
15					
16			Number of Outstanding Invoices	10	
17			Total Amount Due	$4,016.96	
18					
19					
20	Summary Table				
21					
22	Time Period	Amount	Number		
23		Due	Due		
24					
25	0-30 Days (A)	$1,032.65	2		
26	31-60 Days (B)	$88.01	2		
27	61-90 Days (C)	$451.40	4		
28	Over 90 Days (D)	$2,444.90	2		
29					
30	Total	$4,016.96	10		
31					
32	Criterion Table				
33					
34	Age	Age	Age	Age	
35	TRUE	FALSE	FALSE	FALSE	

Working with the Spreadsheet

To work with this spreadsheet, you need to enter the following information.

Col A invoice number
Col B name
Col C date due
Col D amount due you

Accounting Worksheets

When the spreadsheet is complete, it will provide you with the following information.

Col E	age (in days) between date due and current date
B25...B28	amount due you by 30-day period
B30	total amount due you
C30	number of outstanding invoices due you

What It Looks Like

Figure 6.1 shows a pie chart with the relative percentages of outstanding receivables for 0–30 days, 31–60 days, 61–90 days, and over 90 days.

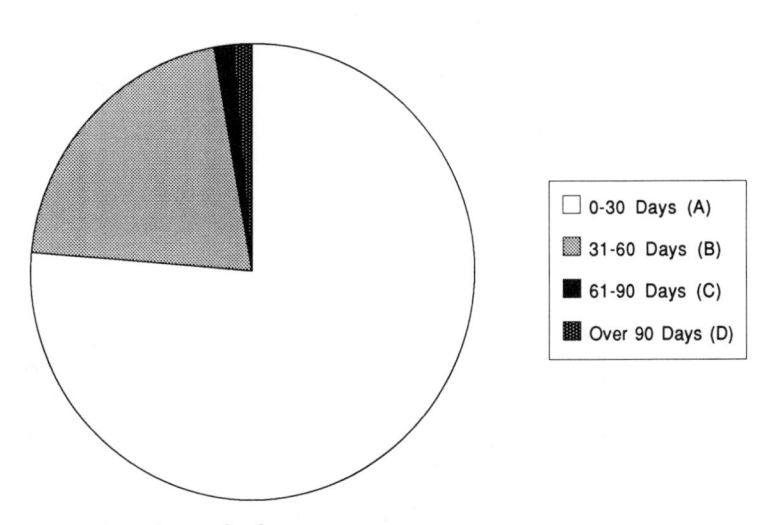

6.1 A pie chart of relative percentages

The Cell Contents and Formulas

	A	B	C	D	E
1	ACCOUNTS RECEIVABL				
2					
3	Invoice	Company	Date Due	Amount	Age
4	31456	Byron's	32530	245.76	=NOW()-C4
5	222	Rusty's	32516	786.89	=NOW()-C5
6	22223	Pickney School	32499	43.78	=NOW()-C6
7	43125	H&H Insurance	32485	44.23	=NOW()-C7
8	3321	Glen's Coins	32470	123.32	=NOW()-C8
9	2311	Mickey's Bikes	32470	223.56	=NOW()-C9
10	13454	Gas	32470	67.98	=NOW()-C10
11	45333	Whel's Lumber	32470	36.54	=NOW()-C11
12	312	A. Smith	32439	2112.45	=NOW()-C12
13	676	L-Mart	32439	332.45	=NOW()-C13
14					
15					
16	Number of Outstanding Invoices			=COUNT(B4:B13)	
17	Total Amount Due			=SUM(D4:D13)	
18					
19					
20	Summary Table				
21					
22	Time Period	Amount Due	Number Due		
23					
24					
25	0-30 Days (A)	=DSUM(Database,4,A34:A35)	=DCOUNTA(Database,5,A34:A35)		
26	31-60 Days (B)	=DSUM(Database,4,B34:B35)	=DCOUNTA(Database,5,B34:B35)		
27	61-90 Days (C)	=DSUM(Database,4,C34:C35)	=DCOUNTA(Database,5,C34:C35)		
28	Over 90 Days (D)	=DSUM(Database,4,D34:D35)	=DCOUNTA(Database,5,D34:D35)		
29					
30	Total	=SUM(B25:B28)	=SUM(C25:C28)		
31					
32	Criterion Table				
33					
34	Age	Age	Age	Age	
35	=AND(E4>0,E4<30)	=AND(E4>=31,E4<=60)	=AND(E4>=61,E4<=90)	=E4>=90	

Accounts Payable

	A	B	C	D	E
1	ACCOUNTS PAYABLE				
2					
3	Invoice	Company	Date Due	Amount	Age
4	345	Bay Leaf	1/5/89	$534.78	27
5	21342	Joe's Bakery	1/10/89	$89.45	22
6	454	Jayhawk Bowl	12/15/88	$213.45	48
7	333	William's	11/15/88	$34.87	78
8	454	R&R	11/1/88	$32.78	92
9	1	Your Child	1/15/89	$221.78	17
10	1232	Tin Pan Alley	1/20/89	$743.09	12
11	56455	Standing Con	12/25/88	$315.77	38
12	677	Leni's Fudge	1/15/89	$314.66	17
13	678	EPR	1/15/89	$50.50	17
14					
15					
16		Number of Outstanding Invoices		10	
17		Total Amount Due		$2,551.13	
18					
19					
20	Summary Table				
21					
22	Time Period	Amount	Number		
23		Due	Due		
24					
25	0-30 Days (A)	$1,954.26	6		
26	31-60 Days (B)	$529.22	2		
27	61-90 Days (C)	$34.87	1		
28	Over 90 Days (D)	$32.78	1		
29					
30	Total	$2,551.13	10		
31					
32	Criterion Table				
33					
34	Age	Age	Age	Age	
35	TRUE	FALSE	FALSE	FALSE	

What the Spreadsheet Does

Every business has invoices that need to be paid. This spreadsheet keeps track of invoices that are due and past due and uses a criterion table to sum up amounts by number of days past due. The criterion table is based on periods of 0–30 days, 31–60 days, 61–90 days, and over 90 days. As in many businesses, this spreadsheet discounts any payments by 2% that are made within 30 days. The spreadsheet uses the **=NOW**, **=DSUM**, and **=DAVG** formulas to compute the age of the bill and the sum.

Excel Business Applications

Working with the Spreadsheet

To work with this spreadsheet, you need to enter the following information.

Col A invoice number
Col B name
Col C date due
Col D amount due

When the spreadsheet is complete, it will provide you with the following information.

Col E   age (in days) between date due and current date
B25...B28   amount due by 30-day period
B30   total amount due
C30   number of outstanding invoices

What It Looks Like

Figure 6.2 shows an exploded pie chart with the relative percentages of outstanding invoices for 0–30 days, 31–60 days, 61–90 days, and over 90 days.

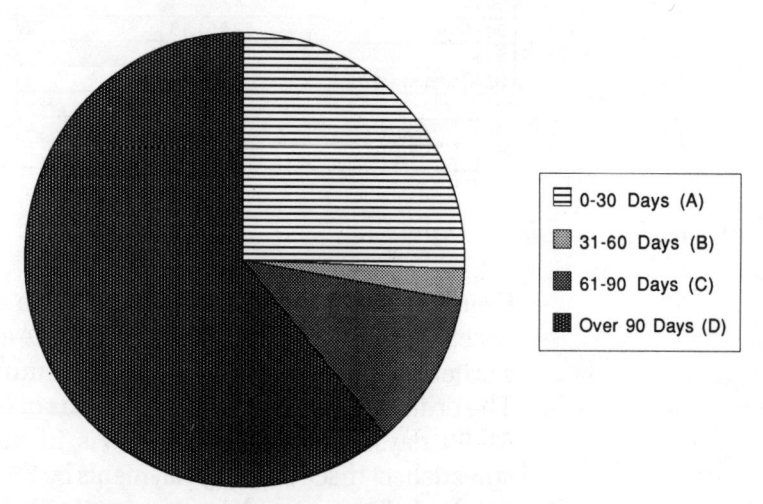

6.2 An exploded pie chart of relative percentages

The Cell Contents and Formulas

	A	B	C	D	E
1	ACCOUNTS PAYABLE				
2					
3	Invoice	Company	Date Due	Amount	Age
4	345	Bay Leaf	32513	534.78	=NOW()-C4
5	21342	Joe's Bakery	32518	89.45	=NOW()-C5
6	454	Jayhawk Bowl	32492	213.45	=NOW()-C6
7	333	William's	32462	34.87	=NOW()-C7
8	454	R&R	32448	32.78	=NOW()-C8
9	1	Your Child	32523	221.78	=NOW()-C9
10	1232	Tin Pan Alley	32528	743.09	=NOW()-C10
11	56455	Standing Con	32502	315.77	=NOW()-C11
12	677	Leni's Fudge	32523	314.66	=NOW()-C12
13	678	EPR	32523	50.5	=NOW()-C13
14					
15					
16		Number of Outstanding Invoices		=COUNTA(B4:B13)	
17		Total Amount Due		=SUM(D4:D13)	
18					
19					
20	Summary Table				
21					
22	Time Period	Amount	Number		
23		Due	Due		
24					
25	0-30 Days (A)	=DSUM(A3:E13,4,A34:A35)	=DCOUNTA(A3:E13,5,A34:A35)		
26	31-60 Days (B)	=DSUM(A3:E13,4,B34:B35)	=DCOUNTA(A3:E13,5,B34:B35)		
27	61-90 Days (C)	=DSUM(A3:E13,4,C34:C35)	=DCOUNTA(A3:E13,5,C34:C35)		
28	Over 90 Days (D)	=DSUM(A3:E13,4,D34:D35)	=DCOUNTA(A3:E13,5,D34:D35)		
29					
30	Total	=SUM(B25:B28)	=SUM(C25:C28)		
31					
32	Criterion Table				
33					
34	Age	Age	Age	Age	
35	=AND(E4>0,E4<30)	=AND(E4>=31,E4<60)	=AND(E4>=61,E4<90)	=E4>=90	

Excel Business Applications

Balance Sheet and Ratio Analyses

	A	B	C	D	E	F	G	H
1	BALANCE SHEET AND RATIO ANALYSES							
2								
3					J&R Manufacturing			
4					101-598 W.57th Street			
5					Seattle, WA 12345			
6					(314)-878-2400			
7								
8				Quarter 1	Quarter 2	Quarter 3	Quarter 4	Total
9	ASSETS							
10								
11	Cash			$899,354	$1,876,453	$987,096	$994,097	$4,757,000
12	Market Securities			$298,576	$372,645	$172,645	$253,456	$1,097,322
13	Bonds			$98,465	$101,987	$100,987	$99,067	$400,506
14	Treasury			$20,000	$40,000	$30,000	$20,000	$110,000
15	Accounts Receivable			$286,756	$354,676	$325,676	$298,765	$1,265,873
16	Inventory Value			$789,465	$867,543	$657,486	$657,887	$2,972,381
17	Prepayments/Taxes			$150,987	$104,987	$135,768	$107,987	$499,729
18								
19	Total Current Assets			$2,543,603	$3,718,291	$2,409,658	$2,431,259	$11,102,811
20								
21	Equipment			$645,978	$645,978	$645,978	$645,978	$2,583,912
22	Property			$1,500,000	$1,500,000	$1,500,000	$1,500,000	$6,000,000
23	Depreciation			($62,800)	($67,196)	($71,900)	($76,933)	($278,828)
24								
25	Total Fixed Assets			$2,083,178	$2,078,782	$2,074,078	$2,069,045	$8,305,084
26								
27	TOTAL ASSETS			$4,626,781	$5,797,073	$4,483,736	$4,500,304	$19,407,895
28								
29	LIABILITIES							
30	Notes Payable			$65,748	$67,345	$90,867	$87,456	$311,416
31	Employee's Retirement			$2,345,756	$2,978,654	$2,876,456	$2,313,453	$10,514,319
32	Taxes On Income			$89,675	$78,454	$84,567	$91,243	$343,939
33	Wages			$213,453	$241,234	$231,456	$243,453	$929,596
34	Mortgage			$5,968	$5,968	$5,968	$5,968	$23,872
35	Loans			$87,456	$65,375	$54,768	$45,654	$253,253
36	Long Term Debt			$354,674	$453,123	$543,234	$453,654	$1,804,685
37								
38	TOTAL LIABILITIES			$3,162,730	$3,890,153	$3,887,316	$3,240,881	$14,181,080
39								
40	STOCKHOLDER'S EQUITY							
41	Common Stock			$1,134,222	$187,657	$165,467	$176,789	$1,664,135
42								
43	TOTAL EQUITY			$1,134,222	$1,875,641	$1,654,345	$1,231,232	$5,895,440
44								
45	TOTAL LIABILITIES AND EQUITY			$4,296,952	$5,765,794	$5,541,661	$4,472,113	$20,076,520
46								
47	RATIOS							
48	Current Ratio			1.46	1.49	1.15	1.39	1.37
49	(Assets/Liabilities)							
50	Equity Ratio			0.25	0.32	0.37	0.27	0.30
51	(Equity/Assets)							
52	Debt/Equity Ratio			2.79	2.07	2.35	2.63	2.46

Accounting Worksheets

What the Spreadsheet Does

Tracking assets and liabilities is a major function that spreadsheets can help perform. This spreadsheet computes assets and liabilities by quarter. In any balancing sheet, the assets should be equal to the sum of the liabilities plus the equities.

This spreadsheet can be easily modified to track months rather than quarters just by adding additional columns and labels where necessary. Ratio analyses, which are sometimes included as part of a consolidated balance sheet, are also computed.

Working with the Spreadsheet

To work with this spreadsheet, you need to enter the following information.

D11...G17	assets listed by quarter
D30...G36	liabilities listed by quarter
D43...G43	equity listed by quarter

When the spreadsheet is complete, it will provide you with the following information.

H19	total current assets
H25	total fixed assets
H27	total assets
H38	total liabilities
H43	total equities
H45	total liabilities plus equities
D48...H48	current ratio
D50...H50	equity ratio
D52...H52	debt/equity ratio

Excel Business Applications

What It Looks Like

Figure 6.3 is a bar chart that shows level of current assets, liabilities, and equities by quarter.

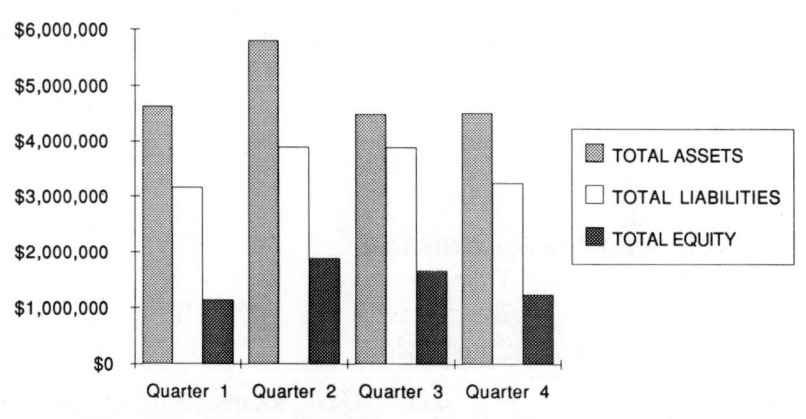

6.3 A bar chart of assets, liabilities, and equities

The Cell Contents and Formulas

	A	B	C	D	E	F
1	BALANCE SHEET AND RATIO ANALYS					
2						
3			J&R Manufacturi			
4			101-598 W.57th			
5			Seattle, WA 123			
6			(314)-878-240			
7						
8			Quarter 2	Quarter 3	Quarter 4	Total
9	ASSETS					
10		Quarter 1				
11	Cash	899354	1876453	987098	994097	=SUM(B11:E11)
12	Market Securities	298576	372845	172845	253456	=SUM(B12:E12)
13	Bonds	98465	101987	100987	99067	=SUM(B13:E13)
14	Treasury	20000	40000	30000	20000	=SUM(B14:E14)
15	Accounts Receivable	286756	354676	325676	298765	=SUM(B15:E15)
16	Inventory Value	789465	867543	657486	657887	=SUM(B16:E16)
17	Prepayments/Taxes	150987	104987	135768	107987	=SUM(B17:E17)
18						
19	Total Current Assets	=SUM(B11:B17)	=SUM(C11:C17)	=SUM(D11:D17)	=SUM(E11:E17)	=SUM(B19:E19)
20						
21	Equipment	645978	645978	645978	645978	=SUM(B21:E21)
22	Property	1500000	1500000	1500000	1500000	=SUM(B22:E22)
23	Depreciation	-62800	=B23*1.07	=C23*1.07	=D23*1.07	=SUM(B23:E23)
24						
25	Total Fixed Assets	=SUM(B21:B23)	=SUM(C21:C23)	=SUM(D21:D23)	=SUM(E21:E23)	=SUM(B25:E25)
26						
27	TOTAL ASSETS	=SUM(B19+B25)	=SUM(C19+C25)	=SUM(D19+D25)	=SUM(E19+E25)	=SUM(B27:E27)
28						
29	LIABILITIES					
30	Notes Payable	65748	67345	90867	87456	=SUM(B30:E30)
31	Employee's Retirement	2345756	2978654	2876456	2313453	=SUM(B31:E31)
32	Taxes On Income	89675	78454	84567	91243	=SUM(B32:E32)
33	Wages	213453	241234	231456	243453	=SUM(B33:E33)
34	Mortgage	5968	5968	5968	5968	=SUM(B34:E34)
35	Loans	87456	65375	54768	45654	=SUM(B35:E35)
36	Long Term Debt	354674	453123	543234	453654	=SUM(B36:E36)
37						
38	TOTAL LIABILITIES	=SUM(B30:B36)	=SUM(C30:C36)	=SUM(D30:D36)	=SUM(E30:E36)	=SUM(B38:E38)
39						
40	STOCKHOLDERS EQUITY					
41	Common Stock	1134222	187857	165467	176789	=SUM(B41:E41)
42						
43	TOTAL EQUITY	=(B41)	1875641	1654345	1231232	=SUM(B43:E43)
44						
45	TOTAL LIABILITIES AND EQUITY	=SUM(B38+B43)	=SUM(C38+C43)	=SUM(D38+D43)	=SUM(E38+E43)	=SUM(B45:E45)
46						
47	RATIOS					
48	Current Ratio	=(B27/B38)	=(C27/C38)	=(D27/D38)	=(E27/E38)	=AVERAGE(B48:E48)
49	(Assets/Liabilities)					
50	Equity Ratio	=(B43/B27)	=(C43/C27)	=(D43/D27)	=(E43/E27)	=AVERAGE(B50:E50)
51	(Equity/Assets)					
52	Debt/Equity Ratio	=(B38/B43)	=(C38/C43)	=(D38/D43)	=(E38/E43)	=AVERAGE(B52:E52)
53	(Liabilities/Equity)					

Excel Business Applications

Consolidated Income

	A	B	C	D
1	CONSOLIDATED INCOME			
2				
3				
4	Number Of Outstanding Shares			$4,546,786.00
5				
6	Net Sales			$54,678,651.18
7	Cost of Goods Sold			$39,456,690.78
8				
9	Gross Margin			$15,221,960.40
10	Administrative Expenses			$4,545,768.12
11				
12	Operating Income			$10,676,192.28
13	Operating Expenses			$243,879.33
14				
15	Income Before Profit Sharing			$10,432,312.95
16	Employee Profit Sharing			$3,465,918.67
17				
18	Income Before Taxes			$6,966,394.28
19	Current Taxes			$1,499,867.45
20	Deferred Taxes			($7,123.98)
21				
22	Net Income			$5,459,402.85
23	Net Sales			$54,678,651.18
24	Income per Share			$1.20

What the Spreadsheet Does

A consolidated income statement is usually the main component of an annual report and appears at the beginning. This spreadsheet computes income total, plus other important factors such as gross margins, net income, and income per share.

Working with the Spreadsheet

To work with this spreadsheet, you need to enter the following information.

- **D4** number of outstanding shares
- **D6** net sales

Accounting Worksheets

D7 costs of goods sold
D10 administrative expenses
D13 operating expenses
D15 income before profit sharing
D16 employee profit-sharing plan
D18 income before taxes
D19 current taxes
D20 deferred taxes

When the spreadsheet is complete, it will provide you with the following information.

D9 gross margins
D12 operating income
D22 net income
D23 net sales
D24 income per share

What It Looks Like

Figure 6.4 is an exploding pie chart that illustrates the important ratio of net sales to net income.

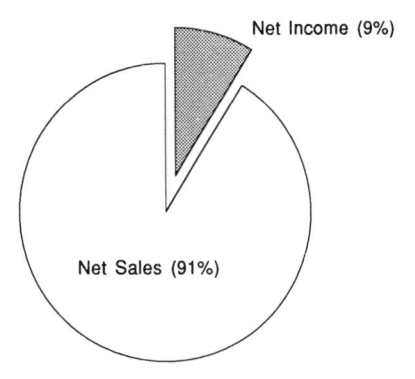

6.4 Net sales to net income

Excel Business Applications

The Cell Contents and Formulas

	A	B	C	D
1	CONSOLIDATED INCOME			
2				
3				
4	Number Of Outstanding Shares			4546786
5				
6	Net Sales			54678651.18
7	Cost of Goods Sold			39456690.78
8				
9	Gross Margin			=D6-D7
10	Administrative Expenses			4545768.12
11				
12	Operating Income			=D9-D10
13	Operating Expenses			243879.33
14				
15	Income Before Profit Sharing			=D12-D13
16	Employee Profit Sharing			3465918.67
17				
18	Income Before Taxes			=D15-D16
19	Current Taxes			1499867.45
20	Deferred Taxes			-7123.98
21				
22	Net Income			=D18-D19+D20
23	Net Sales			=D6
24	Income per Share			=D22/D4

Accounting Worksheets

Fixed Assets Management

	A	B	C	D	E	F	G
1	FIXED ASSETS MANAGEMENT						
2							
3	Depreciation Schedule						
4							
5	Years	Rate					
6	0-3	0.07					
7	4-Apr	0.11					
8	7-Jul	0.15					
9	>9	0.18					
10	-	-	-	-	-	-	-
11	Item	Code	Purchase	Date of	Location	Age	Current
12			Price	Purchase			Value
13	-	-	-	-	-	-	-
14	Car #1	324	$8,798	3/10/79	Bailey	10.24	$7,214
15	Car #2	367	$9,674	4/1/81	Hoch	8.18	$8,223
16	Car #3	321	$11,231	3/27/86	Williams	3.19	$10,445
17	Typewriter	453-6	$399	8/7/83	Gaines	5.83	$355
18	Desk	a23	$125	4/5/85	VanVel	4.16	$111
19	Desk	a25	$250	4/5/85	Monty	4.16	$223
20	Fixtures	12-34	$300	1/3/81	Otts	8.42	$255
21	Cabinets	c34/c66	$240	5/10/85	El	4.07	$214
22	Cooler	4356	$3,000	2/3/85	Dennis	4.33	$2,670
23	Packer	6777	$560	2/4/85	Bob	4.33	$498
24							
25							
26	Total Purchase Value			$34,577			
27	Total Depreciated Value			$30,208			
28	Average Depreciation Time			5.69			

What the Spreadsheet Does

Depreciation is an important part of managing assets as well as keeping track of such factors as age, location, and purchase date. This spreadsheet calculates a depreciated price according to the rates (percentage of depreciation) that you supply. If you want to change the years or rates, you need to rewrite the formula in cell I15 and copy it where appropriate.

Excel Business Applications

Working with the Spreadsheet

To work with this spreadsheet, you need to enter the following information.

Col A	item description
Col B	code for item number, inventory, etc.
A6...B9	rate of depreciation by time
Col C	purchase price
Col D	date of purchase
Col E	location

When the spreadsheet is complete, it will provide you with the following information.

Col F	age in years
Col G	current value
D26	total purchase price
D27	total current value
D28	average age

What It Looks Like

The pie chart in Figure 6.5 examines the relative current versus original values (in dollars) for the fixed assets.

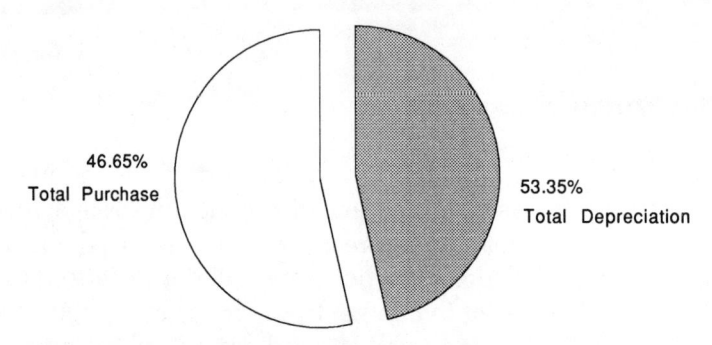

46.65%
Total Purchase

53.35%
Total Depreciation

6.5 Current versus original value

The Cell Contents and Formulas

	A	B	C	D	E	F
1	FIXED ASSETS MANAGEMENT					
2						
3	Depreciation Schedule					
4						
5	Years	Rate				
6	0-3	0.07				
7	4-6	0.11				
8	7-9	0.15				
9	>9	0.18				
10	-			-		
11	Item	Code	Purchase	Date of	Location	Age
12			Price	Purchase		
13	-	-	-	-	-	-
14	Car #1	324	8798	28924	Bailey	=(NOW()-D14)/365
15	Car #2	367	9674	29677	Hoch	=(NOW()-D15)/365
16	Car #3	321	11231	31498	Williams	=(NOW()-D16)/365
17	Typewriter	453-6	399	30535	Gaines	=(NOW()-D17)/365
18	Desk	a23	125	31142	VanVel	=(NOW()-D18)/365
19	Desk	a25	250	31142	Monty	=(NOW()-D19)/365
20	Fixtures	12-34	300	29589	Otts	=(NOW()-D20)/365
21	Cabinets	c34/c66	240	31177	El	=(NOW()-D21)/365
22	Cooler	4356	3000	31081	Dennis	=(NOW()-D22)/365
23	Packer	6777	560	31082	Bob	=(NOW()-D23)/365
24						
25						
26	Total Purchase Value		=SUM(C14:C23)			
27	Total Depreciated Value		=SUM(G14:G23)			
28	Average Depreciation Time		=AVERAGE(F14:F23)			

The Cell Contents and Formulas (Continued)

	G
1	
2	
3	
4	
5	
6	
7	
8	
9	
10	
11	Current
12	Value
13	
14	=IF(F14>9,C14*(1-$B$9),IF(F14>7,C14*(1-$B$8),IF(F14>4,C14*(1-$B$7),IF(F14>0,C14*(1-$B$6),C14))))
15	=IF(F15>9,C15*(1-$B$9),IF(F15>7,C15*(1-$B$8),IF(F15>4,C15*(1-$B$7),IF(F15>0,C15*(1-$B$6),C15))))
16	=IF(F16>9,C16*(1-$B$9),IF(F16>7,C16*(1-$B$8),IF(F16>4,C16*(1-$B$7),IF(F16>0,C16*(1-$B$6),C16))))
17	=IF(F17>9,C17*(1-$B$9),IF(F17>7,C17*(1-$B$8),IF(F17>4,C17*(1-$B$7),IF(F17>0,C17*(1-$B$6),C17))))
18	=IF(F18>9,C18*(1-$B$9),IF(F18>7,C18*(1-$B$8),IF(F18>4,C18*(1-$B$7),IF(F18>0,C18*(1-$B$6),C18))))
19	=IF(F19>9,C19*(1-$B$9),IF(F19>7,C19*(1-$B$8),IF(F19>4,C19*(1-$B$7),IF(F19>0,C19*(1-$B$6),C19))))
20	=IF(F20>9,C20*(1-$B$9),IF(F20>7,C20*(1-$B$8),IF(F20>4,C20*(1-$B$7),IF(F20>0,C20*(1-$B$6),C20))))
21	=IF(F21>9,C21*(1-$B$9),IF(F21>7,C21*(1-$B$8),IF(F21>4,C21*(1-$B$7),IF(F21>0,C21*(1-$B$6),C21))))
22	=IF(F22>9,C22*(1-$B$9),IF(F22>7,C22*(1-$B$8),IF(F22>4,C22*(1-$B$7),IF(F22>0,C22*(1-$B$6),C22))))
23	=IF(F23>9,C23*(1-$B$9),IF(F23>7,C23*(1-$B$8),IF(F23>4,C23*(1-$B$7),IF(F23>0,C23*(1-$B$6),C23))))
24	
25	
26	
27	
28	

Inventory Count, Location, and Control

What the Spreadsheet Does

Inventory is a crucial part of any business, and adequate data about the supply of products needs to be maintained in order for the business to have available what clients and customers need. This spreadsheet maintains a database of inventory items, price, location, availability, and vendor.

Working with the Spreadsheet

To work with this spreadsheet, you need to enter the following information.

Col C	item name
Col D	item number
Col E	item bin location
Col F	item price
Col G	item quantity
Col H	quantity on hand
Col I	quantity needed

When the spreadsheet is complete, it will provide you with the following information.

Col J	signal to reorder
Col K	stock value
H20, H27, H33	total quantity available by category
K36	total value of inventory

	A	B	C	D	E	F	G	H	I	J	K
1	INVENTORY COUNT, LOCATION AND CONTROL										
2											
3				Wilson's Stationery							
4				452 Acton Street							
5				Chicago, Illinois 12345							
6				(312) 123-3456							
7											
8											
9				Item	Bin	Item		Quantity	Quantity	Reorder	Wholesale
10	Category			Number	Location	Price	Lot	On Hand	Needed	(1=y/2=n)	Stock Value
11											
12											
13											
14	Paper		20 lb. bond	P375-01	A7	$5.60	ream	72	60	2	$403.20
15			18 lb. bond	P375-02	A7	$6.20	ream	60	60	2	$372.00
16			15 lb. bond	P376-02	A8	$5.10	ream	62	60	2	$316.20
17			Carbon	P377	A10	$3.80	ream	55	30	2	$209.00
18			Carbonless	P378	A11	$4.87	ream	45	30	2	$219.15
19											
20					Category	Total		294	240		
21											
22											
23	Covers		Plastic	C301	D15	$8.00	doz	124	150	1	$992.00
24			Spiral	C302	D15	$12.00	doz	213	200	2	$2,556.00
25			Clip	C303	D15	$9.50	doz	224	200	2	$2,128.00
26											
27					Category	Total		561	550		
28											
29	Pens		blue	P234	S22	$28.80	gross	28	30	1	$806.40
30			red	P235	S22	$28.80	gross	32	30	2	$921.60
31			black	P236	S23	$28.80	gross	33	30	2	$950.40
32											
33					Category	Total		93	90		
34											
35							Total Value of Inventory				$9,873.95
36											

Accounting Worksheets

The Cell Contents and Formulas

	A	B	C	D
1	INVENTORY COUNT, LOCATION AND CONTROL			
2				
3				Wilson's Stationery
4				452 Acton Street
5				Chicago, Illinois 1234
6				(312) 123-3456
7				
8				
9			Item	Item
10	Category		Name	Number
11				
12				
13				
14	Paper		20 lb. bond	P375-01
15			18 lb. bond	P375-02
16			15 lb. bond	P376-02
17			Carbon	P377
18			Carbonless	P378
19				
20				
21				
22				
23	Covers		Plastic	C301
24			Spiral	C302
25			Clip	C303
26				
27				
28				
29	Pens		blue	P234
30			red	P235
31			black	P236
32				
33				
34				
35				
36				

Excel Business Applications

The Cell Contents and Formulas (Continued)

	E	F	G	H	I	J	K
1							
2							
3							
4							
5							
6							
7							
8							
9	Bin	Item	Lot	Quantity	Quantity	Reorder	Wholesale
10	Location	Price		On Hand	Needed	(1=y/2=n)	Stock Value
11							
12							
13							
14	A7	5.6	ream	72	60	=IF(I14>H14,1,2)	=F14*H14
15	A7	6.2	ream	60	60	=IF(I15>H15,1,2)	=F15*H15
16	A8	5.1	ream	62	60	=IF(I16>H16,1,2)	=F16*H16
17	A10	3.8	ream	55	30	=IF(I17>H17,1,2)	=F17*H17
18	A11	4.87	ream	45	30	=IF(I18>H18,1,2)	=F18*H18
19							
20	Category Total			=SUM(H14:H18)	=SUM(I14:I18)		
21							
22							
23	D15	8	doz	124	150	=IF(I23>H23,1,2)	=F23*H23
24	D15	12	doz	213	200	=IF(I24>H24,1,2)	=F24*H24
25	D15	9.5	doz	224	200	=IF(I25>H25,1,2)	=F25*H25
26							
27	Category Total			=SUM(H23:H25)	=SUM(I23:I25)		
28							
29	S22	28.8	gross	28	30	=IF(I29>H29,1,2)	=F29*H29
30	S22	28.8	gross	32	30	=IF(I30>H30,1,2)	=F30*H30
31	S23	28.8	gross	33	30	=IF(I31>H31,1,2)	=F31*H31
32							
33	Category Total			=SUM(H29:H31)	=SUM(I29:I31)		
34							
35							
36				Total Value of			=SUM(K14:K35)

Accounting Worksheets

Net Worth

	A	B	C	D	E	F
1	NET WORTH					
2						
3		Assets			Liabilities	
4						
5	Cash		$4,512	Mortgage		$110,000
6	Checking Balance		$345	Loans		$2,500
7	Savings Balance		$6,786	Taxes		$4,500
8	Value of Stocks		$0	Charge Account		$450
9	Value of Bonds		$0	Charge Cards		$250
10	Value of Savings			Alimony		$0
11		Bonds	$500	Child Support		$0
12	Life Insurance		$8,894	Other		$0
13	Real Estate		$112,987			
14	Retirement Funds		$35,000	TOTAL		$117,700
15	Household Goods		$35,000			
16	Collectibles		$1,000			
17	Automobile		$7,500			
18	Other Vehicles		$3,500			
19	Personal Property		$2,500			
20	Tax Refunds		$1,500			
21	Cash Owed You		$250			
22	Other Assets		$0			
23						
24	TOTAL		$220,274			
25						
26	NET WORTH		$102,574			

What the Spreadsheet Does

This spreadsheet computes your personal net worth by subtracting total liabilities from total assets. This information is often requested on loan applications and other financial forms.

Excel Business Applications

Working with the Spreadsheet

To work with this spreadsheet, you need to enter the following information.

Col C assets
Col F liabilities

When the spreadsheet is complete, it will provide you with the following information.

C24 total assets
C26 net worth
F14 total liabilities

The Cell Contents and Formulas

	A	B	C	D	E	F
1	NET WORTH					
2						
3		Assets			Liabilities	
4						
5	Cash		4512	Mortgage		110000
6	Checking Balance		345	Loans		2500
7	Savings Balance		6786	Taxes		4500
8	Value of Stocks		0	Charge Accounts		450
9	Value of Bonds		0	Charge Cards		250
10	Value of Savings			Alimony		0
11	Bonds		500	Child Support		0
12	Life Insurance		8894	Other		0
13	Real Estate		112987			
14	Retirement Funds		35000	TOTAL		=SUM(F5:F12)
15	Household Goods		35000			
16	Collectibles		1000			
17	Automobile		7500			
18	Other Vehicles		3500			
19	Personal Property		2500			
20	Tax Refunds		1500			
21	Cash Owed You		250			
22	Other Assets		0			
23						
24	TOTAL		=SUM(C5:C22)			
25						
26	NET WORTH		=C24-F14			

Excel Business Applications

Promissory Note/Loan Application Worksheet

	A	B	C	D	E	F	G	H
1	PROMISSORY NOTE/LOAN APPLICATION WORK SHEET							
2								
3	Client Information			Lender Information				
4								
5	Name	Fed Van		Name		Universal Bank		
6	Address	2713 Tennessee		Address		5319 Wilson Avenue		
7	City/State/Zip	Wison, NV		City/State/Zip		Reno, NV		
8	Phone	(211) 345-6719		Phone		(211) 711-7171		
9								
10	Description of Collateral:							
11	1985 Delta-88 Cutlass							
12	10 $1,000 certificates of deposit							
13								
14	Date Finance Charges		Amount	Interest		Length of		Monthly
15	Begin To Accrue		Borrowed	Rate		Loan (Months)		Payment
16								
17	4/15/87		($5,000.00)	16.00%		12		$453.65
18								
19	Total Balance Refinanced					$5,000.00		
20		New Disbursements To:						
21								
22	Total Proceeds Of Loan					$5,000.00		
23								
24	Additional Charges							
25		1. Credit Life Insurance				$17.15		
26		2. Disability Insurance				$2.58		
27		3. Property Insurance						
28		4. Filing And Releasing Charges				$25.00		
29		5. License, Title And Registration						
30								
31		Total Additional Charges				$44.73		
32								
33	Total Charges					$5,089.46		
34	Finance Charge					$453.65		
35			TOTAL PAYMENTS			$5,443.85		

What the Spreadsheet Does

This spreadsheet is a template for a loan application and requires the completion of information regarding the note, due dates, number of payments, and other necessary information including net worth.

If you want to add specific legal clauses concerning signatures, conditions, and waiver of responsibilities, you could use this form as a loan application itself.

Accounting Worksheets

Working with the Spreadsheet

To work with this spreadsheet, you need to enter the following information.

A10	description of collateral (if any)
A17	date finance charges begin to accrue
B5	client name
B6,B7	client address
B8	client telephone
C17	total borrowed
D17	interest rate
F5	name
F6,F7	lender address
F8	lender telephone
F17	length of loan (months)
F19	total balance refinanced
F21	new disbursements to
F25	credit life insurance
F26	disability insurance
F27	property insurance
F28	filing and releasing charges
F29	license, title, and registration

When the spreadsheet is complete, it will provide you with the following information.

F31	total additional charges
F33	total charges
F34	finance charge
F35	total payments
H17	monthly payment

Excel Business Applications

The Cell Contents and Formulas

	A	B	C
1	PROMISSORY NOTE/LOAN APPLICATION WORK SHEET		
2			
3	Client Information		
4			
5	Name	Fed Van	
6	Address	2713 Tennessee	
7	City/State/Zip	Wison, NV	
8	Phone	(211) 345-6719	
9			
10	Description of Collateral:		
11	1985 Delta-88 Cutlass		
12	10 $1,000 certificates of deposit		
13			
14	Date Finance Charges		Amount
15	Begin To Accrue		Borrowed
16			
17	4/15/87		-5000
18			
19	Total Balance Refinanced		
20		New Disbursements To:	
21			
22	Total Proceeds Of Loan		
23			
24	Additional Charges		
25		1. Credit Life Insurance	
26		2. Disability Insurance	
27		3. Property Insurance	
28		4. Filing And Releasing Charges	
29		5. License, Title And Registration	
30			
31		Total Additional Charges	
32			
33	Total Charges		
34	Finance Charge		
35			TOTAL PAYMENTS

Accounting Worksheets

	D	E	F	G	H
1					
2					
3	Lender Information				
4					
5	Name		Universal Bank		
6	Address		5319 Wilson Avenue		
7	City/State/Zip		Reno, NV		
8	Phone		(211) 711-7171		
9					
10					
11					
12					
13					
14	Interest		Length of		Monthly
15	Rate		Loan (Months)		Payment
16					
17	0.16		12		=PMT(D17/12,F17,C17)
18					
19			5000		
20					
21					
22			5000		
23					
24					
25			17.15		
26			2.58		
27					
28			25		
29					
30					
31			=SUM(F25:F29)		
32					
33			=SUM(F22:F31)		
34			=H17		
35			=H17*F17		

Excel Business Applications

Royalty Computation

	A	B	C	D	E	F
1	Royalty					
2		Selling Price	Net	Royalty Rate	Copies Sold	Income
3	Item #1	$24.95	50%	2.00%	3675	$916.91
4	Item #2	$19.95	50%	10.00%	10023	$9,997.94
5	Item #3	$14.95	50%	12.50%	3321	$3,103.06
6	Item #4	$18.95	50%	10.00%	44213	$41,891.82
7	Item #5	$21.95	50%	10.00%	6788	$7,449.83

What the Spreadsheet Does

This spreadsheet computes the royalty for any item, taking into account important factors such as royalty rate and selling price.

Working with the Spreadsheet

To work with this spreadsheet, you need to enter the following information.

Col B selling price
Col C net price
Col D royalty rate
Col E copies sold

When the spreadsheet is complete, it will provide you with the following information.

Col F income

Accounting Worksheets

The Cell Contents and Formulas

	A	B	C
1	Royalty		
2		Selling Price	Net
3	Item #1	24.95	0.5
4	Item #2	19.95	0.5
5	Item #3	14.95	0.5
6	Item #4	18.95	0.5
7	Item #5	21.95	0.5

	D	E	F
1			
2	Royalty Rate	Copies Sold	Income
3	0.02	3675	=B3*C3*D3*E3
4	0.1	10023	=B4*C4*D4*E4
5	0.125	3321	=B5*C5*D5*E5
6	0.1	44213	=B6*C6*D6*E6
7	0.1	6788	=B7*C7*D7*E7

Excel Business Applications

A Simple Invoice

	A	B	C	D	E	F	G	H	I	J
1	A SIMPLE INVOICE									
2										
3	To: Sunflower Associates									
4	145 Massachusetts Street									
5	Colby, KS 12345									
6										
7	Account # 153-36-0331									
8										
9	Invoice # 12-34-56									
10										
11	Date:									
12										
13										
14	Item #	Quantity	Quantity	Description		Price	Total			
15		Ordered	Sent				This Item			
16										
17	19687	10	9	capacitor		0.85	$7.65			
18	46575	12	11	resistor		0.79	$9.48			
19	43256	9	8	transistors		0.55	$4.95			
20	46478	20	18	coil cord		0.40	$8.00			
21	56544	5	4	boards		1.87	$9.35			
22										
23					CURRENT TOTAL DUE		$39.43			
24					CURRENT PAST DUE		$14.50			
25	Previous Balance Due;				TOTAL DUE		$53.93			
26										
27	30 days	$14.50	60 Days	$0.00		90 Days	$0.00			

What the Spreadsheet Does

This spreadsheet is a template for preparing an invoice. It also carries over from any previous invoices any past accounts for 30, 60, and 90 days.

Accounting Worksheets

Working with the Spreadsheet

To work with this spreadsheet, you need to enter the following information.

B7	the client's account number
B27,D27,G27	past due funds for 30, 60, and 90 days
B11	the date of the invoice
B3,B4,B5	client information (e.g., name, address, etc.)
Col A	item number
Col B	the quantity ordered
Col C	the quantity sent
Col D	item description
Col F	per price piece for the item

When the spreadsheet is complete, it will provide you with the following information.

Col G	total amount per piece ordered
G23	current total due
G24	current past due
G25	total due

The Cell Contents and Formulas

	A	B	C	D	E	F	G
1	A SIMPLE INVOICE						
2							
3	To: Sunflower Associates						
4	145 Massachusetts Str						
5	Colby, KS 12345						
6							
7	Account # 153-36-0331						
8							
9	Invoice # 12-34-56						
10							
11	Date:						
12							
13							
14	Item #	Quantity	Quantity	Description		Price	Total
15		Ordered	Sent				This Item
16							
17	19687	10	9	capacitor		0.85	=C17*F17
18	46575	12	11	resistor		0.79	=B18*F18
19	43256	9	8	transistors		0.55	=B19*F19
20	46478	20	18	coil cord		0.4	=B20*F20
21	56544	5	4	boards		1.87	=B21*F21
22							
23					CURRENT TOTAL DUE		=SUM(G17:G21)
24					CURRENT PAST DUE		=SUM(B27+D27+G27)
25	Previous Balance Due:				TOTAL DUE		=SUM(G23+G24)
26							
27	30 days	14.5	60 Days	0		90 Days	0

108

7

Forecasting Worksheets

Charting Market Trends as a Moving Average

What the Spreadsheet Does

Examining the trend in a market can be done in a variety of ways. One of the most popular is to use a moving average. This spreadsheet computes a three-month moving average over a two-year period, giving you an idea of where the market is headed.

Working with the Spreadsheet

To work with this spreadsheet, you need to enter the following information.

	A	B	C	D	E
1	CHARTING MARKET TRENDS AS A MOVING AVERAGE				
2					
3					
4	Name Of Stock		TRX		
5					
6		Month	Price	3 Month	Average
7				Moving	
8				Average	
9		1	$14.13		$14.31
10		2	$14.25		$14.31
11		3	$14.25	$14.21	$14.31
12		4	$14.38	$14.29	$14.31
13		5	$14.25	$14.29	$14.31
14		6	$14.25	$14.29	$14.31
15		7	$15.00	$14.50	$14.31
16		8	$13.13	$14.13	$14.31
17		9	$13.00	$13.71	$14.31
18		10	$14.38	$13.50	$14.31
19		11	$14.25	$13.88	$14.31
20		12	$14.25	$14.29	$14.31
21		13	$14.25	$14.25	$14.31
22		14	$14.00	$14.17	$14.31
23		15	$14.25	$14.17	$14.31
24		16	$13.50	$13.92	$14.31
25		17	$14.50	$14.08	$14.31
26		18	$14.50	$14.17	$14.31
27		19	$14.50	$14.50	$14.31
28		20	$14.38	$14.46	$14.31
29		21.	$14.75	$14.54	$14.31
30		22	$15.00	$14.71	$14.31
31		23	$15.00	$14.92	$14.31
32		24	$15.25	$15.08	$14.31
33					
34		Average	$14.31	$14.28	
35		Min Price	$13.00		
36		Max Price	$15.25		

    Col B month
    Col C monthly stock/market price for 24 consecutive months
    C4   name of stock

When the spreadsheet is complete, it will provide you with the following information.

    Col D 3-month moving average
    Col E average value of stock (for charting purposes)

Forecasting Worksheets

    C34   average price of stock
    C35   minimum stock price
    C36   maximum stock price

What It Looks Like

Figure 7.1 is a line chart that shows the monthly price, the 3-month moving average, and the two-year average.

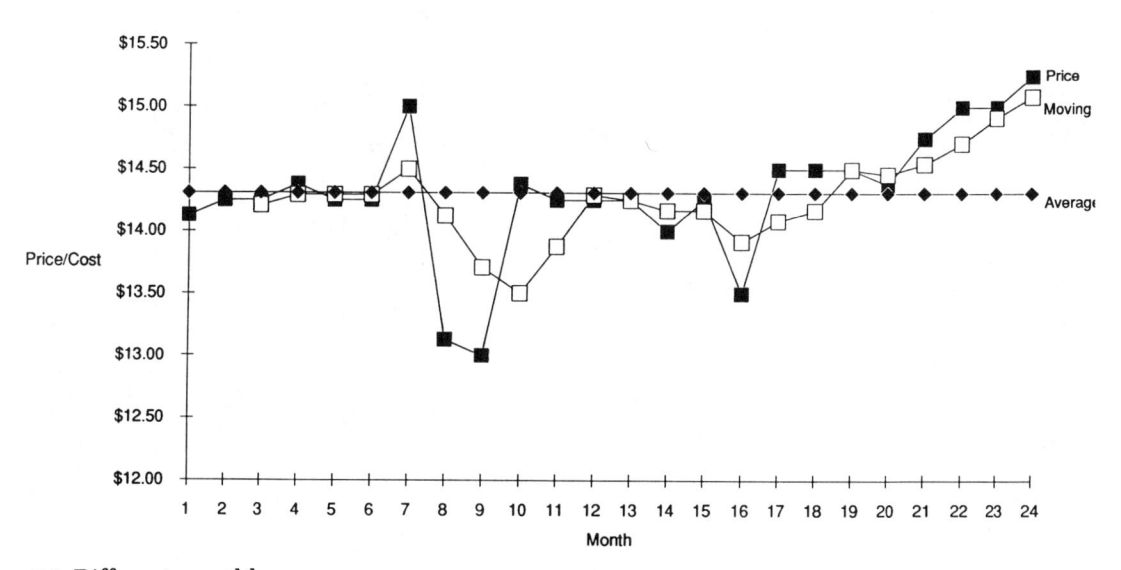

7.1 Different monthly averages

Excel Business Applications

The Cell Contents and Formulas

	A	B	C	D	E
1	CHARTING MARKET TR				
2					
3					
4	Name Of Stock		TRX		
5					
6		Month	Price	3 Month	Average
7				Moving	
8				Average	
9		1	14.13		=AVERAGE($C$9:$C$32)
10		2	14.25		=AVERAGE($C$9:$C$32)
11		3	14.25	=AVERAGE(C9:C11)	=AVERAGE($C$9:$C$32)
12		4	14.38	=AVERAGE(C10:C12)	=AVERAGE($C$9:$C$32)
13		5	14.25	=AVERAGE(C11:C13)	=AVERAGE($C$9:$C$32)
14		6	14.25	=AVERAGE(C12:C14)	=AVERAGE($C$9:$C$32)
15		7	15	=AVERAGE(C13:C15)	=AVERAGE($C$9:$C$32)
16		8	13.13	=AVERAGE(C14:C16)	=AVERAGE($C$9:$C$32)
17		9	13	=AVERAGE(C15:C17)	=AVERAGE($C$9:$C$32)
18		10	14.38	=AVERAGE(C16:C18)	=AVERAGE($C$9:$C$32)
19		11	14.25	=AVERAGE(C17:C19)	=AVERAGE($C$9:$C$32)
20		12	14.25	=AVERAGE(C18:C20)	=AVERAGE($C$9:$C$32)
21		13	14.25	=AVERAGE(C19:C21)	=AVERAGE($C$9:$C$32)
22		14	14	=AVERAGE(C20:C22)	=AVERAGE($C$9:$C$32)
23		15	14.25	=AVERAGE(C21:C23)	=AVERAGE($C$9:$C$32)
24		16	13.5	=AVERAGE(C22:C24)	=AVERAGE($C$9:$C$32)
25		17	14.5	=AVERAGE(C23:C25)	=AVERAGE($C$9:$C$32)
26		18	14.5	=AVERAGE(C24:C26)	=AVERAGE($C$9:$C$32)
27		19	14.5	=AVERAGE(C25:C27)	=AVERAGE($C$9:$C$32)
28		20	14.38	=AVERAGE(C26:C28)	=AVERAGE($C$9:$C$32)
29		21	14.75	=AVERAGE(C27:C29)	=AVERAGE($C$9:$C$32)
30		22	15	=AVERAGE(C28:C30)	=AVERAGE($C$9:$C$32)
31		23	15	=AVERAGE(C29:C31)	=AVERAGE($C$9:$C$32)
32		24	15.25	=AVERAGE(C30:C32)	=AVERAGE($C$9:$C$32)
33					
34		Average	=AVERAGE($C$9:$C$3	=AVERAGE(D9:D32)	
35		Min Price	=MIN(C9:C32)		
36		Max Price	=MAX(C10:C33)		

Exponential Smoothing and Sales Prediction

	A	B	C	D	E	F	G	H
1	EXPONENTIAL SMOOTHING AND SALES PREDICTION							
2								
3								
4			alpha	0.20				
5	seasonal index for period 3			1.10				
6	seasonal index for period 4			1.03				
7								
8								
9					Time Periods			
10								
11			1	2	3	4		
12								
13	Seasonally							
14	Adjusted Sales		3.15	4.17	2.36	3.35		
15	Smoothed Sales		3.35	3.81	2.56			
16	Sales Forecast			3.69	3.92			
17	------------	------------	------------	------------	------------	------------	------------	------------
18	Smoothed Sales (SS) and Forecasted Sales (FS) for Various Alpha Values							
19								
20								
21			Quarter 2	Quarter 3		Quarter 4		
22								
23			SS	SS	FS	SS	FS	
24	Alpha							
25								
26	0.1		3.25	3.99	3.58	2.46	4.11	
27	0.2		3.35	3.81	3.69	2.56	3.92	
28	0.3		3.46	3.63	3.80	2.66	3.74	
29	0.4		3.56	3.45	3.91	2.76	3.55	
30	0.5		3.66	3.27	4.03	2.86	3.36	
31	0.6		3.76	3.08	4.14	2.95	3.18	
32	0.7		3.86	2.90	4.25	3.05	2.99	
33	0.8		3.97	2.72	4.36	3.15	2.80	
34	0.9		4.07	2.54	4.47	3.25	2.62	
35	1.00		4.17	2.36	4.59	3.35	2.43	

What the Spreadsheet Does

This is a sales prediction technique where you specify a value for the smoothing constant between 0 and 1. The lower the value of the constant, the more weight you are giving to the previous period's sales.

The spreadsheet presents an example where the alpha level is set at .2 and then a set of forecasted sales values where the alpha values range from .1 to 1.0, allowing you to observe the

Excel Business Applications

effect of changing the influence of previous sales on forecasts. You will note that to use this spreadsheet you have to supply seasonal indexes for the period for which you want to estimate sales.

Working with the Spreadsheet

To work with this spreadsheet, you need to enter the following information.

D4	smoothing constant
D5	seasonal index for 3rd quarter
D6	seasonal index for 4th quarter
D14...F14	sales for each of the previous 4 quarters

When the spreadsheet is complete, it will provide you with the following information.

Row 15 smoothed sales for periods 2 through 4
Row 16 sales forecasts for periods 2 through 4

What It Looks Like

Figure 7.2 shows a line chart of forecasted sales for the 3rd and 4th quarters using interior labels (making the chart especially easy to read) as well as legends. The chart is based on the summary constructed at the bottom of the spreadsheet.

Forecasting Worksheets

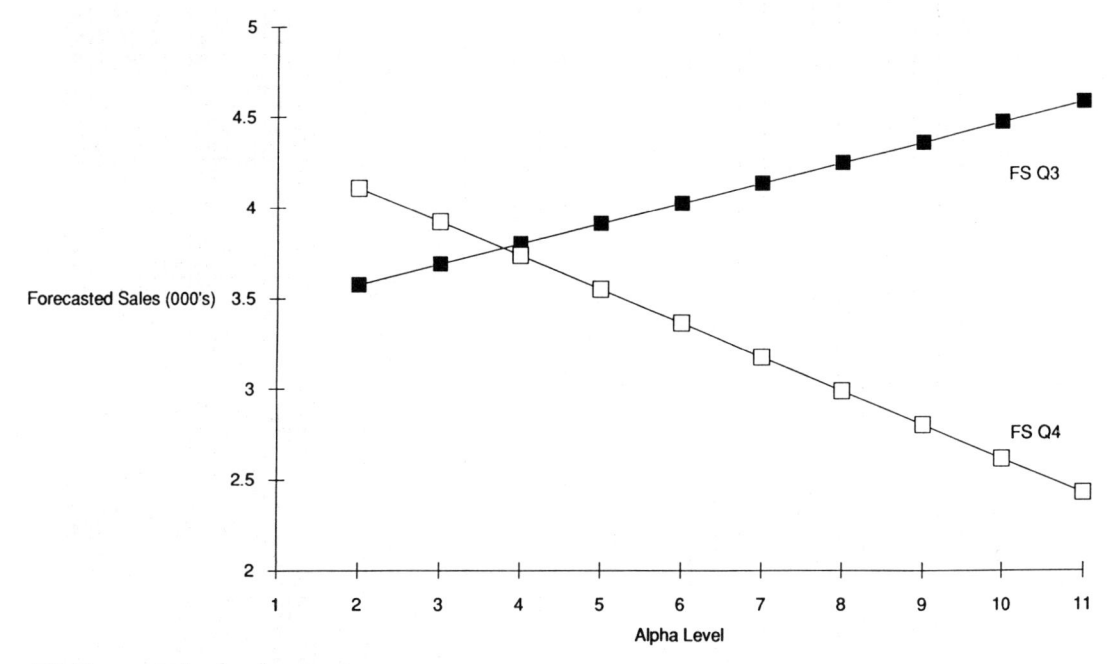

7.2 Forecasted sales by quarter

115

The Cell Contents and Formulas

	A	B	C
1	EXPONENTIAL SMOOTHING AND SALES PREDICTION		
2			
3			
4			alpha
5	seasonal index for period 3		
6	seasonal index for period 4		
7			
8			
9			
10			
11		1	
12			
13	Seasonally		
14	Adjusted Sales		3.15
15	Smoothed Sales		
16	Sales Forecast		
17	-	-	-
18	Smoothed Sales (SS) and Forecasted Sales (FS) for Various Alph		
19			
20			
21		Quarter 2	Quarter 3
22			
23		SS	SS
24	Alpha		
25			
26	0.1	=($D$14*A26)+($C$14*(1-A26))	=($E$14*A26)+($D$14*(1-A26))
27	0.2	=($D$14*A27)+($C$14*(1-A27))	=($E$14*A27)+($D$14*(1-A27))
28	0.3	=($D$14*A28)+($C$14*(1-A28))	=($E$14*A28)+($D$14*(1-A28))
29	0.4	=($D$14*A29)+($C$14*(1-A29))	=($E$14*A29)+($D$14*(1-A29))
30	0.5	=($D$14*A30)+($C$14*(1-A30))	=($E$14*A30)+($D$14*(1-A30))
31	0.6	=($D$14*A31)+($C$14*(1-A31))	=($E$14*A31)+($D$14*(1-A31))
32	0.7	=($D$14*A32)+($C$14*(1-A32))	=($E$14*A32)+($D$14*(1-A32))
33	0.8	=($D$14*A33)+($C$14*(1-A33))	=($E$14*A33)+($D$14*(1-A33))
34	0.9	=($D$14*A34)+($C$14*(1-A34))	=($E$14*A34)+($D$14*(1-A34))
35	1	=($D$14*A35)+($C$14*(1-A35))	=($E$14*A35)+($D$14*(1-A35))

	D	E	F
1			
2			
3			
4	0.2		
5	1.1		
6	1.03		
7			
8		Time Periods	
9			
10			
11	2	3	4
12			
13			
14	4.17	2.36	3.35
15	=$D$4*D14)+((1-$D$4)*C14)	=$D$4*E14)+((1-$D$4)*D14)	=$D$4*F14)+((1-$D$4)*E14)
16		=(D15)*D5	=(E15*D6)
17		-	-
18			
19			
20		Quarter 4	
21			
22			
23	FS	SS	FS
24			
25			
26	=B26*$D$5	=($F$14*A26)+($E$14*(1-A26))	=C26*$D$6
27	=B27*$D$5	=($F$14*A27)+($E$14*(1-A27))	=C27*$D$6
28	=B28*$D$5	=($F$14*A28)+($E$14*(1-A28))	=C28*$D$6
29	=B29*$D$5	=($F$14*A29)+($E$14*(1-A29))	=C29*$D$6
30	=B30*$D$5	=($F$14*A30)+($E$14*(1-A30))	=C30*$D$6
31	=B31*$D$5	=($F$14*A31)+($E$14*(1-A31))	=C31*$D$6
32	=B32*$D$5	=($F$14*A32)+($E$14*(1-A32))	=C32*$D$6
33	=B33*$D$5	=($F$14*A33)+($E$14*(1-A33))	=C33*$D$6
34	=B34*$D$5	=($F$14*A34)+($E$14*(1-A34))	=C34*$D$6
35	=B35*$D$5	=($F$14*A35)+($E$14*(1-A35))	=C35*$D$6

Excel Business Applications

Forecasting Sales Using Linear Regression

	A	B	C	D	E	F
1	FORECASTING SALES USING LINEAR REGRESSION					
2						
3						
4	The Prediction of Sales Based on Time (Month)					
5						
6						
7		Month	Sales	XY	X Squared	Pred
8		(X)	(Y)			Y
9						
10		1	39.80	39.80	1.00	40.90
11		2	40.10	80.20	4.00	42.41
12		3	43.70	131.10	9.00	43.92
13		4	46.70	186.80	16.00	45.43
14		5	50.80	254.00	25.00	46.94
15		6	50.10	300.60	36.00	48.45
16		7	47.80	334.60	49.00	49.96
17		8	51.80	414.40	64.00	51.47
18		9	53.50	481.50	81.00	52.98
19		10	53.60	536.00	100.00	54.49
20		11	56.00	616.00	121.00	56.00
21		12	56.60	679.20	144.00	57.51
22	N		12			
23	Total	78.00	590.50	4054.20	650.00	
24	Average	6.50	49.21	337.85	54.17	
25						
26	Prediction equation (Y = a + bX)					
27			('Y = 1.51X + 39.39)			
28						
29		b =	1.51			
30		a =	39.39			
31						
32						
33						
34						
35						
36						
37						
38						
39						
40						
41						
42						
43						

Forecasting Worksheets

What the Spreadsheet Does

Another way to forecast sales that takes into account the multiple contribution of several variables is linear regression. This spreadsheet computes the important statistical indicators of whether one factor (such as advertising) makes an important contribution in understanding another factor (such as sales). It can also help you determine if a trend is present and if changes can be predicted over time.

Working with the Spreadsheet

To work with this spreadsheet, you need to enter the following information.

- **Col B** the predictor variable (the X variable)
- **Col C** the predicted or criterion variable (the Y variable)

When the spreadsheet is complete, it will provide you with the following information.

- **C29** the slope of the prediction line
- **C30** the Y intercept
- **Col F** the predicted Y scores
- **Col E** X squared
- **D23** the sum of the product of X and Y
- **Row 24** the average of columns B, C, D, and E
- **Row 23** the total of columns B, C, D, and E

Excel Business Applications

What It Looks Like

Figure 7.3 shows you a line chart that compares predicted and actual sales values. The lines are relatively close together, reflecting a good fit. You could be fairly comfortable predicting sales based on the amount of time that has passed.

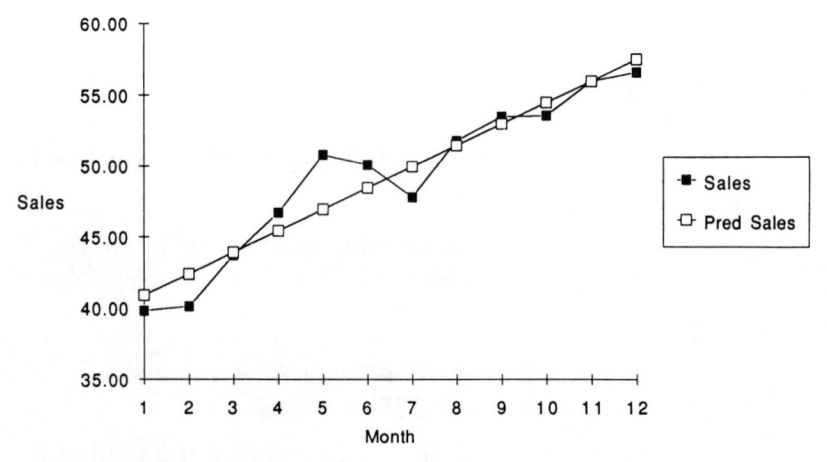

7.3 Predicted and actual sales

The Cell Contents and Formulas

	A	B	C
1	FORECASTING SALES USING LINEAR REGRESSION		
2			
3			
4	The Prediction of Sales Based on Time (Month)		
5			
6			
7		Month	Sales
8		(X)	(Y)
9			
10		1	39.8
11		2	40.1
12		3	43.7
13		4	46.7
14		5	50.8
15		6	50.1
16		7	47.8
17		8	51.8
18		9	53.5
19		10	53.6
20		11	56
21		12	56.6
22	N		=COUNT(B10:B21)
23	Total	=SUM(B10:B21)	=SUM(C10:C21)
24	Average	=AVERAGE(B10:B21)	=AVERAGE(C10:C21)
25			
26	Prediction equation (Y = a + bX)		
27			('Y = 1.51X + 39.39)
28			
29		b =	=(((C22)*D23)-B23*C23)/(((C22)*E23)-B23^2)
30		a =	=C24-(C29*B24)
31			
32			
33			
34			
35			

The Cell Contents and Formulas (Continued)

	D	E	F
1			
2			
3			
4			
5			
6			
7	XY	X Squared	Pred
8			Y
9			
10	=C10*B10	=B10^2	=$C$30+($C$29*B10)
11	=C11*B11	=B11^2	=$C$30+($C$29*B11)
12	=C12*B12	=B12^2	=$C$30+($C$29*B12)
13	=C13*B13	=B13^2	=$C$30+($C$29*B13)
14	=C14*B14	=B14^2	=$C$30+($C$29*B14)
15	=C15*B15	=B15^2	=$C$30+($C$29*B15)
16	=C16*B16	=B16^2	=$C$30+($C$29*B16)
17	=C17*B17	=B17^2	=$C$30+($C$29*B17)
18	=C18*B18	=B18^2	=$C$30+($C$29*B18)
19	=C19*B19	=B19^2	=$C$30+($C$29*B19)
20	=C20*B20	=B20^2	=$C$30+($C$29*B20)
21	=C21*B21	=B21^2	=$C$30+($C$29*B21)
22			
23	=SUM(D10:D21)	=SUM(E10:E21)	
24	=AVERAGE(D10:D21)	=AVERAGE(E10:E21)	
25			
26			
27			
28			
29			
30			
31			
32			
33			
34			
35			

Forecasting Worksheets

Moving Averages Forecasting Accuracy

	A	B	C	D	E	F	G	H	I	J
1	MOVING AVERAGES FORECASTING ACCURACY (24 MONTH PERIOD In $000)									
2										
3										
4	3 Month	Sales	Predicted	Error	3 Month	3 Month	6 Month	6 Month	9 Month	9 Month
5	Period		Sales		Average	Error	Average	Error	Average	Error
6										
7	1	12.70	12.30	-0.40						
8	2	12.90	12.40	-0.50						
9	3	13.20	12.50	-0.70						
10	4	14.30	12.60	-1.70	13.47	-0.87				
11	5	14.10	12.70	-1.40	13.87	-1.17				
12	6	14.30	12.80	-1.50	14.23	-1.43				
13	7	14.40	12.90	-1.50	14.27	-1.37	13.58	-0.68		
14	8	13.90	13.00	-0.90	14.20	-1.20	13.87	-0.87		
15	9	12.90	13.10	0.20	13.73	-0.63	14.03	-0.93		
16	10	13.60	13.20	-0.40	13.47	-0.27	13.98	-0.78	13.63	-0.43
17	11	13.30	13.30	0.00	13.27	0.03	13.87	-0.57	13.73	-0.43
18	12	14.00	13.40	-0.60	13.63	-0.23	13.73	-0.33	13.78	-0.38
19	13	14.50	13.50	-1.00	13.93	-0.43	13.68	-0.18	13.87	-0.37
20	14	14.60	13.60	-1.00	14.37	-0.77	13.70	-0.10	13.89	-0.29
21	15	15.10	13.70	-1.40	14.73	-1.03	13.82	-0.12	13.94	-0.24
22	16	14.30	13.80	-0.50	14.67	-0.87	14.18	-0.38	14.03	-0.23
23	17	14.40	13.90	-0.50	14.60	-0.70	14.30	-0.40	14.02	-0.12
24	18	14.50	14.00	-0.50	14.40	-0.40	14.48	-0.48	14.08	-0.08
25	19	14.30	14.10	-0.20	14.40	-0.30	14.57	-0.47	14.26	-0.16
26	20	15.00	14.20	-0.80	14.60	-0.40	14.53	-0.33	14.33	-0.13
27	21	15.10	14.30	-0.80	14.80	-0.50	14.60	-0.30	14.52	-0.22
28	22	14.50	14.40	-0.10	14.87	-0.47	14.60	-0.20	14.64	-0.24
29	23	14.30	14.50	0.20	14.63	-0.13	14.63	-0.13	14.64	-0.14
30	24	14.50	14.60	0.10	14.43	0.17	14.62	-0.02	14.61	-0.01
31										
32	Average	14.11	13.45	-0.66	14.22	-0.62	14.15	-0.40	14.13	-0.23
33	Error In Prediction			0.30		0.19		0.07		0.02
34										
35										

What the Spreadsheet Does

The ability to predict outcomes may be the most important tool that a business can use to ensure its success. This spreadsheet provides moving averages for 3-, 6-, and 9-month periods and computes the error associated with the prediction (the variance

Excel Business Applications

of the differences between the actual sales and the moving averages). When the error is minimal, as it is for the 9-month cycle, the differences between the lines in the chart that accompanies the spreadsheet are also minimal. The smoother the line, the more accurate the prediction.

Working with the Spreadsheet

To work with this spreadsheet, you need to enter the following information.

Col B actual sales
Col C predicted sales (here the assumption is that sales remain steady each year)

When the spreadsheet is complete, it will provide you with the following information.

Col D errors between actual and predicted sales
Col E 3-month moving average figures
Col F error between 3-month moving average and actual sales
Col G 6-month moving average figures
Col H error between 6-month moving average and actual sales
Col I 9-month moving average figures
Col J error between 9-month moving average and actual sales
Row 32 averages for all columns
Row 33 variance of the errors (a method of standardizing error in prediction)

Forecasting Worksheets

What It Looks Like

Figure 7.4 compares the three moving averages with actual sales using markers and lines, with no grids, and with a customized Y axis to reset the scale to 13 and 15 from 11 and 16.

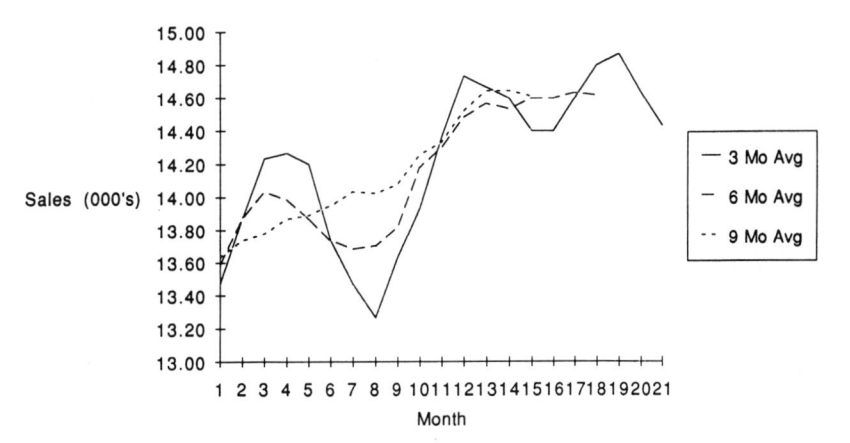

7.4 Three moving averages

Excel Business Applications

The Cell Contents and Formulas

	A	B	C	D	E
1	MOVING AVERAGES				
2					
3					
4	3 Month	Sales	Predicted	Error	3 Month
5	Period		Sales		Average
6					
7	1	12.7	12.3	=C7-B7	
8	2	12.9	=C7+0.1	=C8-B8	
9	3	13.2	=C8+0.1	=C9-B9	
10	4	14.3	=C9+0.1	=C10-B10	=AVERAGE(B8:B10)
11	5	14.1	=C10+0.1	=C11-B11	=AVERAGE(B9:B11)
12	6	14.3	=C11+0.1	=C12-B12	=AVERAGE(B10:B12)
13	7	14.4	=C12+0.1	=C13-B13	=AVERAGE(B11:B13)
14	8	13.9	=C13+0.1	=C14-B14	=AVERAGE(B12:B14)
15	9	12.9	=C14+0.1	=C15-B15	=AVERAGE(B13:B15)
16	10	13.6	=C15+0.1	=C16-B16	=AVERAGE(B14:B16)
17	11	13.3	=C16+0.1	=C17-B17	=AVERAGE(B15:B17)
18	12	14	=C17+0.1	=C18-B18	=AVERAGE(B16:B18)
19	13	14.5	=C18+0.1	=C19-B19	=AVERAGE(B17:B19)
20	14	14.6	=C19+0.1	=C20-B20	=AVERAGE(B18:B20)
21	15	15.1	=C20+0.1	=C21-B21	=AVERAGE(B19:B21)
22	16	14.3	=C21+0.1	=C22-B22	=AVERAGE(B20:B22)
23	17	14.4	=C22+0.1	=C23-B23	=AVERAGE(B21:B23)
24	18	14.5	=C23+0.1	=C24-B24	=AVERAGE(B22:B24)
25	19	14.3	=C24+0.1	=C25-B25	=AVERAGE(B23:B25)
26	20	15	=C25+0.1	=C26-B26	=AVERAGE(B24:B26)
27	21	15.1	=C26+0.1	=C27-B27	=AVERAGE(B25:B27)
28	22	14.5	=C27+0.1	=C28-B28	=AVERAGE(B26:B28)
29	23	14.3	=C28+0.1	=C29-B29	=AVERAGE(B27:B29)
30	24	14.5	=C29+0.1	=C30-B30	=AVERAGE(B28:B30)
31					
32	Average	=AVERAGE(B7:B30)	=AVERAGE(C7:C30)	=AVERAGE(D7:D30)	=AVERAGE(E7:E30)
33	Error In Prediction			=VAR(D7:D30)	
34					
35					

Forecasting Worksheets

	F	G	H	I	J
1					
2					
3					
4	3 Month	6 Month	6 Month	9 Month	9 Month
5	Error	Average	Error	Average	Error
6					
7					
8					
9					
10	=C10-E10				
11	=C11-E11				
12	=C12-E12				
13	=C13-E13	=AVERAGE(B7:B12)	=C13-G13		
14	=C14-E14	=AVERAGE(B8:B13)	=C14-G14		
15	=C15-E15	=AVERAGE(B9:B14)	=C15-G15		
16	=C16-E16	=AVERAGE(B10:B15)	=C16-G16	=AVERAGE(B7:B15)	=C16-I16
17	=C17-E17	=AVERAGE(B11:B16)	=C17-G17	=AVERAGE(B8:B16)	=C17-I17
18	=C18-E18	=AVERAGE(B12:B17)	=C18-G18	=AVERAGE(B9:B17)	=C18-I18
19	=C19-E19	=AVERAGE(B13:B18)	=C19-G19	=AVERAGE(B10:B18)	=C19-I19
20	=C20-E20	=AVERAGE(B14:B19)	=C20-G20	=AVERAGE(B11:B19)	=C20-I20
21	=C21-E21	=AVERAGE(B15:B20)	=C21-G21	=AVERAGE(B12:B20)	=C21-I21
22	=C22-E22	=AVERAGE(B16:B21)	=C22-G22	=AVERAGE(B13:B21)	=C22-I22
23	=C23-E23	=AVERAGE(B17:B22)	=C23-G23	=AVERAGE(B14:B22)	=C23-I23
24	=C24-E24	=AVERAGE(B18:B23)	=C24-G24	=AVERAGE(B15:B23)	=C24-I24
25	=C25-E25	=AVERAGE(B19:B24)	=C25-G25	=AVERAGE(B16:B24)	=C25-I25
26	=C26-E26	=AVERAGE(B20:B25)	=C26-G26	=AVERAGE(B17:B25)	=C26-I26
27	=C27-E27	=AVERAGE(B21:B26)	=C27-G27	=AVERAGE(B18:B26)	=C27-I27
28	=C28-E28	=AVERAGE(B22:B27)	=C28-G28	=AVERAGE(B19:B27)	=C28-I28
29	=C29-E29	=AVERAGE(B23:B28)	=C29-G29	=AVERAGE(B20:B28)	=C29-I29
30	=C30-E30	=AVERAGE(B24:B29)	=C30-G30	=AVERAGE(B21:B29)	=C30-I30
31					
32	=AVERAGE(F7:F30)	=AVERAGE(G7:G30)	=AVERAGE(H7:H30)	=AVERAGE(I7:I30)	=AVERAGE(J7:J30)
33	=VAR(F10:F30)		=VAR(H13:H30)		=VAR(J16:J30)
34					
35					

8

Investment Worksheets

Amortization Schedule

What the Spreadsheet Does

This spreadsheet uses the **=PMT** function, one of Excel's most powerful tools for computing financial data. With it you can predict how changing interest rates will affect monthly payments on a loan.

Working with the Spreadsheet

To work with this spreadsheet, you need to enter the following information.

Investment Worksheets

D3 principal amount of loan
D4 annual interest rate/number of periods per year
D5 length of loan (total number of payment periods)

When the spreadsheet is complete, it will provide you with the following information.

Col B principal due on payment
Col C interest due on payment
Col D total payment
Col E remaining balance to be paid
D7 monthly payment

	A	B	C	D	E
1	AMORTIZATION SCHEDULE				
2					
3	Principal			$50,000.00	
4	Annual Interest			10.00%	
5	Length of Loan (Years)			15	
6					
7	PAYMENT			$537.30	
8					
9	Payment	Principal	Interest	Total	Remaining
10	Number	Due	Due	Payment	Balance
11					
12	1	$120.64	$416.67	$537.30	$49,462.70
13	2	$125.11	$412.19	$537.30	$48,925.39
14	3	$129.59	$407.71	$537.30	$48,388.09
15	4	$134.07	$403.23	$537.30	$47,850.79
16	5	$138.55	$398.76	$537.30	$47,313.49
17	6	$143.02	$394.28	$537.30	$46,776.18
18	7	$147.50	$389.80	$537.30	$46,238.88
19	8	$151.98	$385.32	$537.30	$45,701.58
20	9	$156.46	$380.85	$537.30	$45,164.28
21	10	$160.93	$376.37	$537.30	$44,626.97
22	11	$165.41	$371.89	$537.30	$44,089.67
23	12	$169.89	$367.41	$537.30	$43,552.37
24	13	$174.37	$362.94	$537.30	$43,015.07
25	14	$178.84	$358.46	$537.30	$42,477.76
26	15	$183.32	$353.98	$537.30	$41,940.46
27	16	$187.80	$349.50	$537.30	$41,403.16
28	17	$192.28	$345.03	$537.30	$40,865.86
29	18	$196.75	$340.55	$537.30	$40,328.55
30	19	$201.23	$336.07	$537.30	$39,791.25
31	20	$205.71	$331.59	$537.30	$39,253.95
32	21	$210.19	$327.12	$537.30	$38,716.65
33	22	$214.66	$322.64	$537.30	$38,179.34
34	23	$219.14	$318.16	$537.30	$37,642.04
35	24	$223.62	$313.68	$537.30	$37,104.74

Excel Business Applications

What It Looks Like

Figure 8.1 shows a line chart that illustrates how principal and interest payment approach each other over time.

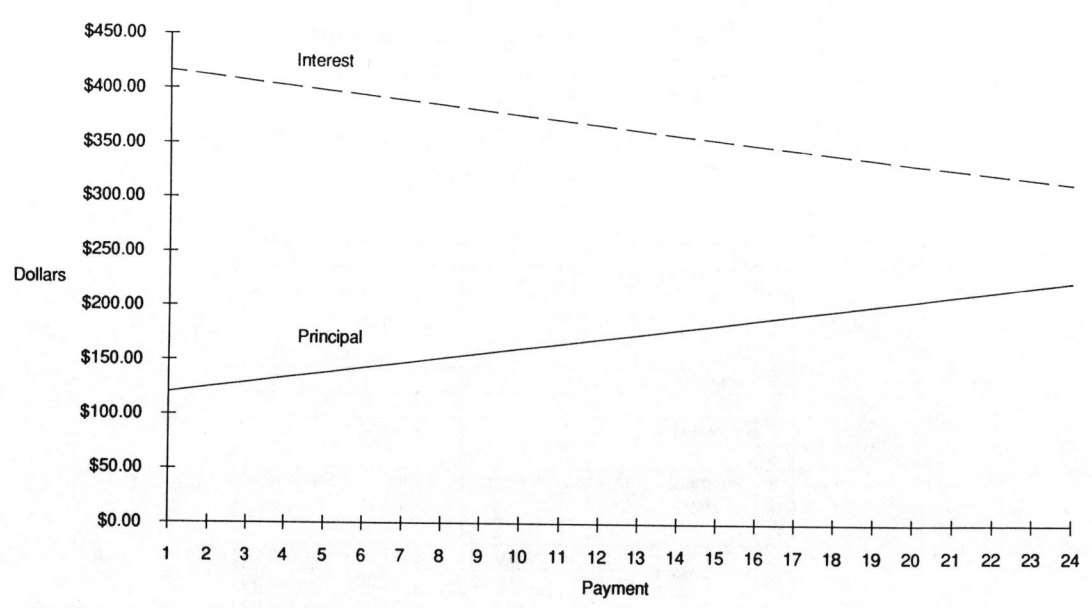

8.1 Principal and interest payments

The Cell Contents and Formulas

	A	B	C	D	E
1	AMORTIZATION SCHEDULE				
2					
3	Principal			50000	
4	Annual Interest			0.1	
5	Length of Loan (Years)			15	
6					
7	PAYMENT			=PMT(D4/12,D5*12,-D3)	
8					
9	Payment	Principal	Interest	Total	Remaining
10	Number	Due	Due	Payment	Balance
11					
12	1	=$D$7-C12	=D3*$D$4/12	=C12+B12	=D3-C12-B12
13	2	=$D$7-C13	=E12*$D$4/12	=C13+B13	=E12-B13-C13
14	3	=$D$7-C14	=E13*$D$4/12	=C14+B14	=E13-B14-C14
15	4	=$D$7-C15	=E14*$D$4/12	=C15+B15	=E14-B15-C15
16	5	=$D$7-C16	=E15*$D$4/12	=C16+B16	=E15-B16-C16
17	6	=$D$7-C17	=E16*$D$4/12	=C17+B17	=E16-B17-C17
18	7	=$D$7-C18	=E17*$D$4/12	=C18+B18	=E17-B18-C18
19	8	=$D$7-C19	=E18*$D$4/12	=C19+B19	=E18-B19-C19
20	9	=$D$7-C20	=E19*$D$4/12	=C20+B20	=E19-B20-C20
21	10	=$D$7-C21	=E20*$D$4/12	=C21+B21	=E20-B21-C21
22	11	=$D$7-C22	=E21*$D$4/12	=C22+B22	=E21-B22-C22
23	12	=$D$7-C23	=E22*$D$4/12	=C23+B23	=E22-B23-C23
24	13	=$D$7-C24	=E23*$D$4/12	=C24+B24	=E23-B24-C24
25	14	=$D$7-C25	=E24*$D$4/12	=C25+B25	=E24-B25-C25
26	15	=$D$7-C26	=E25*$D$4/12	=C26+B26	=E25-B26-C26
27	16	=$D$7-C27	=E26*$D$4/12	=C27+B27	=E26-B27-C27
28	17	=$D$7-C28	=E27*$D$4/12	=C28+B28	=E27-B28-C28
29	18	=$D$7-C29	=E28*$D$4/12	=C29+B29	=E28-B29-C29
30	19	=$D$7-C30	=E29*$D$4/12	=C30+B30	=E29-B30-C30
31	20	=$D$7-C31	=E30*$D$4/12	=C31+B31	=E30-B31-C31
32	21	=$D$7-C32	=E31*$D$4/12	=C32+B32	=E31-B32-C32
33	22	=$D$7-C33	=E32*$D$4/12	=C33+B33	=E32-B33-C33
34	23	=$D$7-C34	=E33*$D$4/12	=C34+B34	=E33-B34-C34
35	24	=$D$7-C35	=E34*$D$4/12	=C35+B35	=E34-B35-C35

Excel Business Applications

Computing the Interest Rate

	A	B	C	D	E	F
1	COMPUTING THE INTEREST RATE					
2						
3	The Current Value of the Investment (CV)					-4000
4	The Future Value of the Investment (FV)					20000
5	Number of Compounding Periods (CP)					10
6						
7	Interest Rate		15.10%			
8						
9						
10						
11		Number of Compounding Periods			10	
12						
13		CV	FV	Interest Rate		
14						
15						
16		-4000	$20,000	15.10%		
17		-4000	$21,000	13.83%		
18		-4000	$22,050	12.61%		
19		-4000	$23,153	11.42%		
20		-4000	$24,310	10.26%		
21		-4000	$25,526	9.13%		
22		-4000	$26,802	8.03%		
23		-4000	$28,142	6.96%		
24		-4000	$29,549	5.92%		
25		-4000	$31,027	4.91%		
26		-4000	$32,578	3.92%		

What the Spreadsheet Does

This spreadsheet computes the interest rate that is necessary to turn a current investment into a particular future value. For example, in order to have $4,000 grow to $20,000, it must be invested at 15.1% for 10 years with annual compounding.

Working with the Spreadsheet

To work with this spreadsheet, you need to enter the following information.

F4 current value of investment (notice that Excel requires investments to be entered as a negative value)

Investment Worksheets

F5 future value of investment

F6 number of compounding periods or term of compounding

When the spreadsheet is complete, it will provide you with the following information.

C7 compound interest rate

What It Looks Like

Figure 8.2 presents a scatter chart that compares interest rate with future value.

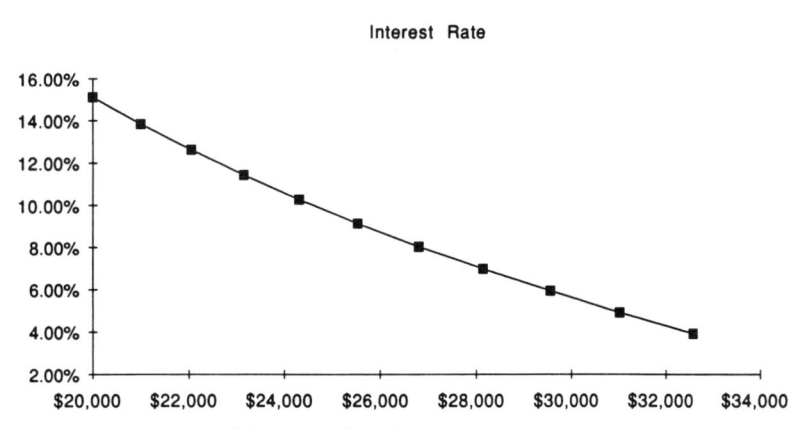

8.2 Interest rate and future value data points

Excel Business Applications

The Cell Contents and Formulas

	A	B	C
1	COMPUTING THE INTEREST RATE		
2			
3	The Current Value of the Investment (CV)		
4	The Future Value of the Investment (FV)		
5	Number of Compounding Periods (CP)		
6			
7	Interest Rate		=RATE(F5,F3,F4)
8			
9			
10			
11		Number of Compounding Pe	
12			
13		CV	FV
14			
15			
16		-4000	=F4
17		-4000	=C16*1.05
18		-4000	=C17*1.05
19		-4000	=C18*1.05
20		-4000	=C19*1.05
21		-4000	=C20*1.05
22		-4000	=C21*1.05
23		-4000	=C22*1.05
24		-4000	=C23*1.05
25		-4000	=C24*1.05
26		-4000	=C25*1.05

Investment Worksheets

	D	E	F
1			
2			
3			-4000
4			20000
5			10
6			
7			
8			
9			
10			
11		=F5	
12			
13	Interest Rate		
14			
15			
16	=RATE($F$5,B16,C16)		
17	=RATE($F$5,B17,C17)		
18	=RATE($F$5,B18,C18)		
19	=RATE($F$5,B19,C19)		
20	=RATE($F$5,B20,C20)		
21	=RATE($F$5,B21,C21)		
22	=RATE($F$5,B22,C22)		
23	=RATE($F$5,B23,C23)		
24	=RATE($F$5,B24,C24)		
25	=RATE($F$5,B25,C25)		
26	=RATE($F$5,B26,C26)		

Excel Business Applications

Future Value of an Annuity

	A	B	C	D	E
1	FUTURE VALUE OF AN ANNUITY				
2					
3					
4				Future Value	
5					
6					
7		Investment	($5,000)	($10,000)	($15,000)
8					
9	Interest	Length of			
10	Rate	Investment			
11		(Years)			
12					
13		6%	1	$5,000.00	$10,000.00	$15,000.00
14			2	$10,300.00	$20,600.00	$30,900.00
15			3	$15,918.00	$31,836.00	$47,754.00
16			4	$21,873.08	$43,746.16	$65,619.24
17			5	$28,185.46	$56,370.93	$84,556.39
18					
19		7%	1	$5,000.00	$10,000.00	$15,000.00
20			2	$10,350.00	$20,700.00	$31,050.00
21			3	$16,074.50	$32,149.00	$48,223.50
22			4	$22,199.72	$44,399.43	$66,599.15
23			5	$28,753.70	$57,507.39	$86,261.09
24					
25		8%	1	$5,000.00	$10,000.00	$15,000.00
26			2	$10,400.00	$20,800.00	$31,200.00
27			3	$16,232.00	$32,464.00	$48,696.00
28			4	$22,530.56	$45,061.12	$67,591.68
29			5	$29,333.00	$58,666.01	$87,999.01
30					
31		9%	1	$5,000.00	$10,000.00	$15,000.00
32			2	$10,450.00	$20,900.00	$31,350.00
33			3	$16,390.50	$32,781.00	$49,171.50
34			4	$22,865.65	$45,731.29	$68,596.94
35			5	$29,923.55	$59,847.11	$89,770.66
36					
37		10%	1	$5,000.00	$10,000.00	$15,000.00
38			2	$10,500.00	$21,000.00	$31,500.00
39			3	$16,550.00	$33,100.00	$49,650.00
40			4	$23,205.00	$46,410.00	$69,615.00
41			5	$30,525.50	$61,051.00	$91,576.50

What the Spreadsheet Does

What an investment will be worth in the future depends on the original amount invested, the percentage rate of return on the investment, and the time period of the investment.

Investment Worksheets

This spreadsheet computes the future value of an investment given these different factors and assumes that you will be investing the same amount of money periodically over a five-year period (an annuity).

Working with the Spreadsheet

To work with this spreadsheet, you need to enter the following information.

A13,A19,A25,A31,A37   interest rates (five values)
Col B   length of investment
C7,D7,E7   annuity amount (three values)

When the spreadsheet is complete, it will provide you with the following information.

Cols C,D,E   total future value of investment

What It Looks Like

Figure 8.3 shows what three equally spaced investments would be worth at 10% from one through five years.

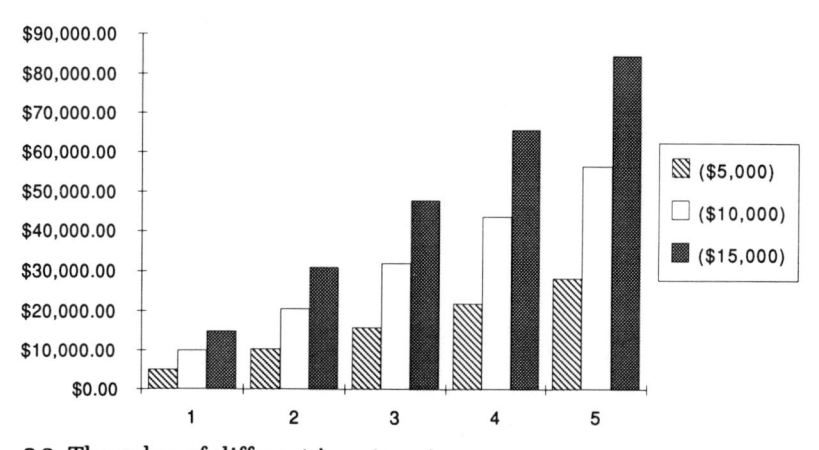

8.3 The value of different investments

Excel Business Applications

The Cell Contents and Formulas

	A	B	C	D	E
1	FUTURE VALUE OF AN ANNUITY				
2					
3					
4				Future Value	
5					
6					
7		Investment	-5000	-10000	-15000
8					
9	Interest	Length of			
10	Rate	Investment			
11		(Years)			
12					
13	0.06	1	=FV($A$13,B13,$C$7)	=FV($A$13,B13,$D$7)	=FV($A$13,B13,$E$7)
14		2	=FV($A$13,B14,$C$7)	=FV($A$13,B14,$D$7)	=FV($A$13,B14,$E$7)
15		3	=FV($A$13,B15,$C$7)	=FV($A$13,B15,$D$7)	=FV($A$13,B15,$E$7)
16		4	=FV($A$13,B16,$C$7)	=FV($A$13,B16,$D$7)	=FV($A$13,B16,$E$7)
17		5	=FV($A$13,B17,$C$7)	=FV($A$13,B17,$D$7)	=FV($A$13,B17,$E$7)
18					
19	0.07	1	=FV($A$19,B19,$C$7)	=FV($A$19,B19,$D$7)	=FV($A$19,B19,$E$7)
20		2	=FV($A$19,B20,$C$7)	=FV($A$19,B20,$D$7)	=FV($A$19,B20,$E$7)
21		3	=FV($A$19,B21,$C$7)	=FV($A$19,B21,$D$7)	=FV($A$19,B21,$E$7)
22		4	=FV($A$19,B22,$C$7)	=FV($A$19,B22,$D$7)	=FV($A$19,B22,$E$7)
23		5	=FV($A$19,B23,$C$7)	=FV($A$19,B23,$D$7)	=FV($A$19,B23,$E$7)
24					
25	0.08	1	=FV($A$25,B25,$C$7)	=FV($A$25,B25,$D$7)	=FV($A$25,B25,$E$7)
26		2	=FV($A$25,B26,$C$7)	=FV($A$25,B26,$D$7)	=FV($A$25,B26,$E$7)
27		3	=FV($A$25,B27,$C$7)	=FV($A$25,B27,$D$7)	=FV($A$25,B27,$E$7)
28		4	=FV($A$25,B28,$C$7)	=FV($A$25,B28,$D$7)	=FV($A$25,B28,$E$7)
29		5	=FV($A$25,B29,$C$7)	=FV($A$25,B29,$D$7)	=FV($A$25,B29,$E$7)
30					
31	0.09	1	=FV($A$31,B31,$C$7)	=FV($A$31,B31,$D$7)	=FV($A$31,B31,$E$7)
32		2	=FV($A$31,B32,$C$7)	=FV($A$31,B32,$D$7)	=FV($A$31,B32,$E$7)
33		3	=FV($A$31,B33,$C$7)	=FV($A$31,B33,$D$7)	=FV($A$31,B33,$E$7)
34		4	=FV($A$31,B34,$C$7)	=FV($A$31,B34,$D$7)	=FV($A$31,B34,$E$7)
35		5	=FV($A$31,B35,$C$7)	=FV($A$31,B35,$D$7)	=FV($A$31,B35,$E$7)
36					
37	0.1	1	=FV($A$37,B37,$C$7)	=FV($A$37,B37,$D$7)	=FV($A$37,B37,$E$7)
38		2	=FV($A$37,B38,$C$7)	=FV($A$37,B38,$D$7)	=FV($A$37,B38,$E$7)
39		3	=FV($A$37,B39,$C$7)	=FV($A$37,B39,$D$7)	=FV($A$37,B39,$E$7)
40		4	=FV($A$37,B40,$C$7)	=FV($A$37,B40,$D$7)	=FV($A$37,B40,$E$7)
41		5	=FV($A$37,B41,$C$7)	=FV($A$37,B41,$D$7)	=FV($A$37,B41,$E$7)

Internal Rate of Return

	A	B	C	D	E	F	G	H
1	INTERNAL RATE OF RETURN							
2								
3			Plan #1		Plan #2		Plan #3	
4								
5	Starting		$3,000	$3,500	$3,000	$3,500	$3,000	$3,500
6	Capital							
7								
8	Estimated							
9	Return							
10			($3,000)	($3,500)	($3,000)	($3,500)	($3,000)	($3,500)
11	0.08		$450	$450	$550	$550	$650	$650
12			$450	$450	$550	$550	$650	$650
13			$450	$450	$550	$550	$650	$650
14			$450	$450	$550	$550	$650	$650
15			$450	$450	$550	$550	$650	$650
16			$450	$450	$550	$550	$650	$650
17			$450	$450	$550	$550	$650	$650
18								
19		IRR	1.23%	-2.57%	6.66%	2.44%	11.65%	7.02%

What the Spreadsheet Does

One measure of the value of an investment is the return it will generate given certain market conditions. This spreadsheet uses what you expect to receive as a function of the investment and calculates the internal rate of return (the **=IRR** Excel function). Here the closest approximation to the estimate of an 8% return is Plan #3, where the cash flow regularly comes in at $650.00 (for a return of 7.02%). Note that the beginning number in each cash flow column is negative, since the initial investment represents a loss.

Excel Business Applications

Working with the Spreadsheet

To work with this spreadsheet, you need to enter the following information.

A11	estimate of the return
Cols C,D,E,F,G,H	cash flow from the investment
Row 5	initial investment amount

When the spreadsheet is complete, it will provide you with the following information.

Row 19 internal rate of return

What It Looks Like

Figure 8.4 compares the cash flow for the three plans, including the starting negative balance.

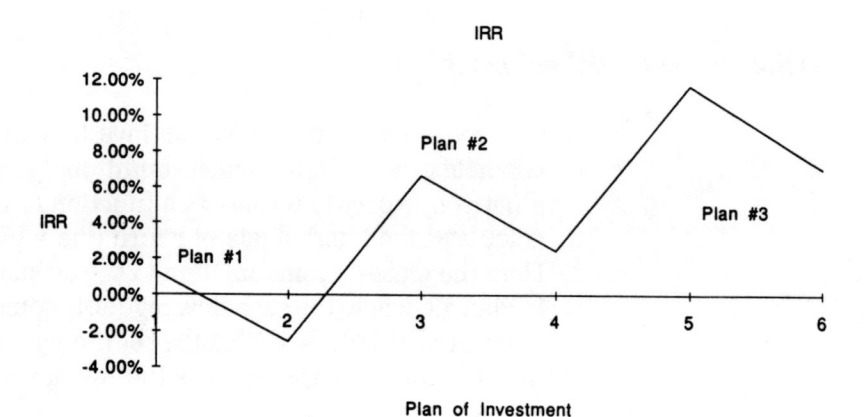

8.4 Cash flow for three plans

Investment Worksheets

The Cell Contents and Formulas

	A	B	C	D
1	INTERNAL RATE OF RETURN			
2				
3			Plan #1	
4				
5	Starting		3000	3500
6	Capital			
7				
8	Estimated			
9	Return			
10			=-C5	=-D5
11	0.08		450	450
12			450	450
13			450	450
14			450	450
15			450	450
16			450	450
17			450	450
18				
19		IRR	=IRR(C10:C17)	=IRR(D10:D17)

	E	F	G	H
1				
2				
3	Plan #2		Plan #3	
4				
5	3000	3500	3000	3500
6				
7				
8				
9				
10	=-E5	=-F5	=-G5	=-H5
11	550	550	650	650
12	550	550	650	650
13	550	550	650	650
14	550	550	650	650
15	550	550	650	650
16	550	550	650	650
17	550	550	650	650
18				
19	=IRR(E10:E17)	=IRR(F10:F17)	=IRR(G10:G17)	=IRR(H10:H17)

Excel Business Applications

Stock Portfolio

What the Spreadsheet Does

Investment in stocks is a very common way of building a financial base for the future. This spreadsheet helps you track stock investments and provides you with detailed information concerning your portfolio's performance as well as its total worth.

Working with the Spreadsheet

To work with this spreadsheet, you need to enter the following information.

Col A	stock name
Col C	code for charting
Col D	date purchased
Col E	quantity purchased
Col F	purchase price per share
Col G	total purchase value
Col H	current price per share
Col I	total dividends paid
Col J	total current value

When the spreadsheet is complete, it will provide you with the following information.

Col K	total percent gain or loss
Col L	annualized gain or loss
Row 19	total for all columns
Row 20	average for all columns

	A	B	C	D	E	F	G	H	I	J	K	L	M
1	STOCK PORTFOLIO												
2													
3													
4							Purchase	Current		Current	Percent	Annualized	
5		Stock	Code	Date	Quantity	Price/	Value	Price	Dividends	Value	gain/loss	gain/loss	
6		Name		Purchased		Share							
7													
8		Alpha Systems	A	28570	350	$30.50	$10,675.00	$37.50	$987.00	$14,112.00	32.2	2.91	
9		Geotech	B	30147	100	$38.50	$3,850.00	$31.25	$435.00	$3,560.00	-7.5	-1.12	
10		Williams R&R	C	31572	200	$125.00	$25,000.00	$110.00	$2,415.00	$24,415.00	-2.3	-0.83	
11		Silicon Prairie	D	29913	430	$42.50	$18,275.00	$65.75	$167.00	$28,439.50	55.6	7.54	
12		Delphi	E	31181	25	$112.00	$2,800.00	$125.00	$112.00	$3,237.00	15.6	4.00	
13		Axon	F	31886	50	$75.50	$3,775.00	$82.50	$8.00	$4,133.00	9.5	4.80	
14		Field Energy	G	31118	125	$34.25	$4,281.25	$25.50	$389.00	$3,576.50	-16.5	-4.04	
15		21st Century	H	30970	50	$56.13	$2,806.25	$38.75	$156.00	$2,093.50	-25.4	-5.67	
16		Ferdinand	I	30970	75	$54.88	$4,115.63	$98.50	$341.00	$7,728.50	87.8	19.58	
17		Baker Systems	J	31049	20	$98.50	$1,970.00	$125.75	$101.00	$2,616.00	32.8	7.69	
18													
19				Total	1425.00	$667.75	$77,548.13	$740.50	$5,111.00	$93,911.00	181.8	34.9	
20				Average	142.5	$66.78	$7,754.81	$74.05	$511.10	$9,391.10	18.2	3.5	

Excel Business Applications

What It Looks Like

Figure 8.5, a bar chart, compares total percent gain with annual percent gain using a range for the Y axis that includes negative numbers.

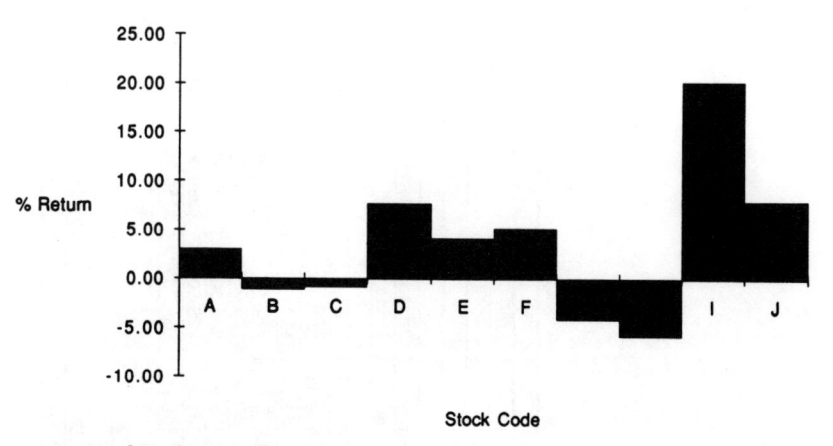

8.5 Total and annual percent gain

The Cell Contents and Formulas

	A	B	C	D	E	F	G
1	STOCK PORTFOLIO						
2							
3							
4							
5	Stock		Code	Date	Quantity	Price/	Purchase
6	Name			Purchased		Share	Value
7							
8	Alpha Systems		A	28570	350	30.5	=F8*E8
9	Geotech		B	30147	100	38.5	=F9*E9
10	Williams R&R		C	31572	200	125	=F10*E10
11	Silicon Prairie		D	29913	430	42.5	=F11*E11
12	Delphi		E	31181	25	112	=F12*E12
13	Axon		F	31886	50	75.5	=F13*E13
14	Field Energy		G	31118	125	34.25	=F14*E14
15	21st Century		H	30970	50	56.125	=F15*E15
16	Ferdinand		I	30970	75	54.875	=F16*E16
17	Baker Systems		J	31049	20	98.5	=F17*E17
18							
19				Total	=SUM(E8:E17)	=SUM(F8:F17)	=SUM(G8:G17)
20				Average	=AVERAGE(E8:E17)	=AVERAGE(F8:F17)	=AVERAGE(G8:G17)

	H	I	J	K	L
1					
2					
3					
4					
5	Current	Dividends	Current	Percent	Annualized
6	Price		Value	gain/loss	gain/loss
7					
8	37.5	987	=H8*E8+I8	=(J8−G8)/G8*100	=+K8/((NOW()−D8)/365)
9	31.25	435	=H9*E9+I9	=(J9−G9)/G9*100	=+K9/((NOW()−D9)/365)
10	110	2415	=H10*E10+I10	=(J10−G10)/G10*100	=+K10/((NOW()−D10)/365)
11	65.75	167	=H11*E11+I11	=(J11−G11)/G11*100	=+K11/((NOW()−D11)/365)
12	125	112	=H12*E12+I12	=(J12−G12)/G12*100	=+K12/((NOW()−D12)/365)
13	82.5	8	=H13*E13+I13	=(J13−G13)/G13*100	=+K13/((NOW()−D13)/365)
14	25.5	389	=H14*E14+I14	=(J14−G14)/G14*100	=+K14/((NOW()−D14)/365)
15	38.75	156	=H15*E15+I15	=(J15−G15)/G15*100	=+K15/((NOW()−D15)/365)
16	98.5	341	=H16*E16+I16	=(J16−G16)/G16*100	=+K16/((NOW()−D16)/365)
17	125.75	101	=H17*E17+I17	=(J17−G17)/G17*100	=+K17/((NOW()−D17)/365)
18					
19	=SUM(H8:H17)	=SUM(I8:I17)	=SUM(J8:J17)	=SUM(K8:K17)	=SUM(L8:L17)
20	=AVERAGE(H8:H17)	=AVERAGE(I8:I17)	=AVERAGE(J8:J17)	=AVERAGE(K8:K17)	=AVERAGE(L8:L17)

9 / Management Worksheets

Analysis of Personnel Referrals

	A	B	C	D	E	F	G	H
1	Analysis of Personnel Referrals							
2								
3	Source of	Code	W	Number	Percent of	Success	Success	
4				Applica	Applications		Ratio	
5								
6								
7	Former Em	Emp	1.0	27	11.54%	18	0.67	
8	Educationa	Ed I	1.0	56	23.93%	26	0.46	
9	Outside N	Out	1.0	32	13.68%	21	0.66	
10	Employmen	Emp	1.0	22	9.40%	11	0.50	
11	Unsolicited	Unso	1.0	16	6.84%	8	0.50	
12	Customers	Cust	1.0	57	24.36%	32	0.56	
13	Personal	Per	1.0	21	8.97%	10	0.48	
14	Other (spe	Othe	1.0	3	1.28%	0	0.00	
15								
16			Tota	234	100.00%	126		

What the Spreadsheet Does

This spreadsheet is used to examine the success of various sources of referrals in predicting the success of job candidates. The number of recruits is the same as the number of applications that have been received by each of the eight referrals listed in the spreadsheet. The number of successes can be defined in a variety of ways, such as longevity (more than five years), sales performance, productivity, and so on.

Working with the Spreadsheet

To work with this spreadsheet, you need to enter the following information.

- **Col A** source of referral
- **Col B** code for charting purposes
- **Col C** weight you assign to each category
- **Col D** number of applicants

When the spreadsheet is complete, it will provide you with the following information.

- **Col E** percent of total applications
- **Col F** successes
- **Col G** success ratio

What It Looks Like

Figure 9.1 is a bar chart indicating the success rate for each type of referral.

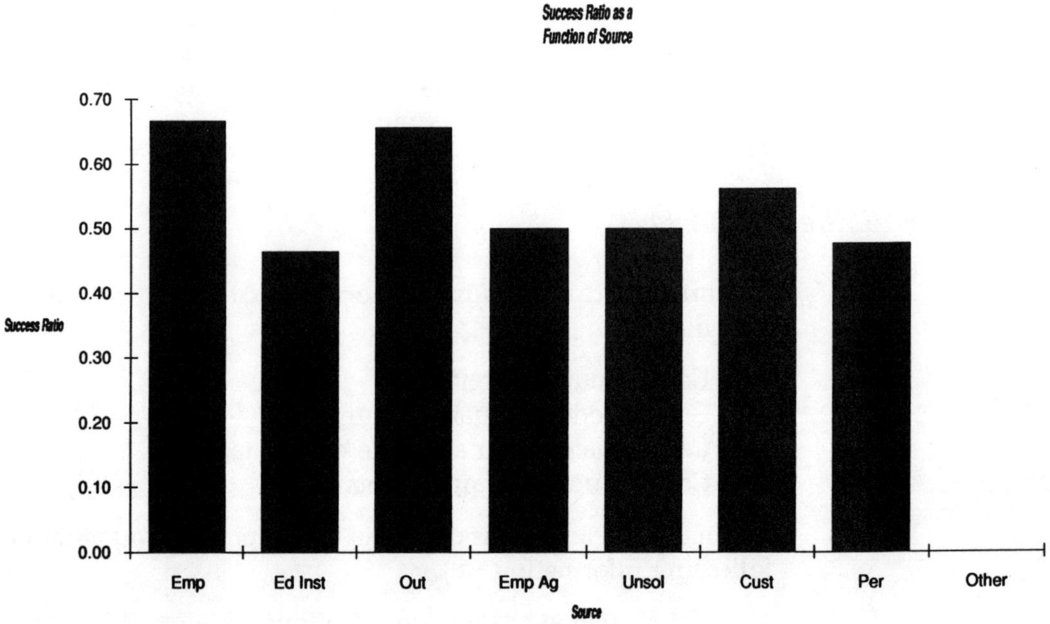
Success Ratio as a
Function of Source
0.70
0.60
0.50
0.40
0.30
0.20
0.10
0.00
Success Ratio
Emp
Ed Inst
Out
Emp Ag
Unsol
Cust
Per
Other
Source

9.1 Success rate by referral

Management Worksheets

The Cell Contents and Formulas

	A	B	C	D
1	Analysis of Personnel Referrals			
2				
3	Source of Referral	Code	Weight	Number of
4				Applications
5				
6				
7	Former Employer	Emp	1	27
8	Educational Institution	Ed Inst	1	56
9	Outside Non-competitor	Out	1	32
10	Employment Agency	Emp Ag	1	22
11	Unsolicited Referral	Unsol	1	16
12	Customers	Cust	1	57
13	Personal	Per	1	21
14	Other (specify)	Other	1	3
15				
16			Total	=SUM(D7:D14)

	E	F	G	H
1				
2				
3	Percent of	Successes	Success	
4	Applications		Ratio	
5				
6				
7	=D7/$D$16	18	=(F7/D7)*C7	
8	=D8/$D$16	26	=(F8/D8)*C8	
9	=D9/$D$16	21	=(F9/D9)*C9	
10	=D10/$D$16	11	=(F10/D10)*C10	
11	=D11/$D$16	8	=(F11/D11)*C11	
12	=D12/$D$16	32	=(F12/D12)*C12	
13	=D13/$D$16	10	=(F13/D13)*C13	
14	=D14/$D$16	0	=(F14/D14)*C14	
15				
16	=SUM(E7:E14)	=SUM(F7:F14)		

Excel Business Applications

Bidding on a Project

	A	B	C	D	E	F
1	BIDDING ON A PROJECT					
2						
3						
4	Hourly Rates				Summary	
5		Steve	$15.00			
6		Mark	$12.50		Materials	$705.67
7		Harold	$5.50		Labor	$1,142.50
8					Deposit	$500.00
9						
10					Total Due	$1,348.17
11	Job Name:	Standing				
12	Address:	1217 Learned				
13	Estimated Date Of Completion:			5/1/88		
14						
15	Job Description:		Expand screened in porch off kitchen			
16						
17	Material Co					
18						
19		Type		Quantity	Cost/Per	Total
20						Cost
21						
22		10' 2"x4"		50	$2.45	$122.50
23		8' 4"x4"		16	$5.80	$92.80
24		8' beadboard		12	$8.96	$107.52
25		16' beadboard		20	$15.17	$303.40
26		roll screen		1	$14.50	$14.50
27		4'x8' 1/2" ply (AC)		5	$12.30	$61.50
28		nails		1	$3.45	$3.45
29						
30				Total Materials		$705.67
31						
32	Labor					
33						
34		Name	Hours	Cost		
35						
36		Steve	35	$525.00		
37		Mark	45	$562.50		
38		Harold	10	$55.00		
39						
40		Total Hours		$1,142.50		

Management Worksheets

What the Spreadsheet Does

Almost every business needs to get bids or to submit them before securing a job. This spreadsheet takes into account materials and labor costs and computes the estimated cost of the job completion.

You can adjust type and number of materials or labor (people and costs) by editing the appropriate cells.

Working with the Spreadsheet

To work with this spreadsheet, you need to enter the following information.

B36...B38	names of laborers
C36...C38	estimated hours of work
C5,C6,C7	hourly labor rates for workers
Col B	material list
Col D	quantity of materials
Col E	cost of material per unit
D13	estimated date of completion
Row 11	job name
Row 12	job address
Row 13	estimated date of collection
Row 15	job description

When the spreadsheet is complete, it will provide you with the following information.

Col F	costs of materials
D36...D38	labor costs by worker
F6	total material costs
F7	total labor costs
F8	deposit
F10	total due upon completion

Excel Business Applications

The Cell Contents and Formulas

	A	B	C
1	Bidding On A Project		
2			
3	Hourly rates		
4		Steve	15
5		Mark	12.5
6		Harold	5.5
7			
8			
9			
10	Job Name:	Standing	
11	Address:	1217 Learned	
12	Estimated Date Of Completion:		
13			
14	Job Description:		Expand screened in porch
15			
16	Materials Costs		
17			
18		Type	
19			
20			
21		10' 2"x4"	
22		8' 4"x4"	
23		8' beadboard	
24		16' beadboard	
25		roll screen	
26		4"x8" 1/2" ply (AC)	
27		nails	
28			
29			
30			
31	Labor		
32			
33		Name	Hours
34			
35		Steve	35
36		Mark	45
37		Harold	10
38			
39		Total Hours	

Management Worksheets

	D	E	F
1			
2			
3		Summary	
4			
5		Materials	=F29
6		Labor	=D39
7		Deposit	500
8			
9		Total Due	=SUM(F5+F6-F7)
10			
11			
12	30802		
13			
14			
15			
16			
17			
18	Quantity	Cost/Per	Total
19			Cost
20			
21	50	2.45	=E21*D21
22	16	5.8	=E22*D22
23	12	8.96	=E23*D23
24	20	15.17	=E24*D24
25	1	14.5	=E25*D25
26	5	12.3	=E26*D26
27	1	3.45	=E27*D27
28			
29	Total Materials		=SUM(F21:F28)
30			
31			
32			
33	Cost		
34			
35	=C35*C4		
36	=C36*C5		
37	=C37*C6		
38			
39	=SUM(D35:D37)		

Excel Business Applications

Breakeven Analysis

	A	B	C	D	E	F
1	BREAKEVEN ANALYSIS					
2						
3	Price of Product		$4.95		Variable Cost	
4	Cost to Produce		$3.98		90000.00	
5	Fixed Expenses					
6		Wages and Salary		$60,000		
7		Rent		$15,000		
8		Depreciation		$5,000		
9						
10		Total		$80,000		
11						
12	Sales Summary					
13		Units Sold		$220,000		
14		Net Sales		$1,089,000		
15		Cost of Goods Sold		$875,600		
16		Gross Margin		$213,400		
17						
18	Ratios					
19		Variable Expense (VER)		$0.08		
20		Gross Margin (GMR)		$0.20		
21		Marginal Income (MIR)		$0.11		
22						
23	Breakeven Point		$705,996.76			
24						
25						
26	Summary Table (for graphing)					
27						
28	Sales	Gross	Total			
29		Margin	Expenses			
30						
31	200	$40	$50			
32	400	$48	$53			
33	600	$58	$55			
34	800	$69	$58			
35	1000	$83	$61			
36	1200	$100	$64			
37						
38						

What the Spreadsheet Does

This spreadsheet does a breakeven analysis, which allows you to examine the effect of certain decisions on future performance in sales. For example, some of the questions that you could answer using breakeven analysis are

- What changes in sales volume would be needed to compensate for an increase in the costs of goods?
- How will changes in variable costs affect gross margin?
- How will a change in production costs affect the breakeven point?

Working with the Spreadsheet

To work with this spreadsheet, you need to enter the following information.

C3	price of product
C4	cost to produce product
D6	wages and salary (including managerial costs, sales support, and clerical expenses)
D7	rent
D8	depreciation
D13	units sold

When the spreadsheet is complete, it will provide you with the following information.

C23	breakeven point in sales volume
D10	total fixed costs
D14	net sales
D15	cost of goods sold
D16	gross margin
D19	variable expense ratio
D20	gross margin of profit
D21	marginal income ratio

Excel Business Applications

What It Looks Like

Figure 9.2 shows a line chart comparing gross margin to total expenses with an estimated breakeven point of between $500 and $600.

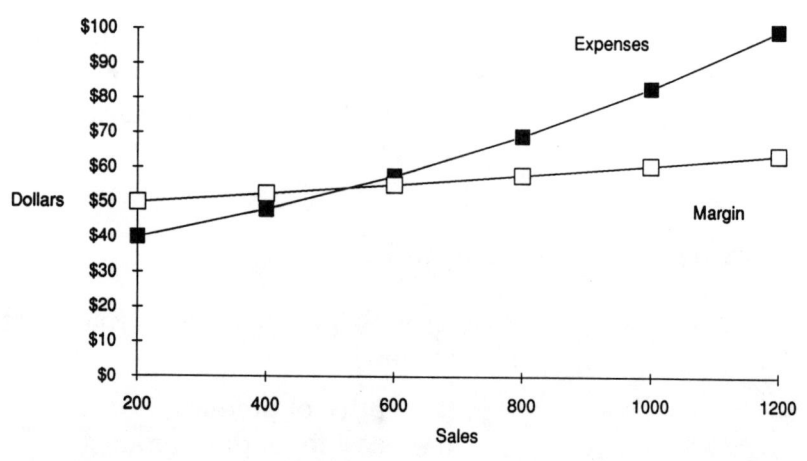

9.2 Gross margin to total expenses

The Cell Contents and Formulas

	A	B	C	D	E
1	BREAKEVEN ANALYSIS				
2					
3	Price of Product		4.95		Variable Cost
4	Cost to Produce		3.9799999999999		90000
5	Fixed Expenses				
6		Wages and Salary		60000	
7		Rent		15000	
8		Depreciation		5000	
9					
10		Total		=SUM(D6:D8)	
11					
12	Sales Summary				
13		Units Sold		220000	
14		Net Sales		=C3*D13	
15		Cost of Goods Sold		=C4*D13	
16		Gross Margin		=D14-D15	
17					
18	Ratios				
19		Variable Expense (VER)		=E4/D14	
20		Gross Margin (GMR)		=D16/D14	
21		Marginal Income (MIR)		=D20-D19	
22					
23	Breakeven Point		=D10/D21		
24					
25					
26	Summary Table (for graphing)				
27					
28	Sales	Gross	Total		
29		Margin	Expenses		
30					
31	200	=A31*0.2	50		
32	400	=B31*1.2	=C31*1.05		
33	600	=B32*1.2	=C32*1.05		
34	800	=B33*1.2	=C33*1.05		
35	1000	=B34*1.2	=C34*1.05		
36	1200	=B35*1.2	=C35*1.05		
37					
38					

Excel Business Applications

Hourly Work Sheet

	A	B	C	D	E	F	G	H	I	J	K
1	HOURLY WORK SHEET										
2											
3	Week Of:	March 21, 1988									
4	Overtime Rate		1.50								
5											
6	Employee	Hourly			Monday	Tuesday	Wednesday	Thursday	Friday	Weekly	Weekly
7		Rate								Total	Salary
8											
9	A	$7.25	In		8:00 AM	8:00 AM	8:12 AM	8:01 AM	8:34 AM		
10			Out		8:00 PM	6:40 PM	5:40 PM	7:30 PM	6:00 PM		
11			Daily Hours		12.00	10.67	9.47	11.48	9.43	53.05	$431.92
12											
13	B	$7.50	In		8:10 AM	8:08 AM	8:11 AM	8:00 AM	8:00 AM		
14			Out		4:20 PM	4:40 PM	4:10 PM	4:30 PM	4:00 PM		
15			Daily Hours		8.17	8.53	7.98	8.50	8.00	41.18	$313.31
16											
17	C	$10.00	In		8:30 AM	8:30 AM	8:30 AM	8:30 AM	8:30 AM		
18			Out		4:20 PM	4:30 PM	4:15 PM	4:20 PM	4:10 PM		
19			Daily Hours		7.83	8.00	7.75	7.83	7.67	39.08	$390.83
20											
21	D	$6.25	In		8:00 AM	8:00 AM	8:05 AM	8:00 AM	8:00 AM		
22			Out		5:30 PM	5:30 PM	5:30 PM	5:30 PM	5:30 PM		
23			Daily Hours		9.50	9.50	9.42	9.50	9.50	47.42	$319.53
24											
25	E	$7.75	In		8:05 AM	8:05 AM	8:05 AM	8:05 AM	8:05 AM		
26			Out		4:15 PM	4:15 PM	4:15 PM	4:15 PM	4:15 PM		
27			Daily Hours		8.17	8.17	8.17	8.17	8.17	40.83	$319.69
28											
29	F	$12.00	In		8:00 AM	8:00 AM	8:00 AM	8:00 AM	8:00 AM		
30			Out		4:30 PM	4:30 PM	4:30 PM	4:30 PM	4:30 PM		
31			Daily Hours		8.50	8.50	8.50	8.50	8.50	42.50	$525.00
32											
33	G	$7.50	In		8:00 AM	9:00 AM	9:00 AM	9:00 AM	9:00 AM		
34			Out		5:00 PM	5:00 PM	5:00 PM	5:00 PM	5:00 PM		
35			Daily Hours		9.00	8.00	8.00	8.00	8.00	41.00	$311.25
36											
37	H	$12.00	In		8:00 AM	8:00 AM	8:00 AM	8:00 AM	8:00 AM		
38			Out		4:30 PM	4:30 PM	4:30 PM	4:30 PM	12:30 PM		
39			Daily Hours		8.50	8.50	8.50	8.50	4.50	38.50	$462.00
40											
41	I	$10.50	In		8:00 AM	8:00 AM	8:00 AM	8:00 AM	8:00 AM		
42			Out		4:10 PM	4:00 PM	4:20 PM	4:00 PM	4:00 PM		
43			Daily Hours		8.17	8.00	8.33	8.00	8.00	40.50	$427.88
44											
45	J	$10.50	In		8:00 AM	8:00 AM	8:12 AM	8:01 AM	8:34 AM		
46			Out		7:20 PM	5:40 PM	5:40 PM	7:20 PM	6:00 PM		
47			Daily Hours		11.33	9.67	9.47	11.32	9.43	51.22	$596.66
48											
49			Daily Average		9.12	8.75	8.56	8.98	8.12		
50			Overtime		1.12	0.75	0.56	0.98	0.12		
51			% Overtime		0.12	0.09	0.07	0.11	0.01		
52											
53										Total	435.28	$3,501.41

Management Worksheets

What the Spreadsheet Does

Payroll generates a significant amount of information during each pay period. This spreadsheet allows you to track daily hourly work times and to use this information to compute payment given a specific hourly rate for regular as well as overtime work (which you define).

The spreadsheet computes the time between in and out by using the **=TIME** function and then multiplies the difference by 24 to adjust for the fractional expression of time using that function. It also adjusts for overtime rate (which you set in cell C4) for anything over 40 hours.

Working with the Spreadsheet

To work with this spreadsheet, you need to enter the following information.

C4	overtime rate
Col A	employee identification
Col B	hourly rate
Col E...I	in and out time

When the spreadsheet is complete, it will provide you with the following information.

Col J	weekly total
Col K	weekly salary
J53	total weekly hours
K53	total payment
Rows 11,15,19,23,etc.	daily hours for each employee
Row 49	daily average hours per employee
Row 50	average overtime
Row 51	overtime as a percentage of workday

Excel Business Applications

What It Looks Like

Figure 9.3 is a pie chart showing percent of total weekly overtime by day.

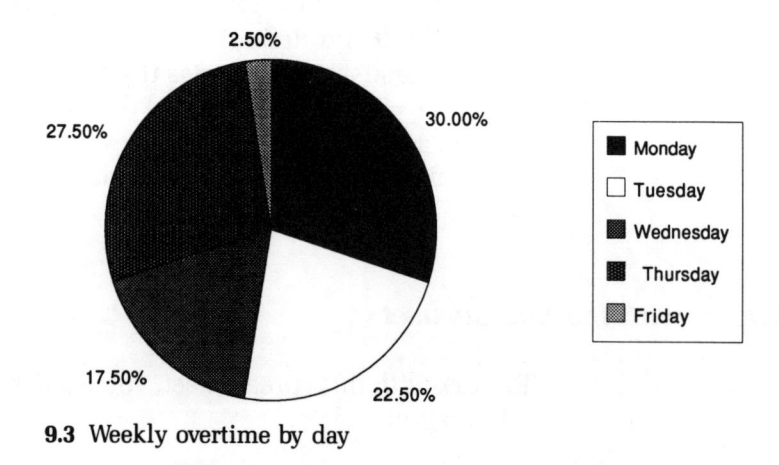

- Monday: 30.00%
- Tuesday: 22.50%
- Wednesday: 17.50%
- Thursday: 27.50%
- Friday: 2.50%

9.3 Weekly overtime by day

Management Worksheets

The Cell Contents and Formulas

	A	B	C	D	E
1	HOURLY WORK SHEET				
2					
3	Week Of:	March 21, 1988			
4	Overtime Rate		1.5		
5					
6	Employee	Hourly			Monday
7		Rate			
8					
9	A	7.25	In		=TIME(8,0,0)
10			Out		=TIME(20,0,0)
11			Daily Hours		=(E10-E9)*24
12					
13	B	7.5	In		=TIME(8,10,0)
14			Out		=TIME(16,20,0)
15			Daily Hours		=(E14-E13)*24
16					
17	C	10	In		=TIME(8,30,0)
18			Out		=TIME(16,20,0)
19			Daily Hours		=(E18-E17)*24
20					
21	D	6.25	In		=TIME(8,0,0)
22			Out		=TIME(17,30,0)
23			Daily Hours		=(E22-E21)*24
24					
25	E	7.75	In		=TIME(8,5,0)
26			Out		=TIME(16,15,0)
27			Daily Hours		=(E26-E25)*24
28					
29	F	12	In		=TIME(8,0,0)
30			Out		=TIME(16,30,0)
31			Daily Hours		=(E30-E29)*24
32					
33	G	7.5	In		=TIME(8,0,0)
34			Out		=TIME(17,0,0)
35			Daily Hours		=(E34-E33)*24
36					
37	H	12	In		=TIME(8,0,0)
38			Out		=TIME(16,30,0)
39			Daily Hours		
40					
41	I	10.5	In		=TIME(8,0,0)
42			Out		=TIME(16,10,0)
43			Daily Hours		=(E42-E41)*24
44					
45	J	10.5	In		=TIME(8,0,0)
46			Out		=TIME(19,20,0)
47			Daily Hours		=(E46-E45)*24
48					
49			Daily Average		=(E11+E15+E19+E23+E27+E31+E35+E39+E43+E47)/10
50			Overtime		=E49-8

Excel Business Applications

The Cell Contents and Formulas (Continued)

	F	G
1		
2		
3		
4		
5		
6	Tuesday	Wednesday
7		
8		
9	=TIME(8,0,0)	=TIME(8,12,0)
10	=TIME(18,40,0)	=TIME(17,40,0)
11	=(F10-F9)*24	=(G10-G9)*24
12		
13	=TIME(8,8,0)	=TIME(8,11,0)
14	=TIME(16,40,0)	=TIME(16,10,0)
15	=(F14-F13)*24	=(G14-G13)*24
16		
17	=TIME(8,30,0)	=TIME(8,30,0)
18	=TIME(16,30,0)	=TIME(16,15,0)
19	=(F18-F17)*24	=(G18-G17)*24
20		
21	=TIME(8,0,0)	=TIME(8,5,0)
22	=TIME(17,30,0)	=TIME(17,30,0)
23	=(F22-F21)*24	=(G22-G21)*24
24		
25	=TIME(8,5,0)	=TIME(8,5,0)
26	=TIME(16,15,0)	=TIME(16,15,0)
27	=(F26-F25)*24	=(G26-G25)*24
28		
29	=TIME(8,0,0)	=TIME(8,0,0)
30	=TIME(16,30,0)	=TIME(16,30,0)
31	=(F30-F29)*24	=(G30-G29)*24
32		
33	=TIME(9,0,0)	=TIME(9,0,0)
34	=TIME(17,0,0)	=TIME(17,0,0)
35	=(F34-F33)*24	=(G34-G33)*24
36		
37	=TIME(8,0,0)	=TIME(8,0,0)
38	=TIME(16,30,0)	=TIME(16,30,0)
39	=(F38-F37)*24	=(G38-G37)*24
40		
41	=TIME(8,0,0)	=TIME(8,0,0)
42	=TIME(16,0,0)	=TIME(16,20,0)
43	=(F42-F41)*24	=(G42-G41)*24
44		
45	=TIME(8,0,0)	=TIME(8,12,0)
46	=TIME(17,40,0)	=TIME(17,40,0)
47	=(F46-F45)*24	=(G46-G45)*24
48		
49	=(F11+F15+F19+F23+F27+F31+F35+F39+F43+F47)/10	=(G11+G15+G19+G23+G27+G31+G35+G39+G43+G47)/10
50	=F49-8	=G49-8

Management Worksheets

	H	I	J
1			
2			
3			
4			
5			
6	Thursday	Friday	Weekly
7			Total
8			
9	=TIME(8,1,0)	=TIME(8,34,0)	
10	=TIME(19,30,0)	=TIME(18,0,0)	
11	=(H10-H9)*24	=(I10-I9)*24	=SUM(E11:I11)
12			
13	=TIME(8,0,0)	=TIME(8,0,0)	
14	=TIME(16,30,0)	=TIME(16,0,0)	
15	=(H14-H13)*24	=(I14-I13)*24	=SUM(E15:I15)
16			
17	=TIME(8,30,0)	=TIME(8,30,0)	
18	=TIME(16,20,0)	=TIME(16,10,0)	
19	=(H18-H17)*24	=(I18-I17)*24	=SUM(E19:I19)
20			
21	=TIME(8,0,0)	=TIME(8,0,0)	
22	=TIME(17,30,0)	=TIME(17,30,0)	
23	=(H22-H21)*24	=(I22-I21)*24	=SUM(E23:I23)
24			
25	=TIME(8,5,0)	=TIME(8,5,0)	
26	=TIME(16,15,0)	=TIME(16,15,0)	
27	=(H26-H25)*24	=(I26-I25)*24	=SUM(E27:I27)
28			
29	=TIME(8,0,0)	=TIME(8,0,0)	
30	=TIME(16,30,0)	=TIME(16,30,0)	
31	=(H30-H29)*24	=(I30-I29)*24	=SUM(E31:I31)
32			
33	=TIME(9,0,0)	=TIME(9,0,0)	
34	=TIME(17,0,0)	=TIME(17,0,0)	
35	=(H34-H33)*24	=(I34-I33)*24	=SUM(E35:I35)
36			
37	=TIME(8,0,0)	=TIME(8,0,0)	
38	=TIME(16,30,0)	=TIME(12,30,0)	
39	=(H38-H37)*24	=(I38-I37)*24	=SUM(E39:I39)
40			
41	=TIME(8,0,0)	=TIME(8,0,0)	
42	=TIME(16,0,0)	=TIME(16,0,0)	
43	=(H42-H41)*24	=(I42-I41)*24	=SUM(E43:I43)
44			
45	=TIME(8,1,0)	=TIME(8,34,0)	
46	=TIME(19,20,0)	=TIME(18,0,0)	
47	=(H46-H45)*24	=(I46-I45)*24	=SUM(E47:I47)
48			
49	=(H11+H15+H19+H23+H27+H31+H35+H39+H43+H47)/10	=(I11+I15+I19+I23+I27+I31+I35+I39+I43+I47)/10	
50	=H49-8	=I49-8	

Excel Business Applications

The Cell Contents and Formulas (Continued)

	K
1	
2	
3	
4	
5	
6	Weekly
7	Salary
8	
9	
10	
11	=IF(J11>40,(J11-40)*(B9*$C$4)+(40*B9),J11*B9)
12	
13	
14	
15	=IF(J15>40,(J15-40)*(B13*$C$4)+(40*B13),J15*B13)
16	
17	
18	
19	=IF(J19>40,(J19-40)*(B17*$C$4)+(40*B17),J19*B17)
20	
21	
22	
23	=IF(J23>40,(J23-40)*(B21*$C$4)+(40*B21),J23*B21)
24	
25	
26	
27	=IF(J27>40,(J27-40)*(B25*$C$4)+(40*B25),J27*B25)
28	
29	
30	
31	=IF(J31>40,(J31-40)*(B29*$C$4)+(40*B29),J31*B29)
32	
33	
34	
35	=IF(J35>40,(J35-40)*(B33*$C$4)+(40*B33),J35*B33)
36	
37	
38	
39	=IF(J39>40,(J39-40)*(B37*$C$4)+(40*B37),J39*B37)
40	
41	
42	
43	=IF(J43>40,(J43-40)*(B41*$C$4)+(40*B41),J43*B41)
44	
45	
46	
47	=IF(J47>40,(J47-40)*(B45*$C$4)+(40*B45),J47*B45)
48	
49	
50	

Management Worksheets

Payroll Ledger

What the Spreadsheet Does

Once a company becomes more than a one-person business, payroll, including various sorts of taxes, has to be paid, and overtime figured.

This spreadsheet allows you to compute these separate values for a set of employees and provides you with a sum for the pay period. You set tax rates as well as overtime payments.

Working with the Spreadsheet

To work with this spreadsheet, you need to enter the following information.

- **Col A** employee identification
- **Col B** number of deductions
- **Col C** FIT rate
- **Col D** hourly wage
- **Col E** number of hours worked
- **Col F** hours overtime
- **Col H** number of hours worked (regular)
- **A3**   FICA rate
- **A4**   state tax
- **A5**   overtime

When the spreadsheet is complete, it will provide you with the following information.

- **Col G** amount of overtime paid
- **Col H** base salary (gross earnings)
- **Col I** total wages paid
- **Col J** FICA withheld (social security tax)
- **Col K** federal income taxes withheld
- **Col L** state taxes withheld
- **Col M** total deductions for this work period
- **Col N** total payment for this work period

165

	A	B	C	D	E	F	G	H	I	J	K	L	M	N
1	PAYROLL LEDGER													
2														
3	FICA value		0.08											
4	State Tax		0.00											
5	Overtime Rate		1.50											
6														
7	Name	# Ded	FIT Rate	Hourly Wage	Hours Worked	Over-time	Over-time ($)	Base Salary	Total Wages	FICA	FIT	State Tax	Total Deductions	Total Payment
8														
9														
10	J.K.	2	0.33	$11.50	51	11	$189.75	$586.50	$776.25	$44.05	$193.55	$32.26	$269.85	$316.65
11	H.G.	2	0.15	$7.50	42	2	$22.50	$315.00	$337.50	$23.66	$47.25	$17.33	$88.23	$226.77
12	W.B.	1	0.15	$8.50	45	5	$63.75	$382.50	$446.25	$28.73	$57.38	$21.04	$107.14	$275.36
13	R.T.	4	0.15	$8.00	41	1	$12.00	$328.00	$340.00	$24.63	$49.20	$18.04	$91.87	$236.13
14	I.O.	2	0.28	$8.50	42	2	$25.50	$357.00	$382.50	$26.81	$99.96	$19.64	$146.41	$210.59
15	F.D.	2	0.28	$7.50	44	4	$45.00	$330.00	$375.00	$24.78	$92.40	$18.15	$135.33	$194.67
16	W.E.	1	0.28	$11.00	48	8	$132.00	$528.00	$660.00	$39.65	$147.84	$29.04	$216.53	$311.47
17	H.T.	2	0.28	$12.00	40	0	$0.00	$480.00	$480.00	$36.05	$134.40	$26.40	$196.85	$283.15
18	W.Q.	2	0.28	$10.00	50	10	$150.00	$500.00	$650.00	$37.55	$140.00	$27.50	$205.05	$294.95
19	T.F.	0	0.28	$8.50	44	4	$51.00	$374.00	$425.00	$28.09	$104.72	$20.57	$153.38	$220.62
20														
21			TOTALS		447			4181.00		313.99	1066.69	229.96	1610.64	2570.36

What It Looks Like

Figure 9.4, a stacked bar chart, compares overtime to base salary.

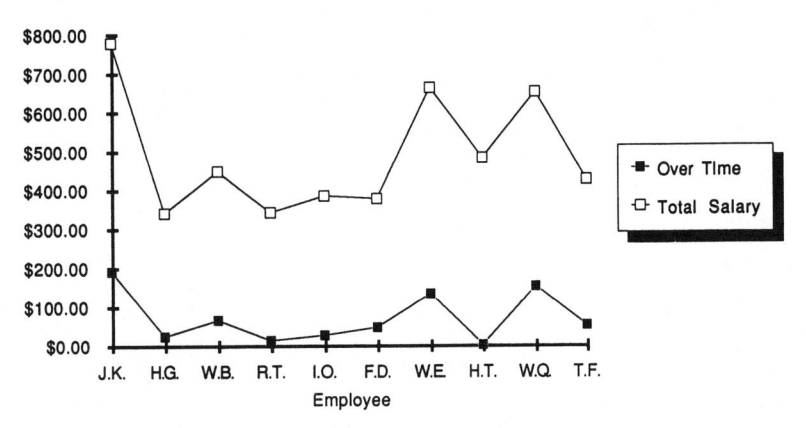

9.4 Overtime to base salary

Excel Business Applications

The Cell Contents and Formulas

	A	B	C	D	E	F	G
1	PAYROLL LEDGER						
2							
3	FICA value		0.0751				
4	State Tax		0.055				
5	Overtime Rate		1.5				
6							
7	Name	# Ded	FIT	Hourly	Hours	Over-	Over-
8			Rate	Wage	Worked	time	time ($)
9							
10	J.K.	2	0.33	11.5	51	=E10-40	=D10*F10*$C$5
11	H.G.	2	0.15	7.5	42	=E11-40	=D11*F11*$C$5
12	W.B.	1	0.15	8.5	45	=E12-40	=D12*F12*$C$5
13	R.T.	4	0.15	8	41	=E13-40	=D13*F13*$C$5
14	I.O.	2	0.28	8.5	42	=E14-40	=D14*F14*$C$5
15	F.D.	2	0.28	7.5	44	=E15-40	=D15*F15*$C$5
16	W.E.	1	0.28	11	48	=E16-40	=D16*F16*$C$5
17	H.T.	2	0.28	12	40	=E17-40	=D17*F17*$C$5
18	W.Q.	2	0.28	10	50	=E18-40	=D18*F18*$C$5
19	T.F.	0	0.28	8.5	44	=E19-40	=D19*F19*$C$5
20							
21			TOTALS		=SUM(E10:E19)		

Management Worksheets

	H	I	J	K	L	M	N
1							
2							
3							
4							
5							
6							
7	Base	Total	FICA	FIT	State	Total	Total
8	Salary	Wages			Tax	Deductions	Payment
9							
10	=D10*E10	=(F10*D10*$C$5)+I	=H10*$C$3	=C10*H10	=$C$4*H10	=SUM(J10:L10)	=H10-M10
11	=D11*E11	=(F11*D11*$C$5)+I	=H11*$C$3	=C11*H11	=$C$4*H11	=SUM(J11:L11)	=H11-M11
12	=D12*E12	=(F12*D12*$C$5)+I	=H12*$C$3	=C12*H12	=$C$4*H12	=SUM(J12:L12)	=H12-M12
13	=D13*E13	=(F13*D13*$C$5)+I	=H13*$C$3	=C13*H13	=$C$4*H13	=SUM(J13:L13)	=H13-M13
14	=D14*E14	=(F14*D14*$C$5)+I	=H14*$C$3	=C14*H14	=$C$4*H14	=SUM(J14:L14)	=H14-M14
15	=D15*E15	=(F15*D15*$C$5)+I	=H15*$C$3	=C15*H15	=$C$4*H15	=SUM(J15:L15)	=H15-M15
16	=D16*E16	=(F16*D16*$C$5)+I	=H16*$C$3	=C16*H16	=$C$4*H16	=SUM(J16:L16)	=H16-M16
17	=D17*E17	=(F17*D17*$C$5)+I	=H17*$C$3	=C17*H17	=$C$4*H17	=SUM(J17:L17)	=H17-M17
18	=D18*E18	=(F18*D18*$C$5)+I	=H18*$C$3	=C18*H18	=$C$4*H18	=SUM(J18:L18)	=H18-M18
19	=D19*E19	=(F19*D19*$C$5)+I	=H19*$C$3	=C19*H19	=$C$4*H19	=SUM(J19:L19)	=H19-M19
20							
21	=SUM(H10:H19)		=SUM(J10:J19)	=SUM(K10:K19)	=SUM(L10:L19)	=SUM(M10:M19)	=SUM(N10:N19)

Excel Business Applications

Property Management

	A	B	C	D	E	F	G
1	PROPERTY MANAGEMENT		Property: 202 Maine				
2							
3							
4	Beginning Cash Balance		$3,675.89				
5	Security Deposit		$1,200.00				
6	Taxes per Annum		$1,345.98				
7	Insurance per Annum		$2,456.98				
8	Mortgage		$1,550.00				
9							
10							
11		Jan	Feb	Mar	April	May	June
12							
13	INCOME	$2,300.00	$2,200.00	$1,800.00	$2,300.00	$2,200.00	$2,300.00
14							
15	EXPENSES						
16	Mortgage	$1,550.00	$1,550.00	$1,550.00	$1,550.00	$1,550.00	$1,550.00
17	Taxes	$112.17	$112.17	$112.17	$112.17	$112.17	$112.17
18	Insurance	$204.75	$204.75	$204.75	$204.75	$204.75	$204.75
19	Maintenance	$657.00	$249.00	$124.00	$435.00	$231.00	$76.00
20							
21	TOTAL	$2,523.91	$2,115.91	$1,990.91	$2,301.91	$2,097.91	$1,942.91
22	GAIN/(LOSS)	($223.91)	$84.09	($190.91)	($1.91)	$102.09	$357.09
23							
24	Available Cash	$2,300.00	$2,200.00	$1,800.00	$2,300.00	$2,200.00	$2,300.00

What the Spreadsheet Does

Managing property means keeping track of many things besides income. For example, management fees, maintenance, and taxes need to be considered as well. This spreadsheet keeps track of income and expenses for any one property and allows you to compare budgeted versus actual expenses over one year.

Working with the Spreadsheet

To work with this spreadsheet, you need to enter the following information.

Management Worksheets

	H	I	J	K	L	M	N
1							
2							
3							
4							
5							
6							
7							
8							
9	Actual Expenses						
10							
11	July	Aug	Sept	Oct	Nov	Dec	Total
12							
13	$1,800.00	$1,800.00	$2,300.00	$2,300.00	$2,200.00	$2,150.00	$25,650.00
14							
15							
16	$1,550.00	$1,550.00	$1,550.00	$1,550.00	$1,550.00	$1,550.00	$18,600.00
17	$112.17	$112.17	$112.17	$112.17	$112.17	$112.17	$1,345.98
18	$204.75	$204.75	$204.75	$204.75	$204.75	$204.75	$2,456.98
19	$221.00	$324.00	$213.00	$312.00	$301.00	$234.00	$3,377.00
20							
21	$2,087.91	$2,190.91	$2,079.91	$2,178.91	$2,167.91	$2,100.91	$25,779.96
22	($287.91)	($390.91)	$220.09	$121.09	$32.09	$49.09	($129.96)
23							
24	$1,800.00	$1,800.00	$2,300.00	$2,300.00	$2,200.00	$2,150.00	$25,650.00

D4	beginning cash balance
D5	security deposit
D6	actual taxes per annum
D7	actual insurance costs per annum
D8	mortgage each month
R13	monthly income
B16...M19	expenses by category

When the spreadsheet is complete, it will provide you with the following information.

Row 21	monthly income
Row 22	gain or loss
Row 24	available cash

Excel Business Applications

What It Looks Like

Figure 9.5 compares income to expenses (for any one property).

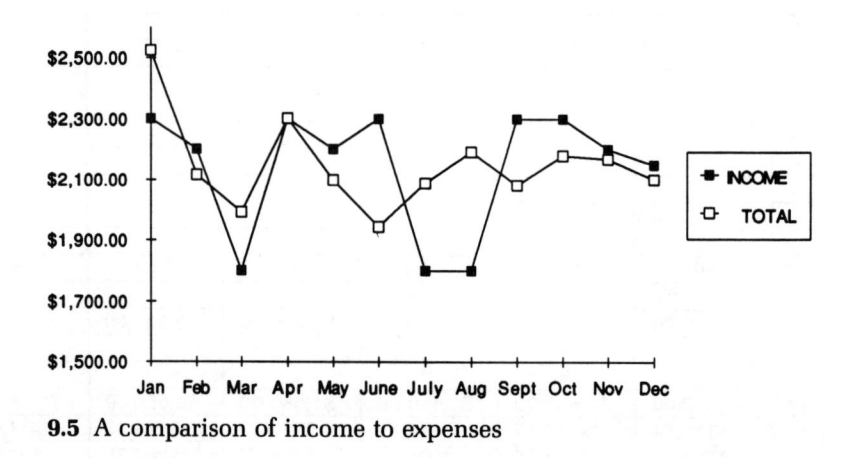

9.5 A comparison of income to expenses

The Cell Contents and Formulas

	A	B	C	D	E	F	G
1	PROPERTY MANAGEMENT		Property: 202 Maine				
2							
3							
4	Beginning Cash Balance		3675.89				
5	Security Deposit		1200				
6	Taxes per Annum		1345.98				
7	Insurance per Annum		2456.98				
8	Mortgage		1550				
9							
10			Jan	Feb	Mar	April	May	June
11							
12							
13	INCOME		2300	2200	1800	2300	2200	2300
14							
15	EXPENSES						
16	Mortgage		=$C$8	=$C$8	=$C$8	=$C$8	=$C$8	=$C$8
17	Taxes		=C6/12	=$C$6/12	=$C$6/12	=$C$6/12	=$C$6/12	=$C$6/12
18	Insurance		=$C$7/12	=$C$7/12	=$C$7/12	=$C$7/12	=$C$7/12	=$C$7/12
19	Maintenance		657	249	124	435	231	76
20							
21	TOTAL	=SUM(B16:B19)	=SUM(C16:C19)	=SUM(D16:D19)	=SUM(E16:E19)	=SUM(F16:F19)	=SUM(G16:G19)
22	GAIN/(LOSS)	=B13-B21	=C13-C21	=D13-D21	=E13-E21	=F13-F21	=G13-G21
23							
24	Available Cash	=B21+B22	=C21+C22	=D21+D22	=E21+E22	=F21+F22	=G21+G22

	H	I	J	K	L	M	N
1							
2							
3							
4							
5							
6							
7							
8							
9	Actual Expenses						
10	July	Aug	Sept	Oct	Nov	Dec	Total
11							
12							
13	1800	1800	2300	2300	2200	2150	=SUM(B13:M13)
14							
15							
16	=$C$8	=$C$8	=$C$8	=$C$8	=$C$8	=$C$8	=SUM(B16:M16)
17	=$C$6/12	=$C$6/12	=$C$6/12	=$C$6/12	=$C$6/12	=$C$6/12	=SUM(B17:M17)
18	=$C$7/12	=$C$7/12	=$C$7/12	=$C$7/12	=$C$7/12	=$C$7/12	=SUM(B18:M18)
19	221	324	213	312	301	234	=SUM(B19:M19)
20							
21	=SUM(H16:H19)	=SUM(I16:I19)	=SUM(J16:J19)	=SUM(K16:K19)	=SUM(L16:L19)	=SUM(M16:M19)	=SUM(B21:M21)
22	=H13-H21	=I13-I21	=J13-J21	=K13-K21	=L13-L21	=M13-M21	=SUM(B22:M22)
23							
24	=H21+H22	=I21+I22	=J21+J22	=K21+K22	=L21+L22	=M21+M22	=N21+N22

Excel Business Applications

Tracking Utility Expenses

	A	B	C	D	E	F	G	H
1	UTILITY EXPENSES							
2								
3							Month	
4			Jan	Feb	March	April	May	June
5								
6	Water		$58.34	$54.67	$67.78	$54.67	$43.67	$65.76
7	Gas		$123.45	$145.67	$103.45	$89.76	$91.34	$78.98
8	Electric		$78.97	$77.89	$87.98	$67.88	$87.76	$98.89
9								
10	Total		$260.76	$278.23	$259.21	$212.31	$222.77	$243.63
11	Average		$86.92	$92.74	$86.40	$70.77	$74.26	$81.21

	I	J	K	L	M	N	O
1							
2							
3							
4	July	August	Sept	Oct	Nov	Dec	Total
5							
6	$66.54	$55.76	$55.89	$49.00	$47.67	$44.67	$664.42
7	$65.78	$69.87	$68.76	$81.24	$91.78	$102.56	$1,112.64
8	$98.78	$78.76	$77.78	$77.89	$81.35	$91.34	$1,005.27
9							
10	$231.10	$204.39	$202.43	$208.13	$220.80	$238.57	
11	$77.03	$68.13	$67.48	$69.38	$73.60	$79.52	

What the Spreadsheet Does

It's often useful to maintain a running average of current utility (or any other operating) costs to get a good idea of what numbers should be considered in future planning. This spreadsheet takes the data for three utilities (although it can be done for more, of course) and computes current, 3-month moving averages, and 6-month moving averages by month.

Management Worksheets

Working with the Spreadsheet

To work with this spreadsheet, you need to enter the following information.

Row 6 costs for water by month
Row 7 costs for gas by month
Row 8 costs for electric by month

When the spreadsheet is complete, it will provide you with the following information.

Row 10 total utility costs by month
Row 11 average utility costs by month

What It Looks Like

Figure 9.6 is bar chart of utility expenses by type by month.

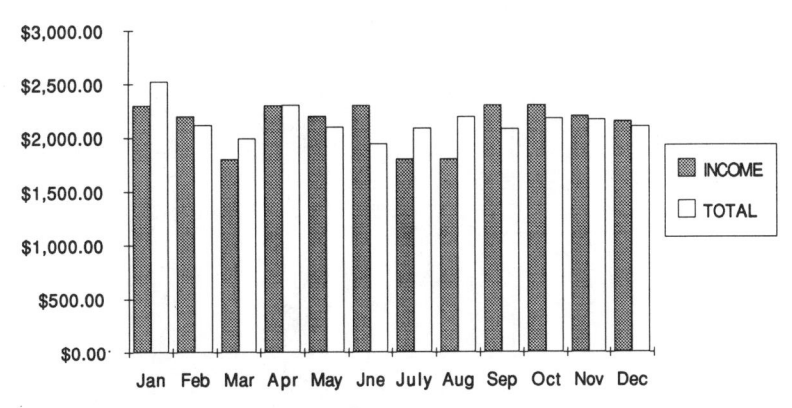

9.6 Expenses by type of month

175

The Cell Contents and Formulas

	A	B	C	D	E	F	G	H
1	UTILITY EXPENSE							
2								
3							Month	
4			Jan	Feb	March	April	May	June
5								
6	Water		58.34	54.67	67.78	54.67	43.67	65.76
7	Gas		123.45	145.67	103.45	89.76	91.34	78.98
8	Electric		78.97	77.89	87.98	67.88	87.76	98.89
9								
10	Total		=SUM(C6:C9)	=SUM(D6:D9)	=SUM(E6:E9)	=SUM(F6:F9)	=SUM(G6:G9)	=SUM(H6:H9)
11	Average		=AVERAGE(C6:C9)	=AVERAGE(D6:D9)	=AVERAGE(E6:E9)	=AVERAGE(F6:F9)	=AVERAGE(G6:G9)	=AVERAGE(H6:H9)

	I	J	K	L	M	N	O
1							
2							
3							
4	July	August	Sept	Oct	Nov	Dec	Total
5							
6	66.54	55.76	55.89	49	47.67	44.67	=SUM(C6:N6)
7	65.78	69.87	68.76	81.24	91.78	102.56	=SUM(C7:N7)
8	98.78	78.76	77.78	77.89	81.35	91.34	=SUM(C8:N8)
9							
10	=SUM(I6:I9)	=SUM(J6:J9)	=SUM(K6:K9)	=SUM(L6:L9)	=SUM(M6:M9)	=SUM(N6:N9)	
11	=AVERAGE(I6:I9)	=AVERAGE(J6:J9)	=AVERAGE(K6:K9)	=AVERAGE(L6:L9)	=AVERAGE(M6:M9)	=AVERAGE(N6:N9)	

Management Worksheets

Weighted Employee Comparison

	A	B	C	D	E	F	G	H	I	J	K	L	M
1	WEIGHTED EMPLOYEE COMPARISON												
2													
3							McCurry Avionics						
4							1608 Strathmore Pk						
5							Witchita, KS 12345						
6							(913) 867-1234						
7													
8													
9							Characteristics						
10													
11				A	B	C	D	E	F	G	H		
12													
13			Weight	1	2	4	4	5	1	2	1		
14												Weighted	Unweighted
15	Name											Score	Score
16													
17	M.O.			4	4	5	5	4	5	3	3	4.13	4.30
18	T.M.			2	2	3	2	3	1	3	3	2.38	2.55
19	R.E.			5	4	3	4	5	2	2	4	3.63	3.80
20	J.I.			4	3	2	3	3	2	3	5	3.13	2.90
21	W.E.			3	5	4	4	4	1	3	4	3.50	3.80
22	Y.U.			2	4	2	3	4	4	2	4	3.13	3.10
23	R.R.			1	3	1	3	5	4	1	4	2.75	2.90
24	Y.Y.			2	2	2	2	4	5	4	5	3.25	3.00
25	B.N.			5	3	2	2	3	1	3	4	2.88	2.65
26	Q.S.			4	4	3	2	3	1	3	5	3.13	2.95
27													
28		Average											
29		Rating		3.20	3.40	2.70	3.00	3.80	2.60	2.70	4.10	3.19	3.19
30													
31													
32	Code for Characteristics						Ratings				Weights		
33													
34	A Appearance						1 Excellent				1 Very Important		
35	B Potential						2 Above Average				2 Somewhat Important		
36	C Enthusiasm						3 Average				3 Undecided		
37	D Product Knowledge						4 Below Average				4 Not Important		
38	E Compatibility with Other Workers						5 Not Acceptable				5 Not At All Important		
39	F Attitude												
40	G Prior Sales record												
41	H Recommendations												

Excel Business Applications

What the Spreadsheet Does

It's often necessary to compare several employees with each other and to make a decision on who might be best to promote, offer additional opportunities, transfer, and so on. This spreadsheet allows you to weigh a number of categories and to derive unweighted and weighted averages given a value assigned on certain characteristics. Although these ratings are subjective, as a weighted score they can provide some assistance in making decisions.

Weights are assigned on a scale of 1 through 5, with 1 the heaviest. Ratings are assigned on a scale of 1 through 5, with 1 being the most important.

Working with the Spreadsheet

To work with this spreadsheet, you need to enter the following information.

>**Col A**   employee identification
>**C17...J26** rating for appearance, potential, enthusiasm, knowledge of product, compatibility with others, attitude, prior sales record, and recommendation
>**Row 13**   weights for appearance, potential, enthusiasm, knowledge of product, compatibility with others, attitude, prior sales record, and recommendation

When the spreadsheet is complete, it will provide you with the following information.

>**Row 29**   average rating per category
>**Col K**   unweighted composite score
>**Col L**   weighted composite score

Management Worksheets

What It Looks Like

Figure 9.7 shows a line chart comparing weighted and unweighted averages as a function of employee identification.

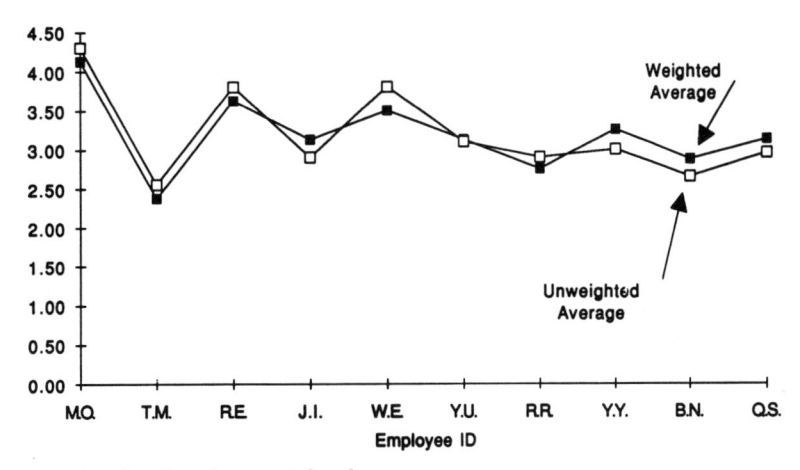

9.7 Weighted and unweighted averages

Excel Business Applications

The Cell Contents and Formulas

	A	B	C	D	E
1	WEIGHTED EMPLOYEE COMPARISON				
2					
3					
4					
5					
6					
7					
8					
9					
10					
11			A	B	C
12					
13		Weight->	1	2	4
14					
15	Name				
16					
17	M.O.		4	4	5
18	T.M.		2	2	3
19	R.E.		5	4	3
20	J.I.		4	3	2
21	W.E.		3	5	4
22	Y.U.		2	4	2
23	R.R.		1	3	1
24	Y.Y.		2	2	2
25	B.N.		5	3	2
26	Q.S.		4	4	3
27					
28		Average			
29		Rating	=AVERAGE(C17:C26)	=AVERAGE(D17:D26)	=AVERAGE(E17:E26)
30					
31					
32	Code for Characteristics				
33					
34	A Appearance				
35	B Potential				
36	C Enthusiasm				
37	D Product Knowledge				
38	E Compatibility with Other Workers				
39	F Attitude				
40	G Prior Sales record				
41	H Recommendations				

	F	G	H	I	J	K
1						
2						
3	McCurry Avionics					
4	1608 Strathmore Pk					
5	Witchita, KS 12345					
6	(913) 867-1234					
7						
8						
9		Characteristics				
10						
11	D	E	F	G	H	
12						
13	4	5	1	2	1	
14						Weighted
15						Score
16						
17	5	4	5	3	3	=AVERAGE(C17:J17)
18	2	3	1	3	3	=AVERAGE(C18:J18)
19	4	5	2	2	4	=AVERAGE(C19:J19)
20	3	3	2	3	5	=AVERAGE(C20:J20)
21	4	4	1	3	4	=AVERAGE(C21:J21)
22	3	4	4	2	4	=AVERAGE(C22:J22)
23	3	5	4	1	4	=AVERAGE(C23:J23)
24	2	4	5	4	5	=AVERAGE(C24:J24)
25	2	3	1	3	4	=AVERAGE(C25:J25)
26	2	3	1	3	5	=AVERAGE(C26:J26)
27						
28						
29	=AVERAGE(F17:F26)	=AVERAGE(G17:G26)	=AVERAGE(H17:H26)	=AVERAGE(I17:I26)	=AVERAGE(J17:J26)	=AVERAGE(K17:K26)
30						
31						
32		Ratings				Weights
33						
34		1 Excellent				1 Very Important
35		2 Above Average				2 Somewhat Important
36		3 Average				3 Undecided
37		4 Below Average				4 Not Important
38		5 Not Acceptable				5 Not At All Important
39						
40						
41						

Excel Business Applications

The Cell Contents and Formulas (Continued)

	L
1	
2	
3	
4	
5	
6	
7	
8	
9	
10	
11	
12	
13	
14	Unweighted
15	Score
16	
17	=((C17*$C$13)+(D17*$D$13)+(E17*$E$13)+(F17*$F$13)+(G17*$G$13)+(H17*$H$13)+(I17*$I$13)+(J17*$J$13))/SUM(C13:J13)
18	=((C18*$C$13)+(D18*$D$13)+(E18*$E$13)+(F18*$F$13)+(G18*$G$13)+(H18*$H$13)+(I18*$I$13)+(J18*$J$13))/20
19	=((C19*$C$13)+(D19*$D$13)+(E19*$E$13)+(F19*$F$13)+(G19*$G$13)+(H19*$H$13)+(I19*$I$13)+(J19*$J$13))/20
20	=((C20*$C$13)+(D20*$D$13)+(E20*$E$13)+(F20*$F$13)+(G20*$G$13)+(H20*$H$13)+(I20*$I$13)+(J20*$J$13))/20
21	=((C21*$C$13)+(D21*$D$13)+(E21*$E$13)+(F21*$F$13)+(G21*$G$13)+(H21*$H$13)+(I21*$I$13)+(J21*$J$13))/20
22	=((C22*$C$13)+(D22*$D$13)+(E22*$E$13)+(F22*$F$13)+(G22*$G$13)+(H22*$H$13)+(I22*$I$13)+(J22*$J$13))/20
23	=((C23*$C$13)+(D23*$D$13)+(E23*$E$13)+(F23*$F$13)+(G23*$G$13)+(H23*$H$13)+(I23*$I$13)+(J23*$J$13))/20
24	=((C24*$C$13)+(D24*$D$13)+(E24*$E$13)+(F24*$F$13)+(G24*$G$13)+(H24*$H$13)+(I24*$I$13)+(J24*$J$13))/20
25	=((C25*$C$13)+(D25*$D$13)+(E25*$E$13)+(F25*$F$13)+(G25*$G$13)+(H25*$H$13)+(I25*$I$13)+(J25*$J$13))/20
26	=((C26*$C$13)+(D26*$D$13)+(E26*$E$13)+(F26*$F$13)+(G26*$G$13)+(H26*$H$13)+(I26*$I$13)+(J26*$J$13))/20
27	
28	
29	=AVERAGE(L17:L26)
30	
31	
32	
33	
34	
35	
36	
37	
38	
39	
40	
41	

10

Personal Worksheets

Comparing Job Opportunities

What the Spreadsheet Does

One needs to consider many different factors when pursuing a new job or contemplating a change in jobs. This spreadsheet helps you compare job alternatives by assigning a weight to different factors in each job and generating a set of indices that reflects an unweighted (the ratings alone) and weighted (ratings plus weights) value for compensation, benefits, and expenses. Remember that expenses need to be factored into the decision, and a high rating on items in this category (such as parking, etc.) represents a high expense associated with a particular job.

Cost indices for living, food, and so on are published regularly for various metropolitan areas in the United States, and these values can be substituted for the weights in the spreadsheet.

Excel Business Applications

	A	B	C	D	E	F	G	H
1	COMPARING JOB OPPORTUNITIES							
2								
3	Weight	Meaning	Ratings	Meaning		Job Description		
4								
5	1	High	1	Very Important		Job A:	NY based sales	
6	2	Medium/High	2	Important		Job B:	LA based sales	
7	3	Medium	3	Somewhat Important		Job C:	Straight sales	
8	4	Low/Medium	4	Not Important				
9	5	Low	5	Not At All Important				
10								
11								
12				Weight	Ratings	Ratings	Ratings	
13					Job A	Job B	Job C	
14	Compensation							
15		Salary		1	1	3	2	
16		Commission Potential		3	1	2	2	
17		Bonus Potential		2	2	2	2	
18								
19	Benefits							
20		Stock Options		1	3	2	4	
21		Health Plan		3	4	2	3	
22		Life Insurance		1	2	3	4	
23		Vacation		2	3	2	3	
24		Sick Leave		3	2	3	2	
25		Retirement Plan		2	2	4	3	
26		Growth Potential		3	2	5	4	
27								
28	Expenses							
29		Parking		5	5	1	1	
30		Commuting		1	5	3	4	
31		Clothes, etc.		2	4	2	3	
32		Cost of Living		1	3	2	1	
33								
34		Weighted Averages						
35								
36		Compensation			1.33	2.25	2.00	
37		Benefits			2.60	2.78	3.33	
38		Expenses			4.56	2.00	2.63	
39								

Remember that if a new category is added, the formulas that compute the weighted averages need to be adjusted to reflect the addition.

Working with the Spreadsheet

To work with this spreadsheet, you need to enter the following information.

Personal Worksheets

Col D   weights for importance of compensation, benefits, and expenses
Row 15 salary
Row 16 commission potential
Row 17 bonus potential
Row 20 stock sharing benefits
Row 21 health benefits
Row 22 life insurance
Row 23 vacation
Row 24 sick leave
Row 25 retirement benefits
Row 26 potential for professional growth
Row 29 cost of parking
Row 30 cost of commuting
Row 31 clothes, etc.
Row 32 cost of living

When the spreadsheet is complete, it will provide you with the following information.

E36...G36 compensation for jobs A, B, and C
E37...G37 benefits for jobs A, B, and C
E38...G38 expenses for jobs A, B, and C

The Cell Contents and Formulas

	A	B	C	D	E
1	COMPARING JOB OPPORTUNITIES				
2					
3	Weight	Meaning	Ratings	Meaning	
4					
5	1	High	1	Very Important	
6	2	Medium/High	2	Important	
7	3	Medium	3	Somewhat Important	
8	4	Low/Medium	4	Not Important	
9	5	Low	5	Not At All Important	
10					
11					Ratings
12				Weight	Job A
13					
14	Compensation				
15		Salary		1	1
16		Commission Potential		3	1
17		Bonus Potential		2	2
18					
19	Benefits				
20		Stock Options		1	3
21		Health Plan		3	4
22		Life Insurance		1	2
23		Vacation		2	3
24		Sick Leave		3	2
25		Retirement Plan		2	2
26		Growth Potential		3	2
27					
28	Expenses				
29		Parking		5	5
30		Commuting		1	5
31		Clothes, etc.		2	4
32		Cost of Living		1	3
33					
34		Weighted Averages			
35					
36		Compensation			=(E15*D15+E16*D16+E17*D17)/SUM(D15:D17)
37		Benefits			=(D20*E20+D21*E21+D22*E22+D23*E23+D24*E24+D25*E25+D26*E26)/SUM(D20:D26)
38		Expenses			=(D29*E29+D30*E30+D31*E31+D32*E32)/SUM(D29:D32)
39					

	F	G
1		
2		
3	Job Description	
4		
5	Job A:	NY based sales
6	Job B:	LA based sales
7	Job C:	Straight sales
8		
9		
10		
11		
12	Ratings	Ratings
13	Job B	Job C
14		
15	3	2
16	2	2
17	2	2
18		
19		
20	2	4
21	2	3
22	3	4
23	2	3
24	3	2
25	4	3
26	5	4
27		
28		
29	1	1
30	3	4
31	2	3
32	2	1
33		
34		
35		
36	=(F15*E15+F16*E16+F17*E17)/SUM(E15:E17)	=(G15*F15+G16*F16+G17*F17)/SUM(F15:F17)
37	=(E20*F20+E21*F21+E22*F22+E23*F23+E24*F24+E25*F25+E26*F26)/SUM(E20:E26)	=(F20*G20+F21*G21+F22*G22+F23*G23+F24*G24+F25*G25+F26*G26)/SUM(F20:F26)
38	=(E29*F29+E30*F30+E31*F31+E32*F32)/SUM(E29:E32)	=(F29*G29+F30*G30+F31*G31+F32*G32)/SUM(F29:F32)
39		

Excel Business Applications

Conversion of Foreign Currency/Dollars and Dollars/Foreign Currency

	A	B	C	D	E	F	G	H	I	J	K	L	M
1	CONVERSION OF FOREIGN CURRENCY												
2													
3			Foreign	Dollars									
4	Country	Unit	Currency	(Foreign		Foreign Currency to Dollars					Dollars to Foreign Currency		
5			(Dollars)	Currency)									
6													
7	Argentina	Austral	0.160400	6.23	25.00	Australs	=	$4.01	$25	=	155.86	Australs	
8	Australia	Dollar	0.733500	1.36	25.00	Dollars	=	$18.34	$25	=	34.08	Dollars	
9	Austria	Schilling	0.084100	11.89	25.00	Schilling	=	$2.10	$25	=	297.27	Schillings	
10	Belgium	Franc	0.028200	35.46	25.00	Francs	=	$0.71	$25	=	886.52	Francs	
11	Brazil	Cruzado	0.009300	107.53	25.00	Cruzados	=	$0.23	$25	=	2688.17	Cruzados	
12	Britain	Pound	1.833000	0.55	25.00	Pounds	=	$45.83	$25	=	13.64	Pounds	
13	Canada	Dollar	0.800000	1.25	25.00	Dollars	=	$20.00	$25	=	31.25	Dollars	
14	Chile	Peso	0.004000	250.00	25.00	Pesos	=	$0.10	$25	=	6250.00	Pesos	
15	Columbia	Peso	0.003350	298.51	25.00	Pesos	=	$0.08	$25	=	7462.69	Pesos	
16	Denmark	Krone	0.154100	6.49	25.00	Krone	=	$3.85	$25	=	162.23	Krones	
17	Egypt	Pound	0.447600	2.24	25.00	Pounds	=	$11.18	$25	=	55.88	Pounds	
18	Finland	Mark	0.246400	4.06	25.00	Marks	=	$6.16	$25	=	101.46	Marks	
19	France	Franc	0.174000	5.75	25.00	Francs	=	$4.35	$25	=	143.68	Francs	
20	Greece	Drachma	0.007400	135.14	25.00	Drachmas	=	$0.19	$25	=	3378.38	Drachmas	
21	Hong Kong	Dollar	0.128200	7.80	25.00	Dollars	=	$3.21	$25	=	195.01	Dollars	
22	India	Rupee	0.077100	12.97	25.00	Rupees	=	$1.93	$25	=	324.25	Rupees	
23	Indonesia	Rupiah	0.000602	1661.13	25.00	Rupiahs	=	$0.02	$25	=	41528.24	Rupiahs	
24	Ireland	Punt	1.579000	0.63	25.00	Punts	=	$39.48	$25	=	15.83	Punts	
25	Israel	Shekel	0.638000	1.57	25.00	Shekels	=	$15.95	$25	=	39.18	Shekels	
26	Italy	Lira	0.007980	125.31	25.00	Liras	=	$0.20	$25	=	3132.83	Liras	
27	Japan	Yen	0.007767	128.75	25.00	Yen	=	$0.19	$25	=	3218.75	Yen	
28	Jordan	Dinar	2.986000	0.33	25.00	Dinar	=	$74.65	$25	=	8.37	Dinar	
29	Kuwait	Dinar	3.646000	0.27	25.00	Dinar	=	$91.15	$25	=	6.86	Dinar	
30	Lebanon	Pound	0.002730	366.30	25.00	Pounds	=	$0.07	$25	=	9157.51	Pounds	
31	Mexico	Peso	0.000436	2293.58	25.00	Pesos	=	$0.01	$25	=	57339.45	Pesos	
32	Netherlands	Guilder	0.526200	1.90	25.00	Guilders	=	$13.16	$25	=	47.51	Guilders	
33	New Zealand	Dollar	0.666500	1.50	25.00	Dollars	=	$16.66	$25	=	37.51	Dollars	
34	Norway	Krone	0.156700	6.38	25.00	Krone	=	$3.92	$25	=	159.54	Krone	
35	Pakistan	Rupee	0.056900	17.57	25.00	Rupees	=	$1.42	$25	=	439.37	Rupees	
36	Peru	Inti	0.030300	33.00	25.00	Intis	=	$0.76	$25	=	825.08	Intis	
37	Philippines	Peso	0.047500	21.05	25.00	Pesos	=	$1.19	$25	=	526.32	Pesos	
38	Portugal	Escudo	0.007727	129.41	25.00	Escudos	=	$0.19	$25	=	3235.28	Escudos	
39	Saudi Arabia	Riyal	0.266600	3.75	25.00	Riyal	=	$6.67	$25	=	93.77	Riyal	
40	Singapore	Dollar	0.495500	2.02	25.00	Dollars	=	$12.39	$25	=	50.45	Dollars	
41	South Korea	Won	0.001334	749.63	25.00	Won	=	$0.03	$25	=	18740.63	Wons	
42	South Africa	Rand	0.465000	2.15	25.00	Rands	=	$11.63	$25	=	53.76	Rands	
43	Spain	Peseta	0.008814	113.46	25.00	Pesetas	=	$0.22	$25	=	2836.40	Pesetas	
44	Sweden	Krona	0.166900	5.99	25.00	Kron	=	$4.17	$25	=	149.79	Kronas	
45	Switzerland	Franc	0.711700	1.41	25.00	Francs	=	$17.79	$25	=	35.13	Francs	
46	Turkey	Lira	0.000833	1200.48	25.00	Liras	=	$0.02	$25	=	30012.00	Liras	
47	Uruguay	Peso	0.003600	277.78	25.00	Pesos	=	$0.09	$25	=	6944.44	Pesos	
48	Venezuela	Bolivar	0.033600	29.76	25.00	Bolivars	=	$0.84	$25	=	744.05	Bolivars	
49	West Germany	Mark	0.590800	1.69	25.00	Marks	=	$14.77	$25	=	42.32	Marks	
50	Yugoslavia	Dinar	0.000791	1264.22	25.00	Dinar	=	$0.02	$25	=	31605.56	Dinars	

Personal Worksheets

What the Spreadsheet Does

This spreadsheet takes the current value of foreign currency in dollars and converts that value into dollars expressed in foreign currency. It also does the reverse. The foreign exchange rates change daily and are readily available in all major newspapers.

To use the spreadsheet, enter the current rate in foreign currency. The rate will automatically be converted to dollars or the dollars be converted into foreign currency. For example, 25 shekels (Israel) is worth 15.95 dollars, while 25 dollars will buy you 886.52 francs (France).

Working with the Spreadsheet

To work with this spreadsheet, you need to enter the following information.

Col C updated as necessary
Col E amount of foreign currency you want converted
Col I amount of dollars you want converted

When the spreadsheet is complete, it will provide you with the following information.

Col H dollars
Col J foreign currency

Excel Business Applications

The Cell Contents and Formulas

	A	B	C	D	E
1	CONVERSION OF FOREIGN CURRENCY				
2					
3			Foreign	Dollars	
4	Country	Unit	Currency	(Foreign	
5			(Dollars)	Currency)	
6					
7	Argentina	Austral	0.1604	=(1/C7)	25
8	Australia	Dollar	0.7335	=(1/C8)	25
9	Austria	Schilling	0.0841	=(1/C9)	25
10	Belgium	Franc	0.0282	=(1/C10)	25
11	Brazil	Cruzado	0.0093	=(1/C11)	25
12	Britain	Pound	1.833	=(1/C12)	25
13	Canada	Dollar	0.8	=(1/C13)	25
14	Chile	Peso	0.004	=(1/C14)	25
15	Columbia	Peso	0.00335	=(1/C15)	25
16	Denmark	Krone	0.1541	=(1/C16)	25
17	Egypt	Pound	0.4474	=(1/C17)	25
18	Finland	Mark	0.2464	=(1/C18)	25
19	France	Franc	0.174	=(1/C19)	25
20	Greece	Drachma	0.0074	=(1/C20)	25
21	Hong Kong	Dollar	0.1282	=(1/C21)	25
22	India	Rupee	0.0771	=(1/C22)	25
23	Indonesia	Rupiah	0.000602	=(1/C23)	25
24	Ireland	Punt	1.579	=(1/C24)	25
25	Israel	Shekel	0.638	=(1/C25)	25
26	Italy	Lira	0.00798	=(1/C26)	25
27	Japan	Yen	0.007767	=(1/C27)	25
28	Jordan	Dinar	2.986	=(1/C28)	25
29	Kuwait	Dinar	3.646	=(1/C29)	25
30	Lebanon	Pound	0.00273	=(1/C30)	25
31	Mexico	Peso	0.000436	=(1/C31)	25
32	Netherlands	Guilder	0.5262	=(1/C32)	25
33	New Zealand	Dollar	0.6665	=(1/C33)	25
34	Norway	Krone	0.1567	=(1/C34)	25
35	Pakistan	Rupee	0.0569	=(1/C35)	25
36	Peru	Inti	0.0303	=(1/C36)	25
37	Philippines	Peso	0.0475	=(1/C37)	25
38	Portugal	Escudo	0.0077273	=(1/C38)	25
39	Saudi Arabia	Riyal	0.2666	=(1/C39)	25
40	Singapore	Dollar	0.4955	=(1/C40)	25
41	South Korea	Won	0.001334	=(1/C41)	25
42	South Africa	Rand	0.465	=(1/C42)	25
43	Spain	Peseta	0.008814	=(1/C43)	25
44	Sweden	Krona	0.1669	=(1/C44)	25
45	Switzerland	Franc	0.7117	=(1/C45)	25
46	Turkey	Lira	0.000833	=(1/C46)	25
47	Uruguay	Peso	0.0036	=(1/C47)	25
48	Venezuela	Bolivar	0.0336	=(1/C48)	25
49	West Germany	Mark	0.5908	=(1/C49)	25
50	Yugoslavia	Dinar	0.000791	=(1/C50)	25

Personal Worksheets

	F	G	H	I	J	K	L
1							
2							
3							
4	Foreign Currency to Dollars					Dollars to Foreign Currency	
5							
6							
7	Australs	=	=(E7*C7)	25	=	=(I7*D7)	Australs
8	Dollars	=	=(E8*C8)	25	=	=(I8*D8)	Dollars
9	Schillings	=	=(E9*C9)	25	=	=(I9*D9)	Schillings
10	Francs	=	=(E10*C10)	25	=	=(I10*D10)	Francs
11	Cruzados	=	=(E11*C11)	25	=	=(I11*D11)	Cruzados
12	Pounds	=	=(E12*C12)	25	=	=(I12*D12)	Pounds
13	Dollars	=	=(E13*C13)	25	=	=(I13*D13)	Dollars
14	Pesos	=	=(E14*C14)	25	=	=(I14*D14)	Pesos
15	Pesos	=	=(E15*C15)	25	=	=(I15*D15)	Pesos
16	Krone	=	=(E16*C16)	25	=	=(I16*D16)	Krones
17	Pounds	=	=(E17*C17)	25	=	=(I17*D17)	Pounds
18	Marks	=	=(E18*C18)	25	=	=(I18*D18)	Marks
19	Francs	=	=(E19*C19)	25	=	=(I19*D19)	Francs
20	Drachmas	=	=(E20*C20)	25	=	=(I20*D20)	Drachmas
21	Dollars	=	=(E21*C21)	25	=	=(I21*D21)	Dollars
22	Rupees	=	=(E22*C22)	25	=	=(I22*D22)	Rupees
23	Rupiahs	=	=(E23*C23)	25	=	=(I23*D23)	Rupiahs
24	Punts	=	=(E24*C24)	25	=	=(I24*D24)	Punts
25	Shekels	=	=(E25*C25)	25	=	=(I25*D25)	Shekels
26	Liras	=	=(E26*C26)	25	=	=(I26*D26)	Liras
27	Yen	=	=(E27*C27)	25	=	=(I27*D27)	Yen
28	Dinar	=	=(E28*C28)	25	=	=(I28*D28)	Dinar
29	Dinar	=	=(E29*C29)	25	=	=(I29*D29)	Dinar
30	Pounds	=	=(E30*C30)	25	=	=(I30*D30)	Pounds
31	Pesos	=	=(E31*C31)	25	=	=(I31*D31)	Pesos
32	Guilders	=	=(E32*C32)	25	=	=(I32*D32)	Guilders
33	Dollars	=	=(E33*C33)	25	=	=(I33*D33)	Dollars
34	Krone	=	=(E34*C34)	25	=	=(I34*D34)	Krone
35	Rupees	=	=(E35*C35)	25	=	=(I35*D35)	Rupees
36	Intis	=	=(E36*C36)	25	=	=(I36*D36)	Intis
37	Pesos	=	=(E37*C37)	25	=	=(I37*D37)	Pesos
38	Escudos	=	=(E38*C38)	25	=	=(I38*D38)	Escudos
39	Riyal	=	=(E39*C39)	25	=	=(I39*D39)	Riyal
40	Dollars	=	=(E40*C40)	25	=	=(I40*D40)	Dollars
41	Won	=	=(E41*C41)	25	=	=(I41*D41)	Wons
42	Rands	=	=(E42*C42)	25	=	=(I42*D42)	Rands
43	Pesetas	=	=(E43*C43)	25	=	=(I43*D43)	Pesetas
44	Kron	=	=(E44*C44)	25	=	=(I44*D44)	Kronas
45	Francs	=	=(E45*C45)	25	=	=(I45*D45)	Francs
46	Liras	=	=(E46*C46)	25	=	=(I46*D46)	Liras
47	Pesos	=	=(E47*C47)	25	=	=(I47*D47)	Pesos
48	Bolivars	=	=(E48*C48)	25	=	=(I48*D48)	Bolivars
49	Marks	=	=(E49*C49)	25	=	=(I49*D49)	Marks
50	Dinar	=	=(E50*C50)	25	=	=(I50*D50)	Dinars

Conversion of Measurement Units

	A	B	C	D	E	F	G	H
1	CONVERSION OF MEASUREMENT UNITS							
2								
3	From (Enter Value)		To		From (Enter Value)		To	
4								
5		150	centimeters	4.92	feet	4.92	feet	150	centimeters
6		150	centimeters	59.06	inches	59.05	inches	150	centimeters
7		150	centimeters	1.50	meters	1.50	meters	150	centimeters
8		25	cubic feet	20.07	bushels	20.07	bushels	25	cubic feet
9		25	cubic feet	0.71	cubic meter	0.71	cubic meters	25	cubic feet
10		100	cubic inches	0.00	cubic feet	0.06	cubic feet	103	cubic inches
11		2000	cubic inches	0.03	cubic meter	0.03	cubic meters	1875	cubic inches
12		250	cubic inches	3.72	dry quarts	3.72	dry quarts	250	cubic inches
13		34	cubic meters	1200.65	cubic feet	1200.65	cubic feet	34	cubic meters
14		28	cubic meters	36.62	cubic yards	36.62	cubic yards	28	cubic meters
15		60	degrees (arc)	1.05	radians	1.05	radians	60	degrees (arc)
16		212	degrees (F)	100.00	degrees (C)	100.00	degrees (C)	212	degrees (F)
17		25	feet	762.00	centimeters	762.00	centimeters	25	feet
18		25	feet	300.00	inches	300.00	inches	25	feet
19		25	feet	16.50	links	16.50	links	25	feet
20		25	feet	7.62	meters	7.62	meters	25	feet
21		25	feet	1.52	rods	1.52	rods	25	feet
22		2000	feet	0.33	miles	0.33	miles	2006	feet
23		1500	feet/sec	888.15	knots	888.15	knots	1500	feet/sec
24		200	furlongs	132000.00	feet	132000.00	feet	200	furlongs
25		300	furlongs	37.50	miles	37.50	miles	300	furlongs
26		10	gallons	1280.00	ounces	1280.00	ounces	10	gallons
27		10	gallons	1.34	cubic feet	1.34	cubic feet	10	gallons
28		10	gallons	8.33	gallons imp	8.33	gallons imp	10	gallons
29		50	grams	49050.00	dynes	49050.00	dynes	50	grams
30		75	grams	2.65	ounces (adv)	2.65	ounces (adv)	75	grams
31		100	grams	0.22	pounds (adv)	0.22	pounds (adv)	100	grams
32		50	inches	127.00	centimeters	127.00	centimeters	50	inches
33		50	inches	4.17	feet	4.17	feet	50	inches
34		50	inches	6.31	links	6.31	links	50	inches
35		50	inches	1.27	meters	1.27	meters	50	inches
36		50	inches	50000.00	mils	50000.00	mils	50	inches
37		50	inches	5.56	spans	5.56	spans	50	inches
38		50	inches	1.39	yards	1.39	yards	50	inches
39		25	kilograms	881.85	ounces	881.85	ounces	25	kilograms
40		25	kilograms	55.12	pounds	55.12	pounds	25	kilograms
41		25	kilograms	0.03	tons	0.03	tons	27	kilograms
42		120	kilometers	393699.96	feet	393699.96	feet	120	kilometers
43		120	kilometers	120000.00	meters	120000.00	meters	120	kilometers
44		120	kilometers	64.75	miles (naut)	64.75	miles (naut)	120	kilometers
45		120	kilometers	74.57	miles (land)	74.57	miles (land)	120	kilometers
46		8	liters	0.28	cubic feet	0.28	cubic feet	8	liters
47		8	liters	2.11	gallons (US)	2.11	gallons (US)	8	liters
48		8	liters	0.91	pecks	0.91	pecks	8	liters
49		8	liters	7.26	quarts (dry)	7.26	quarts (dry)	8	liters
50		500	millimeters	19.69	inches	19.69	inches	500	millimeters
51		500	millimeters	0.50	meters	0.50	meters	500	millimeters
52		500	millimeters	500000.00	microns	500000.00	microns	500	millimeters
53		500	millimeters	19685.00	mils	19685.00	mils	500	millimeters
54		200	watts	686.00	BTU's	686.00	BTU's	200	watts
55									
56									

Personal Worksheets

What the Spreadsheet Does

This spreadsheet takes a unit of measurement and converts it to another unit of measurement.

For example, if you want to convert cubic meters to cubic feet, find the cubic meter entry in the **From (Enter Value)** column and enter the value you want to convert to cubic meters. To convert cubic feet to cubic meters, find the cubic feet entry, enter the value, and make the conversion.

Working with the Spreadsheet

To work with this spreadsheet, you need to enter in the **From (Enter Value)** column, the unit you want to convert from adjacent to the unit you want to convert to. When the spreadsheet is complete, it will provide you with the conversion that you specified.

The Cell Contents and Formulas

	A	B	C	D
1	CONVERSION OF MEASUREMENT UNITS			
2				
3	From (Enter Value)		To	
4				
5	150	centimeters	=(A5*0.0328)	feet
6	150	centimeters	=(A6*0.3937)	inches
7	150	centimeters	=(A7*0.01)	meters
8	25	cubic feet	=(A8*0.8029)	bushels
9	25	cubic feet	=(A9*0.0283)	cubic meters
10	100	cubic inches	=(A10*0.00058)	cubic feet
11	2000	cubic inches	=(A11*0.000016)	cubic meters
12	250	cubic inches	=(A12*0.01488)	dry quarts
13	34	cubic meters	=(A13*35.3133)	cubic feet
14	28	cubic meters	=(A14*1.3079)	cubic yards
15	60	degrees (arc)	=(A15*0.0175)	radians
16	212	degrees (F)	=(5*(A16-32))/9	degrees (C)
17	25	feet	=(A17*30.4801)	centimeters
18	25	feet	=(A18*12)	inches
19	25	feet	=(A19*0.66)	links
20	25	feet	=(A20*0.3048)	meters
21	25	feet	=(A21*0.06061)	rods
22	2000	feet	=(A22*0.0001645)	miles
23	1500	feet/sec	=(A23*0.5921)	knots
24	200	furlongs	=(A24*660)	feet
25	300	furlongs	=(A25*0.125)	miles
26	10	gallons	=(A26*128)	ounces
27	10	gallons	=(A27*0.1337)	cubic feet
28	10	gallons	=(A28*0.8327)	gallons imp
29	50	grams	=(A29*981)	dynes
30	75	grams	=(A30*0.0353)	ounces (adv)
31	100	grams	=(A31*0.0022)	pounds (adv)
32	50	inches	=(A32*2.54)	centimeters
33	50	inches	=(A33*0.08333)	feet
34	50	inches	=(A34*0.12626)	links
35	50	inches	=(A35*0.0254)	meters
36	50	inches	=(A36*1000)	mils
37	50	inches	=(A37*0.1111)	spans
38	50	inches	=(A38*0.02778)	yards
39	25	kilograms	=(A39*35.274)	ounces
40	25	kilograms	=(A40*2.2046)	pounds
41	25	kilograms	=(A41*0.0011)	tons
42	120	kilometers	=(A42*3280.833)	feet
43	120	kilometers	=(A43*1000)	meters
44	120	kilometers	=(A44*0.5396)	miles (naut)
45	120	kilometers	=(A45*0.6214)	miles (land)
46	8	liters	=(A46*0.035313)	cubic feet
47	8	liters	=(A47*0.2641)	gallons (US)
48	8	liters	=(A48*0.1135)	pecks
49	8	liters	=(A49*0.9081)	quarts (dry)
50	500	millimeters	=(A50*0.03937)	inches
51	500	millimeters	=(A51*0.001)	meters
52	500	millimeters	=(A52*1000)	microns
53	500	millimeters	=(A53*39.37)	mils
54	200	watts	=(A54*3.43)	BTU's
55				
56				

	E	F	G	H
1				
2				
3	From (Enter Value)		To	
4				
5	4.92	feet	=(E5*1/0.0328)	centimeters
6	59.05	inches	=(E6*1/0.3937)	centimeters
7	1.5	meters	=(E7*1/0.01)	centimeters
8	20.07	bushels	=(E8*1/0.8029)	cubic feet
9	0.71	cubic meters	=(E9*1/0.0283)	cubic feet
10	0.06	cubic feet	=(E10*1/0.00058)	cubic inches
11	0.03	cubic meters	=(E11*1/0.000016)	cubic inches
12	3.72	dry quarts	=(E12*1/0.01488)	cubic inches
13	1200.65	cubic feet	=(E13*1/35.3133)	cubic meters
14	36.62	cubic yards	=(E14*1/1.3079)	cubic meters
15	1.05	radians	=(E15*1/0.0175)	degrees (arc)
16	100	degrees (C)	=(9/5)*E16+32	degrees (F)
17	762	centimeters	=(E17*1/30.4801)	feet
18	300	inches	=(E18*1/12)	feet
19	16.5	links	=(E19*1/0.66)	feet
20	7.62	meters	=(E20*1/0.3048)	feet
21	1.52	rods	=(E21*1/0.06061)	feet
22	0.33	miles	=(E22*1/0.0001645)	feet
23	888.15	knots	=(E23*1/0.5921)	feet/sec
24	132000	feet	=(E24*1/660)	furlongs
25	37.5	miles	=(E25*1/0.125)	furlongs
26	1280	ounces	=(E26*1/128)	gallons
27	1.34	cubic feet	=(E27*1/0.1337)	gallons
28	8.33	gallons imp	=(E28*1/0.8327)	gallons
29	49050	dynes	=(E29*1/981)	grams
30	2.65	ounces (adv)	=(E30*1/0.0353)	grams
31	0.22	pounds (adv)	=(E31*1/0.0022)	grams
32	127	centimeters	=(E32*1/2.54)	inches
33	4.17	feet	=(E33*1/0.08333)	inches
34	6.31	links	=(E34*1/0.12626)	inches
35	1.27	meters	=(E35*1/0.0254)	inches
36	50000	mils	=(E36*1/1000)	inches
37	5.56	spans	=(E37*1/0.1111)	inches
38	1.39	yards	=(E38*1/0.02778)	inches
39	881.85	ounces	=(E39*1/35.274)	kilograms
40	55.12	pounds	=(E40*1/2.2046)	kilograms
41	0.03	tons	=(E41*1/0.0011)	kilograms
42	393699.96	feet	=(E42*1/3280.833)	kilometers
43	120000	meters	=(E43*1/1000)	kilometers
44	64.75	miles (naut)	=(E44*1/0.5396)	kilometers
45	74.57	miles (land)	=(E45*1/0.6214)	kilometers
46	0.28	cubic feet	=(E46*1/0.035313)	liters
47	2.11	gallons (US)	=(E47*1/0.2641)	liters
48	0.91	pecks	=(E48*1/0.1135)	liters
49	7.26	quarts (dry)	=(E49*1/0.9081)	liters
50	19.69	inches	=(E50*1/0.03937)	millimeters
51	0.5	meters	=(E51*1/0.001)	millimeters
52	500000	microns	=(E52*1/1000)	millimeters
53	19685	mils	=(E53*1/39.37)	millimeters
54	686	BTU's	=(E54*1/3.43)	watts
55				
56				

Excel Business Applications

Personal/Family Budget

	A	B	C	D	E	F	G	H	I
1	Personal/Family Budget								
2									
3	Year: 1987								
4									INCOME
5									
6			Jan	Feb	March	April	May	June	July
7	INCOME								
8	Salary #1		$1,567.00	$1,567.00	$1,567.00	$1,567.00	$1,567.00	$1,567.00	$1,567.00
9	Salary #2		$1,675.00	$1,675.00	$1,675.00	$1,675.00	$1,675.00	$1,675.00	$1,675.00
10	Interest		$56.78	$43.67	$55.78	$56.76	$43.67	$56.67	$43.56
11	Dividends		$287.89	$0.00	$0.00	$0.00	$0.00	$0.00	$0.00
12	Gifts		$25.00	$0.00	$0.00	$0.00	$0.00	$25.00	$0.00
13	Bonuses		$0.00	$0.00	$0.00	$0.00	$0.00	$0.00	$0.00
14	Tax Refunds		$0.00	$0.00	$0.00	$0.00	$0.00	$0.00	$0.00
15	Profits From Sales		$0.00	$0.00	$0.00	$0.00	$143.56	$0.00	$0.00
16	Alimony		$150.00	$150.00	$150.00	$150.00	$150.00	$150.00	$150.00
17	Other #1		$0.00	$0.00	$0.00	$0.00	$0.00	$0.00	$0.00
18	Other #2		$56.00	$0.00	$0.00	$0.00	$0.00	$0.00	$78.00
19									
20	TOTAL		$3,817.67	$3,435.67	$3,447.78	$3,448.76	$3,579.23	$3,473.67	$3,513.56
21									
22			Jan	Feb	Mar	Apr	May	June	July
23									
24	EXPENSES								
25	Rent		$1,250.00	$1,250.00	$1,250.00	$1,250.00	$1,250.00	$1,250.00	$1,250.00
26	Food		$528.77	$546.89	$390.00	$398.00	$534.45	$533.34	$566.76
27	Telephone		$56.67	$45.23	$67.87	$45.55	$65.67	$66.67	$56.34
28	Gas		$101.56	$122.45	$132.78	$103.56	$123.45	$133.32	$109.87
29	Electricity		$67.89	$66.76	$65.89	$76.78	$72.54	$70.98	$69.78
30	Loan Payment #1		$100.36	$100.36	$100.36	$100.36	$100.36	$100.36	$100.36
31	Car Payment		$222.56	$222.56	$222.56	$222.56	$222.56	$222.56	$222.56
32	Education		$567.00	$0.00	$0.00	$0.00	$0.00	$0.00	$0.00
33	Life Insurance		$34.67	$34.67	$34.67	$34.67	$34.67	$34.67	$34.67
34	Auto Insurance		$0.00	$0.00	$0.00	$654.60	$0.00	$0.00	$0.00
35	Medical		$0.00	$124.32	$0.00	$0.00	$0.00	$35.89	$0.00
36	Taxes		$486.30	$486.30	$486.30	$486.30	$486.30	$486.30	$486.30
37	Savings		$25.00	$25.00	$25.00	$25.00	$25.00	$25.00	$25.00
38	Gifts/Misc.		$127.00	$43.00	$56.00	$111.00	$342.00	$67.00	$33.00
39									
40	TOTAL		$3,440.78	$3,024.54	$2,775.43	$3,397.38	$2,915.00	$2,959.09	$2,921.64
41									
42	Monthly Balance	Monthly	$376.89	$411.13	$672.35	$51.38	$664.23	$514.58	$591.92
43	(Discretionary Money)								

Personal Worksheets

	J	K	L	M	N	O	P	Q
1								
2								
3								
4								
5								
6	August	Sept	Oct	Nov	Dec	TOTAL	Category	
7							Average	
8	$1,567.00	$1,567.00	$1,567.00	$1,567.00	$1,567.00	$18,804.00	$1,567.00	
9	$1,675.00	$1,675.00	$1,675.00	$1,675.00	$1,675.00	$20,100.00	$1,675.00	
10	$55.56	$53.67	$54.67	$54.67	$67.87	$643.33	$53.61	
11	$0.00	$0.00	$0.00	$0.00	$0.00	$287.89	$23.99	
12	$0.00	$0.00	$0.00	$0.00	$0.00	$50.00	$4.17	
13	$0.00	$0.00	$0.00	$0.00	$0.00	$0.00	$0.00	
14	$43.50	$0.00	$0.00	$0.00	$0.00	$43.50	$3.63	
15	$32.56	$0.00	$0.00	$0.00	$0.00	$176.12	$14.68	
16	$150.00	$150.00	$150.00	$150.00	$150.00	$1,800.00	$150.00	
17	$0.00	$0.00	$0.00	$0.00	$0.00	$0.00	$0.00	
18	$0.00	$110.00	$0.00	$0.00	$0.00	$244.00	$20.33	
19								
20	$3,523.62	$3,555.67	$3,446.67	$3,446.67	$3,459.87	$42,148.84	$3,512.40	
21								
22	Aug	Sept	Oct	Nov	Dec	Total		
23								
24								
25	$1,250.00	$1,250.00	$1,250.00	$1,250.00	$1,250.00	$15,000.00	$0.00	
26	$555.67	$675.78	$578.76	$455.87	$644.67	$6,408.96	$534.08	
27	$44.56	$56.67	$34.55	$54.56	$54.67	$649.01	$54.08	
28	$122.56	$121.34	$115.67	$111.56	$142.67	$1,440.79	$120.07	
29	$76.78	$77.77	$76.78	$65.53	$61.34	$848.82	$70.74	
30	$100.36	$100.36	$100.36	$100.36	$100.36	$1,204.32	$100.36	
31	$222.56	$222.56	$222.56	$222.56	$222.56	$2,670.72	$222.56	
32	$0.00	$589.00	$0.00	$0.00	$0.00	$1,156.00	$96.33	
33	$34.67	$34.67	$34.67	$34.67	$34.67	$416.04	$34.67	
34	$0.00	$0.00	$0.00	$0.00	$0.00	$654.60	$54.55	
35	$0.00	$0.00	$0.00	$122.56	$0.00	$282.77	$23.56	
36	$486.30	$486.30	$486.30	$486.30	$486.30	$5,835.60	$486.30	
37	$25.00	$25.00	$25.00	$25.00	$25.00	$300.00	$25.00	
38	$78.00	$65.00	$54.00	$23.00	$335.00	$1,334.00	$111.17	
39								
40	$2,918.46	$3,639.45	$2,924.65	$2,928.97	$3,022.24	$38,201.63	$3,183.47	
41								
42	$605.16	($83.78)	$522.02	$517.70	$437.63	$3,947.21		
43								

Excel Business Applications

What the Spreadsheet Does

This spreadsheet keeps track of income, fixed expenses, and variable expenses and provides summary information that can be used in planning.

This is an ideal way to keep track of expenses throughout the year and compare them to income. The spreadsheet that is shown here is for a two-income family with some income from investments (shown as dividends). Their expenses include a car payment, an installment loan, and a regular savings program.

Another use of this spreadsheet is for tax purposes. If you need to modify the spreadsheet to take into account special circumstances (such as a home office, etc.), then create a new column called "Deductible Expenses."

Working with the Spreadsheet

To work with this spreadsheet, you need to enter the following information.

Rows 8...18 income by month from jobs, interest, dividends, gifts, bonuses, tax refunds, profits from sales, alimony, and other

Rows 25...38 expenses by month for rent, food, telephone, gas, electricity, loan payment #1, loan payment #2, education, life insurance, auto insurance, medical costs, taxes, savings, and gifts

When the spreadsheet is complete, it will provide you with the following information.

Row 20 total income by month
Row 40 total expenses by month
Row 42 net balance by month
Col O category totals by year
Col P category yearly average

Personal Worksheets

What It Looks Like

Figure 10.1 shows a line chart illustrating monthly surplus or deficit.

Surplus/Deficit by Month

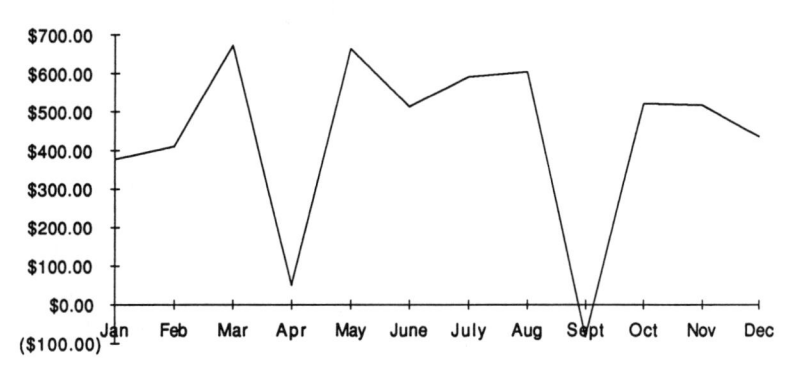

10.1 Monthly surplus or deficit

The Cell Contents and Formulas

	A	B	C	D	E	F	G	H
1	Personal/Family Budget							
2								
3	Year: 1987							
4								
5								
6			Jan	Feb	March	April	May	June
7	INCOME							
8	Salary #1		1567	1567	1567	1567	1567	1567
9	Salary #2		1675	1675	1675	1675	1675	1675
10	Interest		56.78	43.67	55.78	56.76	43.67	56.67
11	Dividends		287.89	0	0	0	0	0
12	Gifts		25	0	0	0	0	25
13	Bonuses		0	0	0	0	0	0
14	Tax Refunds		0	0	0	0	0	0
15	Profits From Sales		0	0	0	0	143.56	0
16	Alimony		150	150	150	150	150	150
17	Other #1		0	0	0	0	0	0
18	Other #2		56	0	0	0	0	0
19								
20	TOTAL		=SUM(C8:C18)	=SUM(D8:D18)	=SUM(E8:E18)	=SUM(F8:F18)	=SUM(G8:G18)	=SUM(H8:H18)
21								
22			Jan	Feb	Mar	Apr	May	June
23								
24	EXPENSES							
25	Rent		1250	1250	1250	1250	1250	1250
26	Food		528.77	546.89	390	398	534.45	533.34
27	Telephone		56.67	45.23	67.87	45.55	65.67	66.67
28	Gas		101.56	122.45	132.78	103.56	123.45	133.32
29	Electricity		67.89	66.76	65.89	76.78	72.54	70.98
30	Loan Payment #1		100.36	100.36	100.36	100.36	100.36	100.36
31	Car Payment		222.56	222.56	222.56	222.56	222.56	222.56
32	Education		567	0	0	0	0	0
33	Life Insurance		34.67	34.67	34.67	34.67	34.67	34.67
34	Auto Insurance		0	0	0	654.6	0	0
35	Medical		0	124.32	0	0	0	35.89
36	Taxes		=(C8+C9)*0.15	=(D8+D9)*0.15	=(E8+E9)*0.15	=(F8+F9)*0.15	=(G8+G9)*0.15	=(H8+H9)*0.15
37	Savings		25	25	25	25	25	25
38	Gifts/Misc.		127	43	56	111	342	67
39								
40	TOTAL		=SUM(C25:C37)	=SUM(D25:D37)	=SUM(E25:E37)	=SUM(F25:F37)	=SUM(G25:G37)	=SUM(H25:H37)
41								
42	Monthly Balance	Monthly Balance	=C20-C40	=D20-D40	=E20-E40	=F20-F40	=G20-G40	=H20-H40
43	(Discretionary Money)							

200

	I	J	K	L	M	N	O	P
1								
2								
3								
4	INCOME							
5								
6	July	August	Sept	Oct	Nov	Dec	TOTAL	Category Average
7								
8	1567	1567	1567	1567	1567	1567	=SUM(C8:N8)	=O8/12
9	1675	1675	1675	1675	1675	1675	=SUM(C9:N9)	=O9/12
10	43.56	55.56	53.67	54.67	54.67	67.87	=SUM(C10:N10)	=O10/12
11	0	0	0	0	0	0	=SUM(C11:N11)	=O11/12
12	0	0	0	0	0	0	=SUM(C12:N12)	=O12/12
13	0	0	0	0	0	0	=SUM(C13:N13)	=O13/12
14	0	43.5	0	0	0	0	=SUM(C14:N14)	=O14/12
15	0	32.56	0	0	0	0	=SUM(C15:N15)	=O15/12
16	150	150	150	150	150	150	=SUM(C16:N16)	=O16/12
17	0	0	0	0	0	0	=SUM(C17:N17)	=O17/12
18	78	0	110	0	0	0	=SUM(C18:N18)	=O18/12
19								
20	=SUM(I8:I18)	=SUM(J8:J18)	=SUM(K8:K18)	=SUM(L8:L18)	=SUM(M8:M18)	=SUM(N8:N18)	=SUM(O8:O18)	=O20/12
21								
22	July	Aug	Sept	Oct	Nov	Dec	Total	
23								
24								
25	1250	1250	1250	1250	1250	1250	=SUM(C25:N25)	=O25/12
26	566.76	555.67	675.78	578.76	455.87	644.67	=SUM(C26:N26)	=O26/12
27	56.34	44.56	56.67	34.55	54.56	54.67	=SUM(C27:N27)	=O27/12
28	109.87	122.56	121.34	115.67	111.56	142.67	=SUM(C28:N28)	=O28/12
29	69.78	76.78	77.77	76.78	65.53	61.34	=SUM(C29:N29)	=O29/12
30	100.36	100.36	100.36	100.36	100.36	100.36	=SUM(C30:N30)	=O30/12
31	222.56	222.56	222.56	222.56	222.56	222.56	=SUM(C31:N31)	=O31/12
32	0	0	589	0	0	0	=SUM(C32:N32)	=O32/12
33	34.67	34.67	34.67	34.67	34.67	34.67	=SUM(C33:N33)	=O33/12
34	0	0	0	0	0	0	=SUM(C34:N34)	=O34/12
35	0	0	0	0	122.56	0	=SUM(C35:N35)	=O35/12
36	=((I8+I9)*0.15	=(J8+J9)*0.15	=(K8+K9)*0.15	=(L8+L9)*0.15	=(M8+M9)*0.15	=(N8+N9)*0.15	=SUM(C36:N36)	=O36/12
37	25	25	25	25	25	25	=SUM(C37:N37)	=O37/12
38	33	78	65	54	23	335	=SUM(C38:N38)	=O38/12
39								
40	=SUM(I25:I37)	=SUM(J25:J37)	=SUM(K25:K37)	=SUM(L25:L37)	=SUM(M25:M37)	=SUM(N25:N37)	=SUM(O25:O38)	=O40/12
41								
42	=I20-I40	=J20-J40	=K20-K40	=L20-L40	=M20-M40	=N20-N40	=O20-O40	
43								

Excel Business Applications

Personal Asset Inventory

	A	B	C	D
1	PERSONAL ASSET INVENTORY			
2				
3	Age	Depreciation		
4				
5	=>1 Year	0.8		
6	>5 Years	0.7		
7	>10 Years	0.5		
8	>20 Years	0.25		
9	>30 Years	0.01	(increase factor)	
10				
11				Date
12				Purchased
13				
14	Living Room			
15		Couch		1983
16		Leather Chair		1981
17		Recliner		1980
18		End Table #1		1975
19		End Table #2		1986
20		Coffee Table		1980
21		Breakfront		1982
22		Upholstered Chair		1987
23				
24	Dining Room			
25		Chairs (8)		1982
26		Table		1982
27		Stemware		1930
28		Silver		1945
29		Buffet		1973
30		Dishes		1985
31				
32	Family Room			
33		Color TV		1983
34		Stereo		1980
35		Bookcases (2)		1979
36		Chair		1981
37		Rug		1983

What the Spreadsheet Does

Even if you are busy all day every day, taking the time to put your personal effects in order always makes life easier. One way to do this is to have complete records about your personal assets, including when they were purchased, what they cost, and their current value.

Personal Worksheets

	A	B	C	D
38		Lamp		1950
39		Couch		1978
40		Chairs (2)		1983
41		Table		1982
42				
43	Master Bedroom			
44		Bed		1910
45		Dresser		1985
46		Tables (2)		1982
47		Lamps (2)		1986
48				
49	Child's Bedroom			
50		Bed		1984
51		Dresser		1984
52		Table		1984
53		Lamp		1985
54		Desk		1983
55		Bookshelf		1975
56				
57	Child's Bedroom			
58		Crib		1980
59		Dresser		1980
60		Table		1980
61		Lamp		1982
62				
63	Garage			
64		Mower		1980
65		Garden Tools		1982
66		Bicycle		1976
67				
68				
69			Total Values	
70				
71			Purchase	
72			Current	

This spreadsheet tracks the value of your personal assets as well as their replacement value based on adjustment factors that you enter for assets that are 1, 5, 10, 20, and greater than 30 years old. It also records which of your assets are included on your insurance policy and which are not.

Excel Business Applications

Working with the Spreadsheet

To work with this spreadsheet, you need to enter the following information.

B5	depreciation rate for assets equal to or more than 1 year old
B6	depreciation rate for assets equal to or more than 5 years old
B7	depreciation rate for assets equal to or more than 10 years old
B8	depreciation rate for assets equal to or more than 20 years old
B9	depreciation rate for assets equal to or more than 30 years old
Col B	items in various rooms
Col D	date of purchase of items (year purchased)
Col E	original purchase cost
Col G	note on whether item is on insurance rider

When the spreadsheet is complete, it will provide you with the following information.

E71	total purchase value
H72	total current value
Col F	age in years
Col H	current value

Personal Worksheets

What It Looks Like

Figure 10.2 is a pie chart that compares the purchase price of your assets with their current value. This chart was intentionally poorly designed to illustrate the effects of chart junk, where too many options were used.

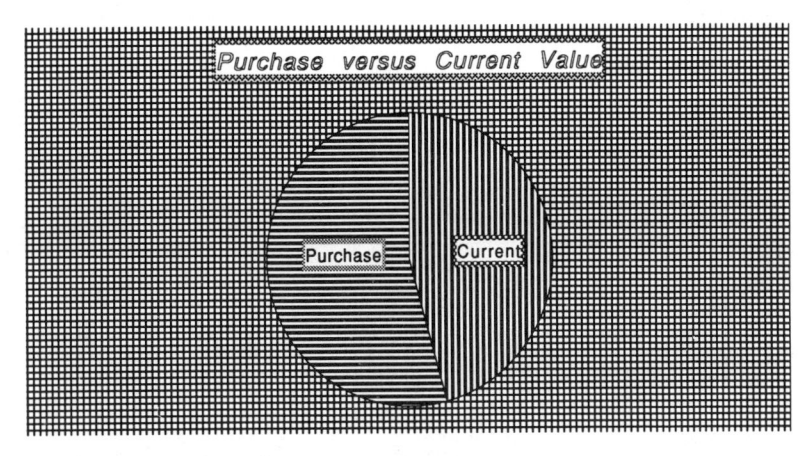

10.2 Relative value of assets

Excel Business Applications

The Cell Contents and Formulas

	A	B	C	D	E	F
1	PERSONAL ASSET INVENTORY				Today's Date	=DATE(89,1,1)
2						
3	Age	Depreciation				
4						
5	=>1 Year	0.8				
6	>5 Years	0.7				
7	>10 Years	0.5				
8	>20 Years	0.25				
9	>30 Years	0.01	(Increase factor)			
10						
11				Date	Cost	Age
12				Purchased		(Yrs.)
13						
14	Living Room					
15		Couch		1983	850	=YEAR($F$1)-1900+27655-D15
16		Leather Chair		1981	525	=YEAR($F$1)-1900+27655-D16
17		Recliner		1980	350	=YEAR($F$1)-1900+27655-D17
18		End Table #1		1975	125	=YEAR($F$1)-1900+27655-D18
19		End Table #2		1986	150	=YEAR($F$1)-1900+27655-D19
20		Coffee Table		1980	225	=YEAR($F$1)-1900+27655-D20
21		Breakfront		1982	575	=YEAR($F$1)-1900+27655-D21
22		Upholstered Chair		1987	400	=YEAR($F$1)-1900+27655-D22
23						
24	Dining Room					
25		Chairs (8)		1982	800	=YEAR($F$1)-1900+27655-D25
26		Table		1982	1200	=YEAR($F$1)-1900+27655-D26
27		Stemware		1930	300	=YEAR($F$1)-1900+27655-D27
28		Silver		1945	1000	=YEAR($F$1)-1900+27655-D28
29		Buffet		1973	425	=YEAR($F$1)-1900+27655-D29
30		Dishes		1985	320	=YEAR($F$1)-1900+27655-D30
31						
32	Family Room					
33		Color TV		1983	350	=YEAR($F$1)-1900+27655-D33
34		Stereo		1980	750	=YEAR($F$1)-1900+27655-D34
35		Bookcases (2)		1979	350	=YEAR($F$1)-1900+27655-D35
36		Chair		1981	225	=YEAR($F$1)-1900+27655-D36
37		Rug		1983	190	=YEAR($F$1)-1900+27655-D37
38		Lamp		1950	50	=YEAR($F$1)-1900+27655-D38
39		Couch		1978	433	=YEAR($F$1)-1900+27655-D39
40		Chairs (2)		1983	425	=YEAR($F$1)-1900+27655-D40
41		Table		1982	120	=YEAR($F$1)-1900+27655-D41
42						
43	Master Bedroom					
44		Bed		1910	125	=YEAR($F$1)-1900+27655-D44
45		Dresser		1985	300	=YEAR($F$1)-1900+27655-D45
46		Tables (2)		1982	100	=YEAR($F$1)-1900+27655-D46
47		Lamps (2)		1986	75	=YEAR($F$1)-1900+27655-D47
48						
49	Child's Bedroom					
50		Bed		1984	125	=YEAR($F$1)-1900+27655-D50
51		Dresser		1984	150	=YEAR($F$1)-1900+27655-D51
52		Table		1984	75	=YEAR($F$1)-1900+27655-D52
53		Lamp		1985	25	=YEAR($F$1)-1900+27655-D53
54		Desk		1983	100	=YEAR($F$1)-1900+27655-D54
55		Bookshelf		1975	150	=YEAR($F$1)-1900+27655-D55
56						
57	Child's Bedroom					
58		Crib		1980	80	=YEAR($F$1)-1900+27655-D58
59		Dresser		1980	75	=YEAR($F$1)-1900+27655-D59
60		Table		1980	40	=YEAR($F$1)-1900+27655-D60
61		Lamp		1982	30	=YEAR($F$1)-1900+27655-D61
62						
63	Garage					
64		Mower		1980	225	=YEAR($F$1)-1900+27655-D64
65		Garden Tools		1982	125	=YEAR($F$1)-1900+27655-D65
66		Bicycle		1976	190	=YEAR($F$1)-1900+27655-D66
67						
68						
69			Total Values			
70						
71			Purchase		=SUM(E15:E66)	
72			Current		=SUM(H15:H66)	

Personal Worksheets

	G	H
1		
2		
3		
4		
5		
6		
7		
8		
9		
10		
11	Insured	Current
12	(1=y/2=n)	Value
13		
14		
15	2	=IF(F15>30,(F15*E15*B9)+E15,(IF(F15>20,E15*B8,IF(F15>10,E15*B7,IF(F15>5,E15*B6,IF(F15>=1,E15*B5,0))))))
16	2	=IF(F16>30,(F16*E16*0.01)+E16,(IF(F16>20,E16*0.25,IF(F16>10,E16*0.5,IF(F16>5,E16*0.7,IF(F16>=1,E16*0.8,0))))))
17	2	=IF(F17>30,(F17*E17*0.01)+E17,(IF(F17>20,E17*0.25,IF(F17>10,E17*0.5,IF(F17>5,E17*0.7,IF(F17>=1,E17*0.8,0))))))
18	2	=IF(F18>30,(F18*E18*0.01)+E18,(IF(F18>20,E18*0.25,IF(F18>10,E18*0.5,IF(F18>5,E18*0.7,IF(F18>=1,E18*0.8,0))))))
19	2	=IF(F19>30,(F19*E19*0.01)+E19,(IF(F19>20,E19*0.25,IF(F19>10,E19*0.5,IF(F19>5,E19*0.7,IF(F19>=1,E19*0.8,0))))))
20	2	=IF(F20>30,(F20*E20*0.01)+E20,(IF(F20>20,E20*0.25,IF(F20>10,E20*0.5,IF(F20>5,E20*0.7,IF(F20>=1,E20*0.8,0))))))
21	2	=IF(F21>30,(F21*E21*0.01)+E21,(IF(F21>20,E21*0.25,IF(F21>10,E21*0.5,IF(F21>5,E21*0.7,IF(F21>=1,E21*0.8,0))))))
22	2	=IF(F22>30,(F22*E22*0.01)+E22,(IF(F22>20,E22*0.25,IF(F22>10,E22*0.5,IF(F22>5,E22*0.7,IF(F22>=1,E22*0.8,0))))))
23		
24		
25	2	=IF(F25>30,(F25*E25*0.01)+E25,(IF(F25>20,E25*0.25,IF(F25>10,E25*0.5,IF(F25>5,E25*0.7,IF(F25>=1,E25*0.8,0))))))
26	2	=IF(F26>30,(F26*E26*0.01)+E26,(IF(F26>20,E26*0.25,IF(F26>10,E26*0.5,IF(F26>5,E26*0.7,IF(F26>=1,E26*0.8,0))))))
27	1	=IF(F27>30,(F27*E27*0.01)+E27,(IF(F27>20,E27*0.25,IF(F27>10,E27*0.5,IF(F27>5,E27*0.7,IF(F27>=1,E27*0.8,0))))))
28	1	=IF(F28>30,(F28*E28*0.01)+E28,(IF(F28>20,E28*0.25,IF(F28>10,E28*0.5,IF(F28>5,E28*0.7,IF(F28>=1,E28*0.8,0))))))
29	2	=IF(F29>30,(F29*E29*0.01)+E29,(IF(F29>20,E29*0.25,IF(F29>10,E29*0.5,IF(F29>5,E29*0.7,IF(F29>=1,E29*0.8,0))))))
30	1	=IF(F30>30,(F30*E30*0.01)+E30,(IF(F30>20,E30*0.25,IF(F30>10,E30*0.5,IF(F30>5,E30*0.7,IF(F30>=1,E30*0.8,0))))))
31		
32		
33	2	=IF(F33>30,(F33*E33*0.01)+E33,(IF(F33>20,E33*0.25,IF(F33>10,E33*0.5,IF(F33>5,E33*0.7,IF(F33>=1,E33*0.8,0))))))
34	2	=IF(F34>30,(F34*E34*0.01)+E34,(IF(F34>20,E34*0.25,IF(F34>10,E34*0.5,IF(F34>5,E34*0.7,IF(F34>=1,E34*0.8,0))))))
35	2	=IF(F35>30,(F35*E35*0.01)+E35,(IF(F35>20,E35*0.25,IF(F35>10,E35*0.5,IF(F35>5,E35*0.7,IF(F35>=1,E35*0.8,0))))))
36	2	=IF(F36>30,(F36*E36*0.01)+E36,(IF(F36>20,E36*0.25,IF(F36>10,E36*0.5,IF(F36>5,E36*0.7,IF(F36>=1,E36*0.8,0))))))
37	2	=IF(F37>30,(F37*E37*0.01)+E37,(IF(F37>20,E37*0.25,IF(F37>10,E37*0.5,IF(F37>5,E37*0.7,IF(F37>=1,E37*0.8,0))))))
38	2	=IF(F38>30,(F38*E38*0.01)+E38,(IF(F38>20,E38*0.25,IF(F38>10,E38*0.5,IF(F38>5,E38*0.7,IF(F38>=1,E38*0.8,0))))))
39	2	=IF(F39>30,(F39*E39*0.01)+E39,(IF(F39>20,E39*0.25,IF(F39>10,E39*0.5,IF(F39>5,E39*0.7,IF(F39>=1,E39*0.8,0))))))
40	2	=IF(F40>30,(F40*E40*0.01)+E40,(IF(F40>20,E40*0.25,IF(F40>10,E40*0.5,IF(F40>5,E40*0.7,IF(F40>=1,E40*0.8,0))))))
41	2	=IF(F41>30,(F41*E41*0.01)+E41,(IF(F41>20,E41*0.25,IF(F41>10,E41*0.5,IF(F41>5,E41*0.7,IF(F41>=1,E41*0.8,0))))))
42		
43		
44	1	=IF(F44>30,(F44*E44*0.01)+E44,(IF(F44>20,E44*0.25,IF(F44>10,E44*0.5,IF(F44>5,E44*0.7,IF(F44>=1,E44*0.8,0))))))
45	2	=IF(F45>30,(F45*E45*0.01)+E45,(IF(F45>20,E45*0.25,IF(F45>10,E45*0.5,IF(F45>5,E45*0.7,IF(F45>=1,E45*0.8,0))))))
46	2	=IF(F46>30,(F46*E46*0.01)+E46,(IF(F46>20,E46*0.25,IF(F46>10,E46*0.5,IF(F46>5,E46*0.7,IF(F46>=1,E46*0.8,0))))))
47	2	=IF(F47>30,(F47*E47*0.01)+E47,(IF(F47>20,E47*0.25,IF(F47>10,E47*0.5,IF(F47>5,E47*0.7,IF(F47>=1,E47*0.8,0))))))
48		
49		
50	2	=IF(F50>30,(F50*E50*0.01)+E50,(IF(F50>20,E50*0.25,IF(F50>10,E50*0.5,IF(F50>5,E50*0.7,IF(F50>=1,E50*0.8,0))))))
51	2	=IF(F51>30,(F51*E51*0.01)+E51,(IF(F51>20,E51*0.25,IF(F51>10,E51*0.5,IF(F51>5,E51*0.7,IF(F51>=1,E51*0.8,0))))))
52	2	=IF(F52>30,(F52*E52*0.01)+E52,(IF(F52>20,E52*0.25,IF(F52>10,E52*0.5,IF(F52>5,E52*0.7,IF(F52>=1,E52*0.8,0))))))
53	2	=IF(F53>30,(F53*E53*0.01)+E53,(IF(F53>20,E53*0.25,IF(F53>10,E53*0.5,IF(F53>5,E53*0.7,IF(F53>=1,E53*0.8,0))))))
54	2	=IF(F54>30,(F54*E54*0.01)+E54,(IF(F54>20,E54*0.25,IF(F54>10,E54*0.5,IF(F54>5,E54*0.7,IF(F54>=1,E54*0.8,0))))))
55	2	=IF(F55>30,(F55*E55*0.01)+E55,(IF(F55>20,E55*0.25,IF(F55>10,E55*0.5,IF(F55>5,E55*0.7,IF(F55>=1,E55*0.8,0))))))
56		
57		
58	2	=IF(F58>30,(F58*E58*0.01)+E58,(IF(F58>20,E58*0.25,IF(F58>10,E58*0.5,IF(F58>5,E58*0.7,IF(F58>=1,E58*0.8,0))))))
59	2	=IF(F59>30,(F59*E59*0.01)+E59,(IF(F59>20,E59*0.25,IF(F59>10,E59*0.5,IF(F59>5,E59*0.7,IF(F59>=1,E59*0.8,0))))))
60	2	=IF(F60>30,(F60*E60*0.01)+E60,(IF(F60>20,E60*0.25,IF(F60>10,E60*0.5,IF(F60>5,E60*0.7,IF(F60>=1,E60*0.8,0))))))
61	2	=IF(F61>30,(F61*E61*0.01)+E61,(IF(F61>20,E61*0.25,IF(F61>10,E61*0.5,IF(F61>5,E61*0.7,IF(F61>=1,E61*0.8,0))))))
62		
63		
64	2	=IF(F64>30,(F64*E64*0.01)+E64,(IF(F64>20,E64*0.25,IF(F64>10,E64*0.5,IF(F64>5,E64*0.7,IF(F64>=1,E64*0.8,0))))))
65	2	=IF(F65>30,(F65*E65*0.01)+E65,(IF(F65>20,E65*0.25,IF(F65>10,E65*0.5,IF(F65>5,E65*0.7,IF(F65>=1,E65*0.8,0))))))
66	2	=IF(F66>30,(F66*E66*0.01)+E66,(IF(F66>20,E66*0.25,IF(F66>10,E66*0.5,IF(F66>5,E66*0.7,IF(F66>=1,E66*0.8,0))))))
67		
68		
69		
70		
71		
72		

Personal Finances

	A	B	C	D	E	F	H	I	K	M	N	O	P	Q	R	S
1	PERSONAL FINANCES															
2																
3				Savings Balance		$3,547.56										
4				Checking Balance		$1,159.76										
5																
6	Month of December, 1987															
7																
8				Savings		Checking										
9																
10	Account Number			1015687-3		213-687										
11																
12	Beginning Balance			$2,387.76		$356.89										
13	Total Checks					$2,271.09										
14	Total Deposits			$1,590.87		$3,089.63										
15	Total Withdrawals			$600.00												
16	Interest On Savings (%)			0.05												
17	Interest Earned			$168.93												
18	Bank Charges					$15.67										
19	Current Balance			$3,378.63		$1,159.76										
20	Adjusted Balance			$3,547.56		$1,159.76										
21																
22	Total Deductions This Month					$548.42										
23	Total Deductions up to This Month					$5,463.00										
24	Total Deductions to Date					$6,011.42										
25																
26																
27																
28	Checking Summary															
29																
30	ID															
31	Number			Date		Description	Amount	Deposits	Balance		Deductible		Deductible			
32											1=yes/2=no		Totals			
33																
34				12/2		deposit	$0.00	$2,654.65	3011.54		2		$0.00			
35	146			12/3		Jim's Engine	$24.95	$0.00	2986.59		1		$24.95			
36	147			12/4		Hall's	$245.78	$0.00	2740.81		2		$0.00			
37	148			12/5		Hall's	$22.31	$0.00	2718.50		2		$0.00			
38				12/5		deposit	$0.00	$45.00	2763.50		2		$0.00			
39	149			12/7		Standing Const.	$324.66	$0.00	2438.84		2		$0.00			
40	150			12/8		Ace	$43.78	$0.00	2395.06		2		$0.00			
41	151			12/10		Nat'l Bank	$657.87	$0.00	1737.19		2		$0.00			
42	152			12/11		Adventure Books	$7.95	$0.00	1729.24		1		$7.95			
43	153			12/11		Warner's	$13.67	$0.00	1715.57		2		$0.00			
44	154			12/14		Warner's	$34.88	$0.00	1680.69		2		$0.00			
45	155			12/15		Hall's	$44.45	$0.00	1636.24		2		$0.00			
46				12/17		deposit	$0.00	$27.98	1664.22		2		$0.00			
47	156			12/18		Warner's	$25.95	$0.00	1638.27		2		$0.00			
48	157			12/18		Water	$55.78	$0.00	1582.49		2		$0.00			
49	158			12/19		MM Music	$15.86	$0.00	1566.63		1		$15.86			
50	159			12/20		Warner's	$4.78	$0.00	1561.85		2		$0.00			
51				12/20		deposit	$0.00	$100.00	1661.85		2		$0.00			
52	160			12/21		School	$105.00	$0.00	1556.85		1		$105.00			
53	161			12/22		Dr. Laird	$35.00	$0.00	1521.85		1		$35.00			
54	162			12/22		Dr. Laird	$35.00	$0.00	1486.85		1		$35.00			
55	163			12/22		Electric	$124.87	$0.00	1361.98		2		$0.00			
56	164			12/23		A&T Inc.	$43.89	$0.00	1318.09		2		$0.00			
57				12/24		deposit	$0.00	$212.00	1530.09		2		$0.00			
58	165			12/26		Jack	$45.00	$0.00	1485.09		2		$0.00			
59	166			12/28		LINK	$35.00	$0.00	1450.09		2		$0.00			
60	167			12/28		Taxes	$324.66	$0.00	1125.43		1		$324.66			
61				12/30		deposit	$0.00	$50.00	1175.43		2		$0.00			
62																
63						Totals	$2,271.09	$3,089.63					$548.42			
64																
65	Savings Summary															
66																
67	Date		Deposit		Withdrawal		Balance									
68																
69	12/3		$300.00		$0.00		$2,687.76									
70	12/6		$0.00		$500.00		$2,187.76									
71	12/10		$312.00		$0.00		$2,499.76									
72	12/15		$234.00				$2,733.76									
73	12/17		$543.87				$3,277.63									
74	12/20		$0.00		$100.00		$3,177.63									
75	12/26		$201.00				$3,378.63									
76																
77	TOTAL		$1,590.87		$600.00											

Personal Worksheets

What the Spreadsheet Does

This spreadsheet helps you keep track of your savings and checking transactions, allows you to keep track of expenses that are deductible, and provides you with a sum of that amount for the month as well as for the year.

The spreadsheet should give you a good idea of where your income is going and what your month-end balances will be. The **=DATE** function is used to enter the date of the transaction as a label. The **Ctrl->D** key combination can also be used.

Working with the Spreadsheet

To work with this spreadsheet, you need to enter the following information.

A69...F75	summary of savings activity
Col A	transaction id (usually check number)
Col C	transaction date
Col E	transaction description
Col H	amount of transaction
Col J	amount of deposit
Col O	whether transaction is deductible
D12	beginning savings balance
D16	interest rate on savings
D17	total interest earned
F12	beginning checking balance
F23	total deductibles for this month
Row 10	checking and savings account numbers
Row 18	bank charges

When the spreadsheet is complete, it will yield the following.

Col K	a running balance of savings
Col P	cost of deductible items
D14	total savings deposit
D15	total savings withdrawal
D17	interest earned
D19	current savings balance
D20	adjusted savings balance
F13	total checks

Excel Business Applications

F14	total checking deposits
F19	current checking balance
F20	adjusted savings balance
F22	total deductibles this month
F23	total deductibles up to this month
F24	total deductibles this year
F3	beginning savings balance
F4	beginning checking balance
J63	total savings deposits
P63	total deductibles for month

What It Looks Like

Figure 10.3 shows a pie chart (with one exploding slice) that reveals the relative percentage of savings and checking balances.

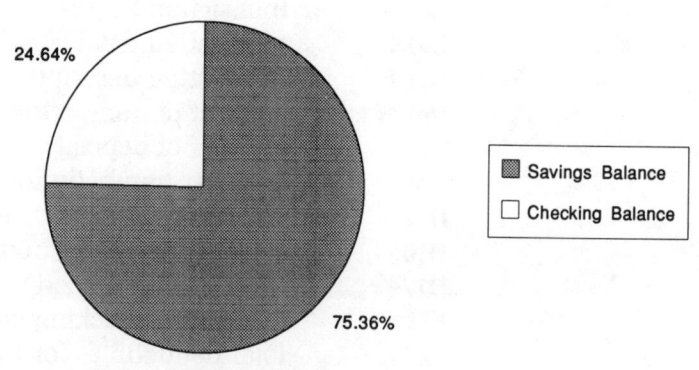

10.3 Saving versus checking

The Cell Contents and Formulas

	A	B	C	D	E	F
1	PERSONAL FINANCES					
2						
3				Savings Balance		=D20
4				Checking Balance		=F20
5						
6	Month of December, 1987					
7						
8				Savings		Checking
9						
10	Account Number			1015687-3		213-687
11						
12	Beginning Balance			2387.76		356.89
13	Total Checks					=(H63)
14	Total Deposits			=(B77)		=(I63)
15	Total Withdrawals			=(D77)		
16	Interest On Savings (%)			0.05		
17	Interest Earned			=(D19)*(D16)		
18	Bank Charges					15.669999999999
19	Current Balance			=(F75)		=F12-F13+F14-F18
20	Adjusted Balance			=(D17)+(D19)		=(F19)
21						
22	Total Deductions This Month					=(P63)
23	Total Deductions up to This Mon					5463
24	Total Deductions to Date					=F22+F23
25						
26						
27						
28	Checking Summary					
29						
30	ID					
31	Number		Date		Description	
32						
33						
34			12/2		deposit	
35	146		12/3		Jim's Engine	
36	147		12/4		Hall's	
37	148		12/5		Hall's	
38			12/5		deposit	
39	149		12/7		Standing Const.	
40	150		12/8		Ace	
41	151		12/10		Nat'l Bank	
42	152		12/11		Adventure Books	
43	153		12/11		Warner's	
44	154		12/14		Warner's	
45	155		12/15		Hall's	
46			12/17		deposit	
47	156		12/18		Warner's	
48	157		12/18		Water	
49	158		12/19		MM Music	
50	159		12/20		Warner's	
51			12/20		deposit	
52	160		12/21		School	
53	161		12/22		Dr. Laird	
54	162		12/22		Dr. Laird	
55	163		12/22		Electric	
56	164		12/23		A&T Inc.	
57			12/24		deposit	
58	165		12/26		Jack	
59	166		12/28		LINK	
60	167		12/28		Taxes	
61			12/30		deposit	
62						
63					Totals	
64						
65	Savings Summary					
66						
67	Date	Deposit		Withdrawal		Balance
68						
69	12/3	300		0		=D12+B69-D69
70	12/6	0		500		=F69+B70-D70
71	12/10	312		0		=F70+B71-D71
72	12/15	234				=F71+B72-D72
73	12/17	543.87				=F72+B73-D73
74	12/20	0		100		=F73+B74-D74
75	12/26	201				=F74+B75-D75
76						
77	TOTAL	=SUM(B69:B75)		=SUM(D69:D75)		

The Cell Contents and Formulas (Continued)

	H	I	K	M	N	O	P
1							
2							
3							
4							
5							
6							
7							
8							
9							
10							
11							
12							
13							
14							
15							
16							
17							
18							
19							
20							
21							
22							
23							
24							
25							
26							
27							
28							
29							
30							
31	Amount	Deposits	Balance		Deductible		Deductible
32					1=yes/2=no		Totals
33							
34	0	2654.65	=F12-H34+I34		2		=IF(N34=1,H34,0)
35	24.95	0	=K34-H35+I35		1		=IF(N35=1,H35,0)
36	245.78	0	=K35-H36+I36		2		=IF(N36=1,H36,0)
37	22.31	0	=K36-H37+I37		2		=IF(N37=1,H37,0)
38	0	45	=K37-H38+I38		2		=IF(N38=1,H38,0)
39	324.66	0	=K38-H39+I39		2		=IF(N39=1,H39,0)
40	43.78	0	=K39-H40+I40		2		=IF(N40=1,H40,0)
41	657.87	0	=K40-H41+I41		2		=IF(N41=1,H41,0)
42	7.95	0	=K41-H42+I42		1		=IF(N42=1,H42,0)
43	13.6699999999	0	=K42-H43+I43		2		=IF(N43=1,H43,0)
44	34.88	0	=K43-H44+I44		2		=IF(N44=1,H44,0)
45	44.45	0	=K44-H45+I45		2		=IF(N45=1,H45,0)
46	0	27.98	=K45-H46+I46		2		=IF(N46=1,H46,0)
47	25.95	0	=K46-H47+I47		2		=IF(N47=1,H47,0)
48	55.78	0	=K47-H48+I48		2		=IF(N48=1,H48,0)
49	15.86	0	=K48-H49+I49		1		=IF(N49=1,H49,0)
50	4.78	0	=K49-H50+I50		2		=IF(N50=1,H50,0)
51	0	100	=K50-H51+I51		2		=IF(N51=1,H51,0)
52	105	0	=K51-H52+I52		1		=IF(N52=1,H52,0)
53	35	0	=K52-H53+I53		1		=IF(N53=1,H53,0)
54	35	0	=K53-H54+I54		1		=IF(N54=1,H54,0)
55	124.87	0	=K54-H55+I55		2		=IF(N55=1,H55,0)
56	43.89	0	=K55-H56+I56		2		=IF(N56=1,H56,0)
57	0	212	=K56-H57+I57		2		=IF(N57=1,H57,0)
58	45	0	=K57-H58+I58		2		=IF(N58=1,H58,0)
59	35	0	=K58-H59+I59		2		=IF(N59=1,H59,0)
60	324.66	0	=K59-H60+I60		1		=IF(N60=1,H60,0)
61	0	50	=K60-H61+I61		2		=IF(N61=1,H61,0)
62							
63	=SUM(H35:H61)	=SUM(I34:I61)					=SUM(P34:P61)

Starting a Business

	A	B	C	D	E	F	G	H	I
1	STARTING A BUSINESS (FIRST THREE MONTHS)								
2									
3	Expenses By Category								
4					Unit	# Hours	Total		
5					Cost		Cost		
6	BUILDING								
7		Labor for construction			$13	300	$3,750		
8		Materials for construction			$2,000	0	$2,000		
9									
10	ADVERTISING								
11		Bulk Mail Permit			$40		$40		
12		Designer			$25	5	$125		
13		Mail consultant			$50	3	$150		
14		Printing			$350		$350		
15		Postage			$125		$125		
16		Classified			$100		$100		
17									
18	EMPLOYEE								
19		Sales #1			$5	480	$2,520		
20		Sales #2			$5	480	$2,520		
21		Manager (fixed salary/mo.)			$5,000	0	$5,000		
22									
23	OPERATION								
24		Rent			$1,500		$1,500		
25		Utilities			$350		$350		
26		Insurance			$225		$225		
27		Office Supplies			$300		$300		
28		Furniture			$560		$560		
29									
30	LICENSING								
31		Local			$35		$35		
32		State			$15		$15		
33									
34									
35				TOTAL STARTUP COSTS			$19,665		

What the Spreadsheet Does

This spreadsheet contains a list of factors to consider when starting a business and allows you to input values and examine the effects on total startup costs.

It provides estimates for a three-month period for the categories of initial necessary construction, advertising, employee costs (including a manager and two salespeople), operations, and licensing.

Excel Business Applications

Working with the Spreadsheet

To work with this spreadsheet, you need to enter the following information.

    E11...E16   advertising costs
    E19...E21   employee costs
    E24...E28   operating costs
    E31...E32   licensing costs
    E7...E9   building costs
    Col F   unit costs

When the spreadsheet is complete, it will provide you with the following information.

    G35   total startup costs
    Col G total item costs

The Cell Contents and Formulas

	A	B	C	D	E	F	G
1	STARTING A BUSINESS						
2							
3	Expenses By Category						
4					Unit	# Hours	Total
5					Cost		Cost
6	BUILDING						
7		Labor for construction			12.5	300	=IF(F7=0,E7,F7*E7)
8		Materials for construction			2000	0	=IF(F8=0,E8,F8*E8)
9							
10	ADVERTISING						
11		Bulk Mail Permit			40		=IF(F11=0,E11,F11*E11)
12		Designer			25	5	=IF(F12=0,E12,F12*E12)
13		Mail consultant			50	3	=IF(F13=0,E13,F13*E13)
14		Printing			350		=IF(F14=0,E14,F14*E14)
15		Postage			125		=IF(F15=0,E15,F15*E15)
16		Classified			100		=IF(F16=0,E16,F16*E16)
17							
18	EMPLOYEE						
19		Sales #1			5.25	480	=IF(F19=0,E19,F19*E19)
20		Sales #2			5.25	480	=IF(F20=0,E20,F20*E20)
21		Manager (fixed salary/mo)			5000	0	=IF(F21=0,E21,F21*E21)
22							
23	OPERATION						
24		Rent			1500		=IF(F24=0,E24,F24*E24)
25		Utilities			350		=IF(F25=0,E25,F25*E25)
26		Insurance			225		=IF(F26=0,E26,F26*E26)
27		Office Supplies			300		=IF(F27=0,E27,F27*E27)
28		Furniture			560		=IF(F28=0,E28,F28*E28)
29							
30	LICENSING						
31		Local			35		=IF(F31=0,E31,F31*E31)
32		State			15		=IF(F32=0,E32,F32*E32)
33							
34				TOTAL STARTUP COSTS			=SUM(G7:G32)
35							

11 / Retail Worksheets

Advertisement Analysis

	A	B	C	D	E	F	G
1	ADVERTISEMENT ANALYSIS			(*classified advertisements)			
2							
3	Source	Cost of	Number of	Number of	% Draw on Ad	Sales	Sales/Adv $
4	Code	Ad	Pieces Mailed	Inquiries		Confirmed	
5							
6	PS1	$1,250.00	1536	45	2.93%	38	$32.89
7	C1	$700.00	870	20	2.30%	12	$58.33
8	SA1*	$675.00		15		13	$51.92
9	V1	$625.00	604	15	2.48%	12	$52.08
10	PM1	$600.00	815	10	1.23%	9	$66.67
11	PM2*	$550.00		6		6	$91.67
12	SN1	$525.00	354	8	2.26%	5	$105.00
13	CJ2	$450.00	1234	30	2.43%	18	$25.00
14	ST1*	$435.00		5		3	$145.00
15	B1	$325.00	490	6	1.22%	1	$325.00
16							
17	Total	$6,135.00	5903	160		117	
18	Average	$613.50	843	16	2.12%	11.7	$95.36

Retail Worksheets

What the Spreadsheet Does

In any retail business one needs to know the effectiveness of different advertising strategies. One way this is measured is in terms of "draw" (the percentage of inquiries) generated by an ad, but it can also be measured based on a ratio of the cost of advertising per sale. The more sales, the lower the cost of the advertising per sales dollar.

Working with the Spreadsheet

To work with this spreadsheet, you need to enter the following information.

Col A source code or some location of where the ad appeared
Col B cost of advertising
Col C number of pieces of direct mail
Col D number of inquiries (draw)
Col F confirmed sales

When the spreadsheet is complete, it will provide you with the following information.

Col E percent draw
Col G sales per advertising dollar
Row 17 totals
Row 18 averages

What It Looks Like

Figure 11.1 is a line chart that examines the sales level per dollar of advertising.

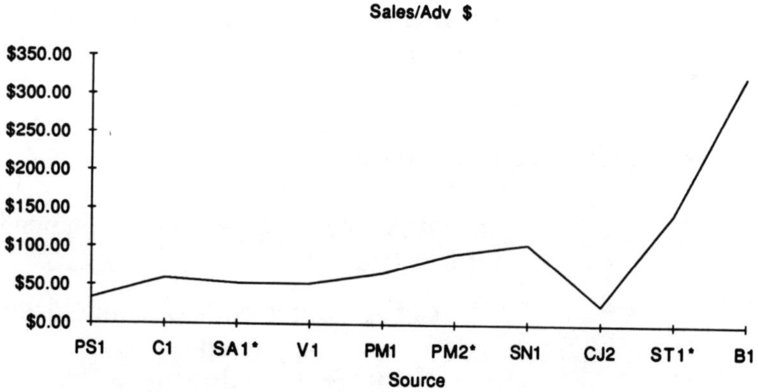
Sales/Adv $
$350.00
$300.00
$250.00
$200.00
$150.00
$100.00
$50.00
$0.00
PS1
C1
SA1*
V1
PM1
PM2*
SN1
CJ2
ST1*
B1
Source

11.1 Sales per dollar

The Cell Contents and Formulas

	A	B	C	D
1	ADVERTISEMENT ANALYSIS			(*classified advertisements)
2				
3	Source	Cost of	Number of	Number of
4	Code	Ad	Pieces Mailed	Inquiries
5				
6	PS1	1250	1536	45
7	C1	700	870	20
8	SA1*	675		15
9	V1	625	604	15
10	PM1	600	815	10
11	PM2*	550		6
12	SN1	525	354	8
13	CJ2	450	1234	30
14	ST1*	435		5
15	B1	325	490	6
16				
17	Total	=SUM(B6:B15)	=SUM(C6:C15)	=SUM(D6:D15)
18	Average	=AVERAGE(B6:B15)	=AVERAGE(C6:C15)	=AVERAGE(D6:D15)

	E	F	G
1			
2			
3	% Draw on Ad	Sales	Sales/Adv $
4		Confirmed	
5			
6	=D6/C6	38	=B6/F6
7	=D7/C7	12	=B7/F7
8		13	=B8/F8
9	=D9/C9	12	=B9/F9
10	=D10/C10	9	=B10/F10
11		6	=B11/F11
12	=D12/C12	5	=B12/F12
13	=D13/C13	18	=B13/F13
14		3	=B14/F14
15	=D15/C15	1	=B15/F15
16			
17		=SUM(F6:F15)	
18	=AVERAGE(E6:E15)	=AVERAGE(F6:F15)	=AVERAGE(G6:G15)

Excel Business Applications

Analysis of Productivity—Products

	A	B	C	D	E
1	ANALYSIS OF PRODUCTIVITY - PRODUCTS				
2					
3	Employee	Input	Output	Productivity	% Share
4		(Units)	(Units)	Ratio	Output
5					
6	1	13	8	0.62	0.07
7	2	15	17	1.13	0.16
8	3	13	14	1.08	0.13
9	4	16	13	0.81	0.12
10	5	12	10	0.83	0.09
11	6	11	8	0.73	0.07
12	7	9	9	1.00	0.08
13	8	10	11	1.10	0.10
14	9	16	13	0.81	0.12
15	10	7	6	0.86	0.06
16					
17		Total	109		

What the Spreadsheet Does

Productivity is not measured by simply counting the production of any one individual, but as a ratio of that individual's output as compared with input.

This spreadsheet provides such information and computes a productivity ratio as well as the percentage of an individual's output compared with all other workers.

Working with the Spreadsheet

To work with this spreadsheet, you need to enter the following information.

Col A employee
Col B input in units
Col C output in units

When the spreadsheet is complete, it will provide you with the following information.

C17 total output
Col D productivity (output/input)
Col E percentage share of output

Retail Worksheets

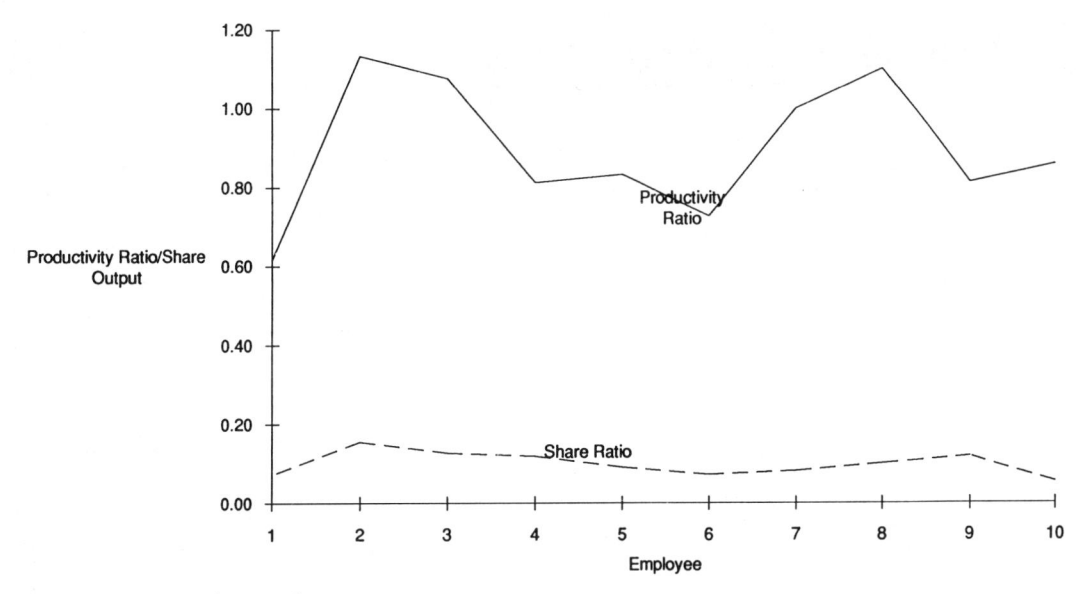

11.2 Productivity by employee

What It Looks Like

Figure 11.2 shows a line chart, compares the productivity and share ratios of all the employees for which this information is available.

The Cell Contents and Formulas

	A	B	C	D	E
1	ANALYSIS OF PRODUCTIVITY - PRODUCTS				
2					
3	Employee	Input	Output	Productivity	% Share
4		(Units)	(Units)	Ratio	Output
5					
6	1	13	8	=C6/B6	=C6/$C$17
7	2	15	17	=C7/B7	=C7/$C$17
8	3	13	14	=C8/B8	=C8/$C$17
9	4	16	13	=C9/B9	=C9/$C$17
10	5	12	10	=C10/B10	=C10/$C$17
11	6	11	8	=C11/B11	=C11/$C$17
12	7	9	9	=C12/B12	=C12/$C$17
13	8	10	11	=C13/B13	=C13/$C$17
14	9	16	13	=C14/B14	=C14/$C$17
15	10	7	6	=C15/B15	=C15/$C$17
16					
17		Total	=SUM(C6:C15)		

Excel Business Applications

Analysis of Productivity—Sales

	A	B	C	D	E	F	G	H	I	J
1	ANALYSIS OF PRODUCTIVITY - SALES									
2										
3	Time Period: April 4-8, 1988									
4										
5										
6	Employe	Hours	# Customer	Number of	%Sales/	Gross	Sales/	Returns	Net	% Total
7		Worked	Contacts	Transactions	Contact	Sales	Contact	On Sales	Sales	Sales
8										
9	15	30	33	25	75.76%	$2,000	$60.61	$1,450	$550	1.55%
10	12	32	25	15	60.00%	$2,700	$108.00	$1,350	$1,350	3.80%
11	13	32	28	13	46.43%	$2,100	$75.00	$1,200	$900	2.53%
12	04	35	30	19	63.33%	$3,200	$106.67	$650	$2,550	7.17%
13	06	38	19	10	52.63%	$2,100	$110.53	$350	$1,750	4.92%
14	09	39	23	12	52.17%	$2,800	$121.74	$1,000	$1,800	5.06%
15	11	41	31	25	80.65%	$3,800	$122.58	$1,000	$2,800	7.87%
16	14	41	31	20	64.52%	$3,550	$114.52	$2,100	$1,450	4.08%
17	06	42	28	20	71.43%	$4,100	$146.43	$560	$3,540	9.95%
18	03	44	36	24	66.67%	$5,100	$141.67	$2,298	$2,802	7.88%
19	05	46	31	20	64.52%	$4,680	$150.97	$550	$4,130	11.61%
20	10	49	26	12	46.15%	$4,200	$161.54	$1,500	$2,700	7.59%
21	01	51	25	17	68.00%	$4,500	$180.00	$1,230	$3,270	9.19%
22	02	52	18	12	66.67%	$3,700	$205.56	$970	$2,730	7.67%
23	06	53	26	21	80.77%	$4,500	$173.08	$1,250	$3,250	9.14%
24										
25	Total	625	410	265		$53,030	$1,978.87	$17,458	$35,572	100.00%
26	Average	41.67	27.33	17.67	63.98%	$3,535	$131.92	$1,164	$2,371	

What the Spreadsheet Does

It's often difficult to measure the value of an employee or an employee group. A frequently used method is productivity analysis, which compares various measures of input and output.

This spreadsheet calculates some basic measures of productivity, such as sales per contact and percent of sales per contact, and can be used to help identify the most efficient use of time for sales.

Retail Worksheets

Working with the Spreadsheet

To work with this spreadsheet, you need to enter the following information.

Col A employee identification
Col B hours worked
Col C number of customer contacts
Col D number of transactions
Col F gross sales
Col H returns on sales

When the spreadsheet is complete, it will provide you with the following information.

Col E percentage of sales per contact
Col G sales per contact
Col I net sales
Col J percentage of total sales
Row 25 column totals
Row 26 column averages

Excel Business Applications

What It Looks Like

Figure 11.3 is a scatter chart that shows that relationship between the number of hours worked and sales per contact, illustrating that the more hours worked, the higher the level of sales per contact. When the information is charted, hours worked (column B) was sorted in ascending order so that one of the two dimensions plotted as a scatter chart was ordered. Otherwise the chart becomes a series of intersecting lines that make little sense. An arrow and some unattached text were also added.

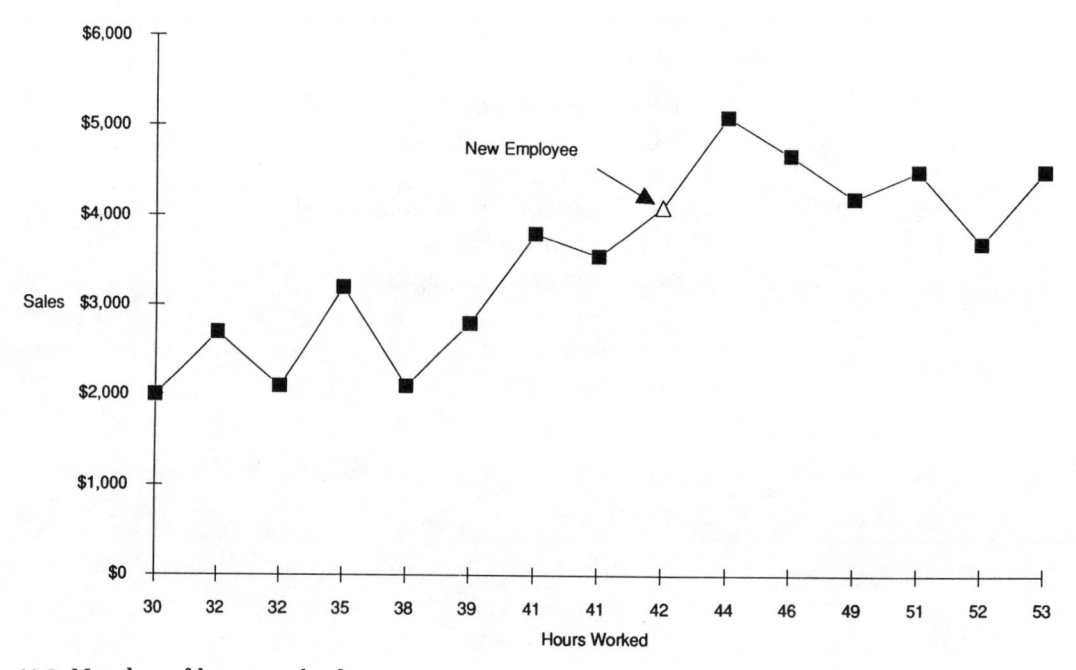

11.3 Number of hours and sales contacts

Retail Worksheets

The Cell Contents and Formulas

	A	B	C	D	E
1	ANALYSIS OF PRODUCTIVITY - SALES				
2					
3	Time Period: April 4-8, 1988				
4					
5					
6	Employee	Hours	# Customer	Number of	%Sales/
7		Worked	Contacts	Transactions	Contact
8					
9	15	30	33	25	=D9/C9
10	12	32	25	15	=D10/C10
11	13	32	28	13	=D11/C11
12	04	35	30	19	=D12/C12
13	06	38	19	10	=D13/C13
14	09	39	23	12	=D14/C14
15	11	41	31	25	=D15/C15
16	14	41	31	20	=D16/C16
17	06	42	28	20	=D17/C17
18	03	44	36	24	=D18/C18
19	05	46	31	20	=D19/C19
20	10	49	26	12	=D20/C20
21	01	51	25	17	=D21/C21
22	02	52	18	12	=D22/C22
23	06	53	26	21	=D23/C23
24					
25	Total	=SUM(B9:B23)	=SUM(C9:C23)	=SUM(D9:D23)	
26	Average	=AVERAGE(B9:B23)	=AVERAGE(C9:C23)	=AVERAGE(D9:D23)	=AVERAGE(E9:E23)

	F	G	H	I	J	K
1						
2						
3						
4						
5						
6	Gross	Sales/	Returns	Net	% Total	
7	Sales	Contact	On Sales	Sales	Sales	
8						
9	2000	=F9/C9	1450	=F9-H9	=I9/$I$25	
10	2700	=F10/C10	1350	=F10-H10	=I10/$I$25	
11	2100	=F11/C11	1200	=F11-H11	=I11/$I$25	
12	3200	=F12/C12	650	=F12-H12	=I12/$I$25	
13	2100	=F13/C13	350	=F13-H13	=I13/$I$25	
14	2800	=F14/C14	1000	=F14-H14	=I14/$I$25	
15	3800	=F15/C15	1000	=F15-H15	=I15/$I$25	
16	3550	=F16/C16	2100	=F16-H16	=I16/$I$25	
17	4100	=F17/C17	560	=F17-H17	=I17/$I$25	
18	5100	=F18/C18	2298	=F18-H18	=I18/$I$25	
19	4680	=F19/C19	550	=F19-H19	=I19/$I$25	
20	4200	=F20/C20	1500	=F20-H20	=I20/$I$25	
21	4500	=F21/C21	1230	=F21-H21	=I21/$I$25	
22	3700	=F22/C22	970	=F22-H22	=I22/$I$25	
23	4500	=F23/C23	1250	=F23-H23	=I23/$I$25	
24						
25	=SUM(F9:F23)	=SUM(G9:G23)	=SUM(H9:H23)	=SUM(I9:I23)	=SUM(J9:J23)	
26	=AVERAGE(F9:F23)	=AVERAGE(G9:G23)	=AVERAGE(H9:H23)	=AVERAGE(I9:I23)		

Excel Business Applications

Cash Flow Analysis

	A	B	C	D	E	F	G	H
1	CASH FLOW ANALYSIS							
2								
3								
4	Yearly Growth Rate of S					12		
5	Costs of Go	Goods (% of Total Sales)				45		
6	Receivables (% of Total Sales)					75		
7								
8				Jan	Feb	March	April	May
9								
10	Cash			$6,758.00	$7,463.00	$5,647.00	$4,253.00	$6,435.00
11	Total Sales			$25,675.00	$24,124.00	$23,546.00	$33,123.00	$31,234.00
12	Receivables			$19,256.25	$18,093.00	$17,659.50	$24,842.25	$23,425.50
13								
14	Total Income			$26,014.25	$25,556.00	$23,306.50	$29,095.25	$29,860.50
15								
16	Operating Expenses							
17		Costs of Goods		$11,706.41	$11,500.20	$10,487.93	$13,092.86	$13,437.23
18		Advertising		$750.00	$750.00	$750.00	$750.00	$750.00
19		Rent		$1,000.00	$1,000.00	$1,000.00	$1,000.00	$1,000.00
20		Utilities		$350.00	$350.00	$350.00	$350.00	$350.00
21		Wages and			$750.00	$750.00	$750.00	$750.00
22		Salaries		$2,500.00	$2,500.00	$2,500.00	$2,500.00	$2,500.00
23		Unpaid			$750.00	$750.00	$750.00	$750.00
24		Payables		$4,814.06	$4,523.25	$4,414.88	$6,210.56	$5,856.38
25		Income Tax Payment		$200.00	$200.00	$200.00	$200.00	$200.00
26		Money Borrowed		$1,000.00	$1,000.00	$1,000.00	$1,000.00	$1,000.00
27		Loan Payme	ents	$450.00	$450.00	$450.00	$450.00	$450.00
28								
29	Total Costs			$22,770.48	$23,773.45	$22,652.80	$27,053.43	$27,043.60
30								
31	Total Cash			$3,243.78	$1,782.55	$653.70	$2,041.82	$2,816.90

What the Spreadsheet Does

This spreadsheet computes a cash flow analysis for a project over a 12-month period. The entire spreadsheet can be copied as many times as necessary if you want to track the cash flow of more than one product/service.

The estimates for yearly growth, and for costs of goods and receivables should be changed to fit your own situation.

Retail Worksheets

	I	J	K	L	M	N	O
1							
2							
3							
4							
5							
6							
7							
8	June	July	Aug	Sept	Oct	Nov	Dec
9							
10	$4,111.00	$5,347.00	$6,567.00	$3,411.00	$5,436.00	$5,443.00	$6,452.00
11	$27,456.00	$24,333.00	$26,546.00	$21,111.00	$31,243.00	$34,123.00	$45,313.00
12	$20,592.00	$18,249.75	$19,909.50	$15,833.25	$23,432.25	$25,592.25	$33,984.75
13							
14	$24,703.00	$23,596.75	$26,476.50	$19,244.25	$28,868.25	$31,035.25	$40,436.75
15							
16							
17	$11,116.35	$10,618.54	$11,914.43	$8,659.91	$12,990.71	$13,965.86	$18,196.54
18	$750.00	$750.00	$750.00	$750.00	$750.00	$750.00	$750.00
19	$1,000.00	$1,000.00	$1,000.00	$1,000.00	$1,000.00	$1,000.00	$1,000.00
20	$350.00	$350.00	$350.00	$350.00	$350.00	$350.00	$350.00
21	$750.00	$750.00	$750.00	$750.00	$750.00	$750.00	$750.00
22	$2,500.00	$2,500.00	$2,500.00	$2,500.00	$2,500.00	$2,500.00	$2,500.00
23	$750.00	$750.00	$750.00	$750.00	$750.00	$750.00	$750.00
24	$5,148.00	$4,562.44	$4,977.38	$3,958.31	$5,858.06	$6,398.06	$8,496.19
25	$200.00	$200.00	$200.00	$200.00	$200.00	$200.00	$200.00
26	$1,000.00	$1,000.00	$1,000.00	$1,000.00	$1,000.00	$1,000.00	$1,000.00
27	$450.00	$450.00	$450.00	$450.00	$450.00	$450.00	$450.00
28							
29	$24,014.35	$22,930.98	$24,641.80	$20,368.23	$26,598.78	$28,113.93	$34,442.73
30							
31	$688.65	$665.78	$1,834.70	($1,123.97)	$2,269.47	$2,921.32	$5,994.02

Working with the Spreadsheet

To work with this spreadsheet, you need to enter the following information on a monthly basis.

Row 10 cash on hand
Row 11 total sales
Row 12 receivables

Excel Business Applications

Row 18 advertising costs
Row 19 rent
Row 20 utility cost
Row 21 wages and salary
Row 23 unpaids
Row 25 income tax payment
Row 26 money borrowed
Row 27 loan payment

When the spreadsheet is complete, it will provide you with the following information.

Row 14 total income
Row 17 costs of goods
Row 24 unpaid receivables
Row 29 total costs
Row 31 available cash

What It Looks Like

Figure 11.4 is a line chart with unattached text showing total costs and income.

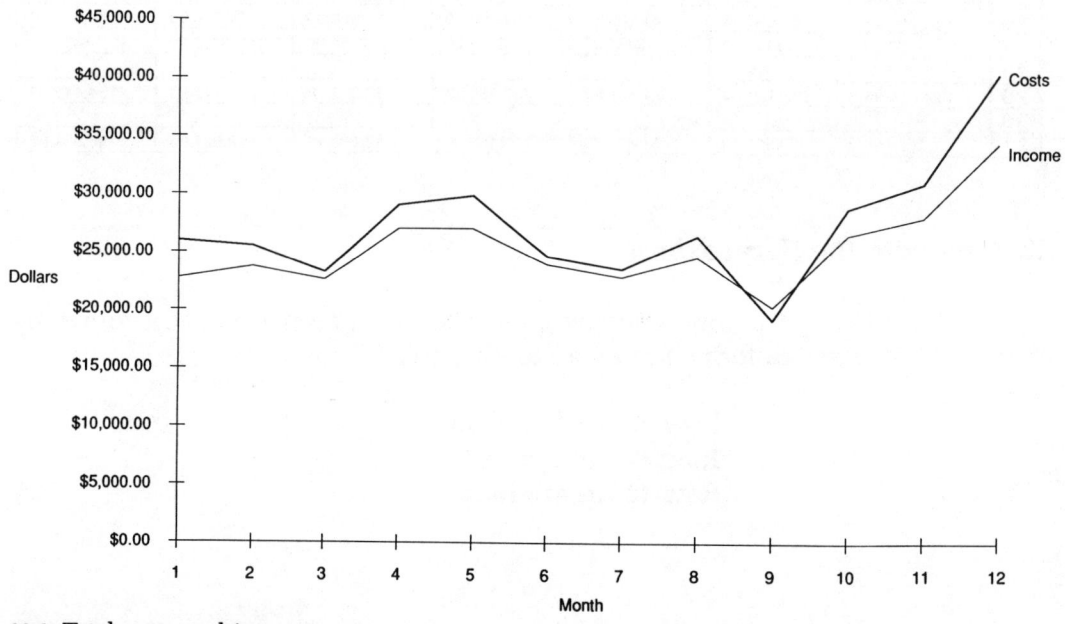

11.4 Total costs and income

Retail Worksheets

The Cell Contents and Formulas

	A	B	C	D
1	CASH FLOW ANALYSIS			
2				
3				
4	Yearly Growth Rate of Sales			12
5	Costs of Goods	(% of Total Sales)		45
6	Receivables (% of Total Sales)			75
7				
8			Jan	Feb
9				
10	Cash		6758	7463
11	Total Sales		25675	24124
12	Receivables		=($D$6/100)*C11	=($D$6/100)*D11
13				
14	Total Income		=C10+C12	=D10+D12
15				
16	Operating Expenses			
17		Costs of Goods	=($D$5/100)*C14	=($D$5/100)*D14
18		Advertising	750	750
19		Rent	1000	1000
20		Utilities	350	350
21		Wages and Salaries		750
22		Salaries	2500	2500
23		Unpaid		750
24		Payables	=(1-$D$6/100)*C12	=(1-$D$6/100)*D12
25		Income Tax Payment	200	200
26		Money Borrowed	1000	1000
27		Loan Payment	450	450
28				
29	Total Costs		=SUM(C17:C27)	=SUM(D17:D27)
30				
31	Total Cash		=C14-C29	=D14-D29

	E	F	G	H	I
1					
2					
3					
4					
5					
6					
7					
8	March	April	May	June	July
9					
10	5647	4253	6435	4111	5347
11	23546	33123	31234	27456	24333
12	=($D$6/100)*E11	=($D$6/100)*F11	=($D$6/100)*G11	=($D$6/100)*H11	=($D$6/100)*I11
13					
14	=E10+E12	=F10+F12	=G10+G12	=H10+H12	=I10+I12
15					
16					
17	=($D$5/100)*E14	=($D$5/100)*F14	=($D$5/100)*G14	=($D$5/100)*H14	=($D$5/100)*I14
18	750	750	750	750	750
19	1000	1000	1000	1000	1000
20	350	350	350	350	350
21	750	750	750	750	750
22	2500	2500	2500	2500	2500
23	750	750	750	750	750
24	=(1-$D$6/100)*E12	=(1-$D$6/100)*F12	=(1-$D$6/100)*G12	=(1-$D$6/100)*H12	=(1-$D$6/100)*I12
25	200	200	200	200	200
26	1000	1000	1000	1000	1000
27	450	450	450	450	450
28					
29	=SUM(E17:E27)	=SUM(F17:F27)	=SUM(G17:G27)	=SUM(H17:H27)	=SUM(I17:I27)
30					
31	=E14-E29	=F14-F29	=G14-G29	=H14-H29	=I14-I29

Excel Business Applications

The Cell Contents and Formulas (Continued)

	J	K	L	M	N
1					
2					
3					
4					
5					
6					
7					
8	Aug	Sept	Oct	Nov	Dec
9					
10	6567	3411	5436	5443	6452
11	26546	21111	31243	34123	45313
12	=($D$6/100)*J11	=($D$6/100)*K11	=($D$6/100)*L11	=($D$6/100)*M11	=($D$6/100)*N11
13					
14	=J10+J12	=K10+K12	=L10+L12	=M10+M12	=N10+N12
15					
16					
17	=($D$5/100)*J14	=($D$5/100)*K14	=($D$5/100)*L14	=($D$5/100)*M14	=($D$5/100)*N14
18	750	750	750	750	750
19	1000	1000	1000	1000	1000
20	350	350	350	350	350
21	750	750	750	750	750
22	2500	2500	2500	2500	2500
23	750	750	750	750	750
24	=(1-$D$6/100)*J12	=(1-$D$6/100)*K12	=(1-$D$6/100)*L12	=(1-$D$6/100)*M12	=(1-$D$6/100)*N12
25	200	200	200	200	200
26	1000	1000	1000	1000	1000
27	450	450	450	450	450
28					
29	=SUM(J17:J27)	=SUM(K17:K27)	=SUM(L17:L27)	=SUM(M17:M27)	=SUM(N17:N27)
30					
31	=J14-J29	=K14-K29	=L14-L29	=M14-M29	=N14-N29

Retail Worksheets

Determining a Markup Based on Retail Price

	A	B	C	D	E	F
1	DETERMINING A PRICE					
2						
3	Department:	Jewelry				
4						
5	Product		Markup	Cost	Markup	Selling Price
6	Description		%		$	
7						
8	jewelry-#453		120%	$3.48	$4.18	$7.66
9	jewelry-#453		80%	$13.25	$10.60	$23.85
10	jewelry-#453		90%	$36.78	$33.10	$69.88
11	jewelry-#453		90%	$66.78	$60.10	$126.88
12	watch-#213		75%	$45.00	$33.75	$78.75
13	watch-#213		67%	$60.00	$40.20	$100.20
14	watch-#213		72%	$66.00	$47.52	$113.52
15	accessories-#243		56%	$13.00	$7.28	$20.28
16	accessories-#433		70%	$6.00	$4.20	$10.20
17	accessories-#555		82%	$3.00	$2.46	$5.46
18			---------	---------	---------	---------
19	Average		80%	$31.33	$24.34	$55.67

What the Spreadsheet Does

An application similar to determining what the price of a product is, given a specific markup, is the determination of the percent of the markup.

This spreadsheet computes the percent markup for a certain product given the cost of the item and the selling price. It computes values for one product based on manufacturer's, wholesaler's, and retailer's figures. You can compute all of these figures or just one.

Working with the Spreadsheet

To work with this spreadsheet, you need to enter the following information.

Row D cost of the item
Row E markup of the item in dollars
Row F total costs of the item including markup

Excel Business Applications

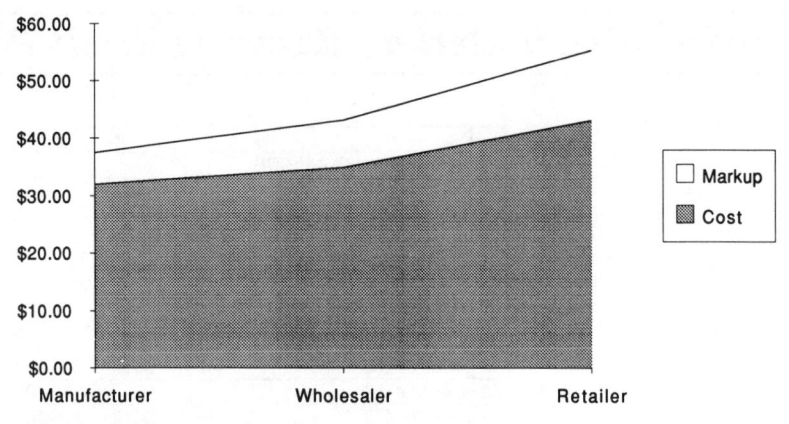

11.5 Cost to markup

When the spreadsheet is complete, it will provide you with the following information.

Row C	percent markup
E9	total dollar markup
G9	total percent markup

What It Looks Like

Figure 11.5 shows an area chart comparing cost to markup at different sales levels.

The Cell Contents and Formulas

	A	B	C	D	E	F
1	DETERMINING A PRICE					
2						
3	Department:	Jewelry				
4						
5	Product		Markup	Cost	Markup	Selling Price
6	Description		%		$	
7						
8	jewelry-#453		1.2	3.48	=C8*D8	=IF(C8=1,D8*2,D8*(1+C8))
9	jewelry-#453		0.8	13.25	=C9*D9	=IF(C9=1,D9*2,D9*(1+C9))
10	jewelry-#453		0.9	36.78	=C10*D10	=IF(C10=1,D10*2,D10*(1+C10))
11	jewelry-#453		0.9	66.78	=C11*D11	=IF(C11=1,D11*2,D11*(1+C11))
12	watch-#213		0.75	45	=C12*D12	=IF(C12=1,D12*2,D12*(1+C12))
13	watch-#213		0.67	60	=C13*D13	=IF(C13=1,D13*2,D13*(1+C13))
14	watch-#213		0.72	66	=C14*D14	=IF(C14=1,D14*2,D14*(1+C14))
15	accessories-#243		0.56	13	=C15*D15	=IF(C15=1,D15*2,D15*(1+C15))
16	accessories-#433		0.7	6	=C16*D16	=IF(C16=1,D16*2,D16*(1+C16))
17	accessories-#555		0.82	3	=C17*D17	=IF(C17=1,D17*2,D17*(1+C17))
18						
19	Average		=AVERAGE(C8:C17)	=AVERAGE(D8:D17)	=AVERAGE(E8:E17)	=AVERAGE(F8:F17)

Determining a Retail Price Based on Markup

	A	B	C	D	E	F	G
1	DETERMINING A MARKUP BASED ON PRICE						
2							
3				Cost	Markup	Selling	% Markup
4						Price	
5							
6		Manufacturer		$32.00	$5.47	$37.47	18.00%
7		Wholesaler		$34.87	$8.23	$43.10	24.00%
8		Retailer		$43.10	$12.35	$55.45	35.00%
9							
10			Total		$26.05		77.00%

What the Spreadsheet Does

In order to be profitable, you must determine the correct markup for your products. This spreadsheet calculates the price of a product for a given markup (expressed as a percent, e.g., 12 equals 12%).

Working with the Spreadsheet

To work with this spreadsheet, you need to enter the following information.

Row G percent of markup
Row D cost of item for manufacturer, wholesaler, and retailer
Row E markup ($)
B3 name of department

When the spreadsheet is complete, it will provide you with the following information.

Row F selling price

Excel Business Applications

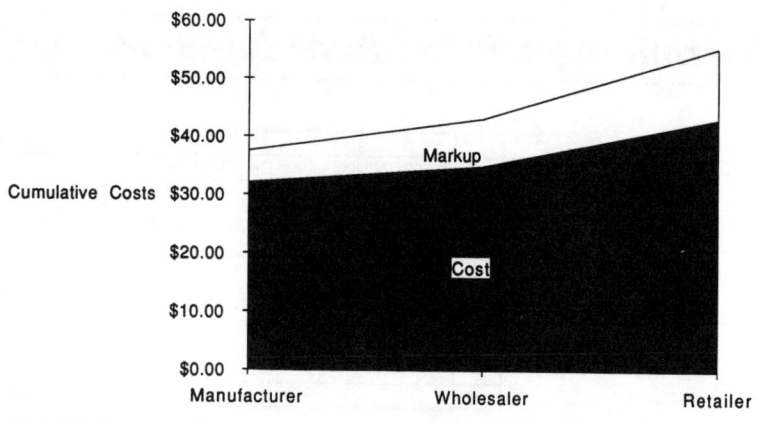

11.6 Markup to costs

What It Looks Like

Figure 11.6 is a chart showing the percentage of markup to costs.

The Cell Contents and Formulas

	A	B	C	D	E	F	G
1	DETERMINING A MARKUP BASED ON PRICE						
2							
3				Cost	Markup	Selling	% Markup
4						Price	
5							
6		Manufacturer		32	5.47	=D6+E6	0.18
7		Wholesaler		34.87	8.23	=D7+E7	0.24
8		Retailer		=D7+E7	12.35	=D8+E8	0.35
9							
10			Total		=SUM(E6:E8)		=SUM(G6:G8)

234

Retail Worksheets

Estimating Size of Salesforce

	A	B	C	D	E	F	G	H
1	STIMATING SIZE OF SALESFORCE							
2								
3	Existing Customer Base			1200		Growth Rate	10.00%	
4	Potential Customers			100		Growth Rate	10.00%	
5	Frequency of Calls/Month			2				
6	Length of Call/Month			0.5				
7	Available Selling Time/Month			30				
8	Estimated Number of P° ple			43				
9	----------	----------	----------	----------	----------	----------	----------	----------
10	Hypothetical Situation							
11								
12		Customer	Potential	Total	#			
13		Base	Customers	Customers	Salespeople			
14		----------	----------	----------	----------			
15		1200	100	1300	43			
16		1320	110	1430	48			
17		1452	121	1573	52			
18		1597	133	1730	58			
19		1757	146	1903	63			
20		1933	161	2094	70			
21		2126	177	2303	77			
22		2338	195	2533	84			
23		2572	214	2787	93			
24		2830	236	3065	102			
25		3112	259	3372	112			
26		3424	285	3709	124			
27		3766	314	4080	136			
28		4143	345	4488	150			
29		4557	380	4937	165			
30		5013	418	5430	181			

What the Spreadsheet Does

The number of salespeople needed by a business depends on a variety of factors. Using the traditional workload method, this spreadsheet estimates how many salespeople are necessary to cover an established or potential customer base.

Working with the Spreadsheet

To work with this spreadsheet, you need to enter the following information.

- D3 existing customer base
- D4 potential customer base
- D5 frequency of calls per month

Excel Business Applications

D6 length of calls per month
D7 selling time

When the spreadsheet is complete, it will provide you with the following information.

D8 estimated number of salespeople needed

What It Looks Like

Figure 11.7 is a combined lines-and-markers chart that shows the number of salespeople needed as the number of potential clients changes by a factor of 10%.

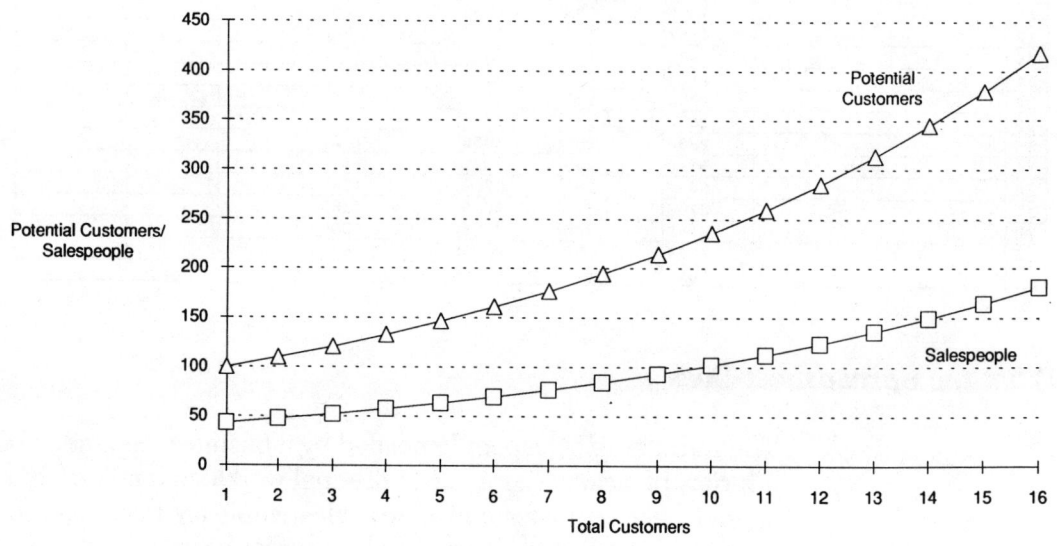

11.7 Salespeople estimate

The Cell Contents and Formulas

	A	B	C	D	E	F	G
1	ESTIMATING SIZE OF SALESFORCE						
2							
3	Existing Customer Base			1200		Growth Rate	0.1
4	Potential Customers			100		Growth Rate	0.1
5	Frequency of Calls/Month			2			
6	Length of Call/Month			0.5			
7	Available Selling Time/Month			30			
8	Estimated Number of People			=((D3+D4)*			
9							
10	Hypothetical Situation						
11							
12		Customer	Potential		Total	#	
13		Base	Customers		Customers	Salespeople	
14							
15		=D3	=D4		=C15+B15	=((B15+C15)*2*0.5)/30	
16		=B15*(1+$G$3)	=C15*(1+$G$4)		=C16+B16	=((B16+C16)*2*0.5)/30	
17		=B16*(1+$G$3)	=C16*(1+$G$4)		=C17+B17	=((B17+C17)*2*0.5)/30	
18		=B17*(1+$G$3)	=C17*(1+$G$4)		=C18+B18	=((B18+C18)*2*0.5)/30	
19		=B18*(1+$G$3)	=C18*(1+$G$4)		=C19+B19	=((B19+C19)*2*0.5)/30	
20		=B19*(1+$G$3)	=C19*(1+$G$4)		=C20+B20	=((B20+C20)*2*0.5)/30	
21		=B20*(1+$G$3)	=C20*(1+$G$4)		=C21+B21	=((B21+C21)*2*0.5)/30	
22		=B21*(1+$G$3)	=C21*(1+$G$4)		=C22+B22	=((B22+C22)*2*0.5)/30	
23		=B22*(1+$G$3)	=C22*(1+$G$4)		=C23+B23	=((B23+C23)*2*0.5)/30	
24		=B23*(1+$G$3)	=C23*(1+$G$4)		=C24+B24	=((B24+C24)*2*0.5)/30	
25		=B24*(1+$G$3)	=C24*(1+$G$4)		=C25+B25	=((B25+C25)*2*0.5)/30	
26		=B25*(1+$G$3)	=C25*(1+$G$4)		=C26+B26	=((B26+C26)*2*0.5)/30	
27		=B26*(1+$G$3)	=C26*(1+$G$4)		=C27+B27	=((B27+C27)*2*0.5)/30	
28		=B27*(1+$G$3)	=C27*(1+$G$4)		=C28+B28	=((B28+C28)*2*0.5)/30	
29		=B28*(1+$G$3)	=C28*(1+$G$4)		=C29+B29	=((B29+C29)*2*0.5)/30	
30		=B29*(1+$G$3)	=C29*(1+$G$4)		=C30+B30	=((B30+C30)*2*0.5)/30	

Excel Business Applications

Keeping Track of Auto Expenses

What the Spreadsheet Does

A primary business expense for many people is their car. This spreadsheet records your automotive expenses, including mileage and maintenance, and computes the per mile deduction according to 1988 IRS standards.

Working with the Spreadsheet

To work with this spreadsheet, you need to provide the following information.

D1	month
E3	total mileage form last month
E4	total mileage this month
F10,11,12	maintenance costs
I11	cost per mile business
I12	cost per mile medical
Col A	date
Col B	destination
Col D	category (1 = business/2 = medical)
Col E	beginning odometer setting
Col F	ending odometer setting
Col J	gas used
Col K	gas cost
Col L	parking cost

When the spreadsheet is complete, it will yield the following information.

E5	total mileage year to date
E7	total deductible mileage this month
E14	total maintenance costs
E8	total transportation costs per month
D16	average cost per mile
Col G	miles per trip
Col I	cumulative miles

238

	A	B	C	D	E	F	G	H	I	J	K	L	M	N
1	AUTO EXPENSE	Month of April, 1988				Car: Company #2								
2														
3		Total Mileage From Last Month			8902	Average Miles								
4		Total Mileage This Month			1250	Per Gallon		19.38						
5		Total Mileage Year to Date			10152									
6														
7		Total Deductible			$272.75									
8		Total Costs			$351.67									
9		Maintenance												
10			Oil Change and Lube		$12.00				Deductible Costs (IRS)					
11			Repair		$53.75				1. Business	$0.23				
12			Other		$4.67				2. Medical	$0.09				
13														
14			Total		$70.42									
15														
16		Average Costs per Mile		$0.28										
17														
18	Date	Destination		Category	Beginning Odometer	Ending Odometer	Total Miles	Cumulative Mileage		Gas (Gal)	Gas ($)	Parking	Deductible Business	Deductible Medical
19														
20														
21	4/1	Store A		1	8902	8953	51	51					$11.48	$0.00
22	4/4	Main Office		1	8953	9011	58	109					$13.05	$0.00
23	4/5	Store B		1	9020	9099	79	188				$4.50	$17.78	$0.00
24	4/5	Red Cross		2	9150	9213	63	251					$0.00	$5.67
25	4/6	Store C		1	9316	9327	11	262					$2.48	$0.00
26	4/8	Office		1	9351	9402	51	313					$11.48	$0.00
27	4/8	Meeting		1	9453	9476	23	336		21.5	$23.65		$5.18	$0.00
28	4/11	Store A		1	9476	9502	26	362					$5.85	$0.00
29	4/11	Store B		1	9502	9555	53	415					$11.93	$0.00
30	4/12	Store C		1	9601	9672	71	486				$4.75	$15.98	$0.00
31	4/12	Meeting		1	9781	9903	122	608		22	$24.20		$27.45	$0.00
32	4/14	Airport		1	10003	10015	12	620					$2.70	$0.00
33	4/14	Supply Center		1	10111	10213	102	722				$5.25	$22.95	$0.00
34	4/15	Meeting		1	10333	10387	54	776					$12.15	$0.00
35	4/19	Store A		1	10402	10453	51	827					$11.48	$0.00
36	4/21	Store A		1	10453	10504	51	878					$11.48	$0.00
37	4/21	Meeting		1	10554	10578	24	902					$5.40	$0.00
38	4/22	Airport		1	10622	10700	78	980		21	$23.10	$6.50	$17.55	$0.00
39	4/25	Office		1	10710	10781	71	1051					$15.98	$0.00
40	4/26	Store A		1	11067	11102	35	1086					$7.88	$0.00
41	4/27	Office		1	11111	11199	88	1174					$19.80	$0.00
42	4/28	Store A		1	12023	12099	76	1250					$17.10	$0.00
43														
44						Total Mileage	1250		TOTALS Gallons	64.50			$267.08	$5.67
45									Cost		$70.95	$21.00		
46														

Excel Business Applications

Col M	deductible business mileage
Col N	deductible medical mileage
G45	total miles
H4	average miles per gallon
J45	gallons of gas used
K46	cost of gas used
L46	cost of parking
M44	total deductible business costs
N48	total deductible medical costs

What It Looks Like

Figure 11.8 is a pie chart of actual versus deductible automobile expenses for the month.

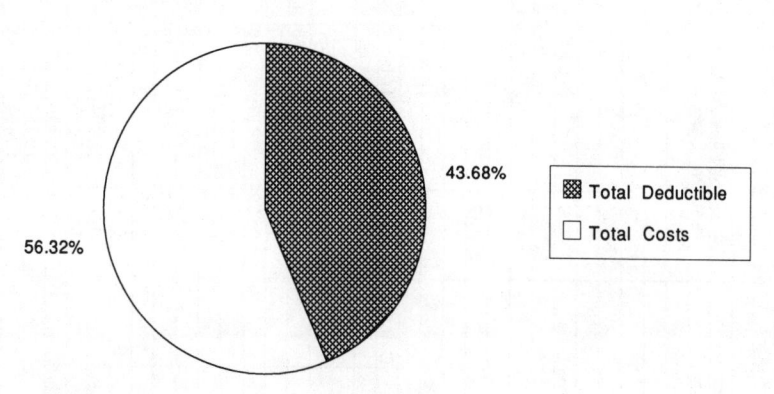

11.8 Actual versus deductible auto expenses

Retail Worksheets

The Cell Contents and Formulas

	A	B	C	D	E	F	G
1	AUTO EXPENSES		Month	April, 1988		Car: Company #2	
2							
3	Total Mileage From Last Month				8902	Average Miles	
4	Total Mileage This Month				=G45	Per Gallon	
5	Total Mileage Year to Date				=E3+E4		
6							
7	Total Deductible				=M44+N44		
8	Total Costs				=(G45*0.225+E14)		
9	Maintenance						
10		Oil Change and Lub			12		Deductible Costs (IRS)
11		Repair			53.75		1. Business
12		Other			4.67		2. Medical
13							
14		Total			=SUM(E10:E12)		
15							
16	Average Costs per Mile			=E8/G45			
17							
18	Date	Destination		Category	Beginning	Ending	Total
19					Odometer	Odometer	Miles
20							
21	4/1	Store A		1	8902	8953	=F21-E21
22	4/4	Main Office		1	8953	9011	=F22-E22
23	4/5	Store B		1	9020	9099	=F23-E23
24	4/5	Red Cross		2	9150	9213	=F24-E24
25	4/6	Store C		1	9316	9327	=F25-E25
26	4/8	Office		1	9351	9402	=F26-E26
27	4/8	Meeting		1	9453	9476	=F27-E27
28	4/11	Store A		1	9476	9502	=F28-E28
29	4/11	Store B		1	9502	9555	=F29-E29
30	4/12	Store C		1	9601	9672	=F30-E30
31	4/12	Meeting		1	9781	9903	=F31-E31
32	4/14	Airport		1	10003	10015	=F32-E32
33	4/14	Supply Center		1	10111	10213	=F33-E33
34	4/15	Meeting		1	10333	10387	=F34-E34
35	4/19	Store A		1	10402	10453	=F35-E35
36	4/21	Store A		1	10453	10504	=F36-E36
37	4/21	Meeting		1	10554	10578	=F37-E37
38	4/22	Airport		1	10622	10700	=F38-E38
39	4/25	Office		1	10710	10781	=F39-E39
40	4/26	Store A		1	11067	11102	=F40-E40
41	4/27	Office		1	11111	11199	=F41-E41
42	4/28	Store A		1	12023	12099	=F42-E42
43							
44						Total	
45						Mileage	=SUM(G21:G42)
46							

Excel Business Applications

The Cell Contents and Formulas (Continued)

	H	I	J	K	L	M	N
1							
2							
3							
4	=H42/J45						
5							
6							
7							
8							
9							
10							
11		0.225					
12		0.09					
13							
14							
15							
16							
17							
18	Cumulative		Gas	Gas		Deductible		Deductible
19	Mileage		(Gal)	($)	Parking	Business	Medical
20							
21	=G21					=IF(D21=1,G21*$I$11,0)	=IF(D21=2,H21*$I$12,0)
22	=H21+G22					=IF(D22=1,G22*$I$11,0)	=IF(D22=2,H22*$I$12,0)
23	=H22+G23				4.5	=IF(D23=1,G23*$I$11,0)	=IF(D23=2,H23*$I$12,0)
24	=H23+G24					=IF(D24=1,G24*$I$11,0)	=IF(D24=2,H24*$I$12,0)
25	=H24+G25					=IF(D25=1,G25*$I$11,0)	=IF(D25=2,H25*$I$12,0)
26	=H25+G26					=IF(D26=1,G26*$I$11,0)	=IF(D26=2,H26*$I$12,0)
27	=H26+G27		21.5	23.65		=IF(D27=1,G27*$I$11,0)	=IF(D27=2,H27*$I$12,0)
28	=H27+G28					=IF(D28=1,G28*$I$11,0)	=IF(D28=2,H28*$I$12,0)
29	=H28+G29				4.75	=IF(D29=1,G29*$I$11,0)	=IF(D29=2,H29*$I$12,0)
30	=H29+G30					=IF(D30=1,G30*$I$11,0)	=IF(D30=2,H30*$I$12,0)
31	=H30+G31		22	24.2		=IF(D31=1,G31*$I$11,0)	=IF(D31=2,H31*$I$12,0)
32	=H31+G32				5.25	=IF(D32=1,G32*$I$11,0)	=IF(D32=2,H32*$I$12,0)
33	=H32+G33					=IF(D33=1,G33*$I$11,0)	=IF(D33=2,H33*$I$12,0)
34	=H33+G34					=IF(D34=1,G34*$I$11,0)	=IF(D34=2,H34*$I$12,0)
35	=H34+G35					=IF(D35=1,G35*$I$11,0)	=IF(D35=2,H35*$I$12,0)
36	=H35+G36					=IF(D36=1,G36*$I$11,0)	=IF(D36=2,H36*$I$12,0)
37	=H36+G37					=IF(D37=1,G37*$I$11,0)	=IF(D37=2,H37*$I$12,0)
38	=H37+G38		21	23.1	6.5	=IF(D38=1,G38*$I$11,0)	=IF(D38=2,H38*$I$12,0)
39	=H38+G39					=IF(D39=1,G39*$I$11,0)	=IF(D39=2,H39*$I$12,0)
40	=H39+G40					=IF(D40=1,G40*$I$11,0)	=IF(D40=2,H40*$I$12,0)
41	=H40+G41					=IF(D41=1,G41*$I$11,0)	=IF(D41=2,H41*$I$12,0)
42	=H41+G42					=IF(D42=1,G42*$I$11,0)	=IF(D42=2,H42*$I$12,0)
43							
44			TOTALS			=SUM(M21:M42)	=SUM(N21:N42)
45			Gallons	=SUM(J21:J42)			
46			Cost		=SUM(K21:K42)	=SUM(L21:L42)		

Making Seasonal Adjustments

	A	B	C	D	E	F	G
1	COMPUTING A SEASONAL INDEX						
2							
3							
4							
5			Sales/Year			Average	Seasonal
6						Sales	Index
7		1983	1984	1985	1986		
8							
9	Quarter						
10							
11	1	$30,100	$37,500	$41,200	$38,000	$36,700	0.97
12	2	$38,000	$29,000	$41,000	$32,000	$35,000	0.93
13	3	$26,000	$31,000	$49,800	$53,200	$40,000	1.06
14	4	$34,500	$34,700	$41,000	$48,000	$39,550	1.05
15							
16	Average	$32,150	$33,050	$43,250	$42,800	$37,813	
17							
18							
19							
20	Corrected Sales Data						
21							
22			Sales/Year				
23							
24		1983	1984	1985	1986		
25							
26	Quarter						
27							
28	1	$31,012	$38,637	$42,449	$39,152		
29	2	$41,054	$40,513	$44,511	$41,054		
30	3	$24,578	$29,305	$47,077	$50,291		
31	4	$32,984	$33,176	$39,199	$45,891		
32							
33	Average	$38,805	$40,938	$43,703	$44,097		

What the Spreadsheet Does

Since product sales are often heavily influenced by seasonal effects, you need more than just straight sales figures to properly understand your sales situation.

This spreadsheet provides you with a seasonal index—a measure of the effect of seasonality on sales. For example, a seasonal index of .83 means that 17% of the decrease of sales during the first quarter may be attributable to seasonal factors. Perhaps the most valuable part of the spreadsheet is the matrix that provides sales for seasonal factors.

Excel Business Applications

Working with the Spreadsheet

To work with this spreadsheet, you need to enter the following information.

Col B sales for year 1 by quarter
Col C sales for year 2 by quarter
Col D sales for year 3 by quarter
Col E sales for year 4 by quarter

When the spreadsheet is complete, it will provide you with the following information.

B28...E31 seasonally adjusted sales figures
Col F quarterly average sales
Col G seasonal index
F16 average quarterly sales across four years
Row 16 average unadjusted sales by year
Row 33 average adjusted sales by year

What It Looks Like

Figure 11.9 shows a line chart illustrating both unadjusted and adjusted sales trends.

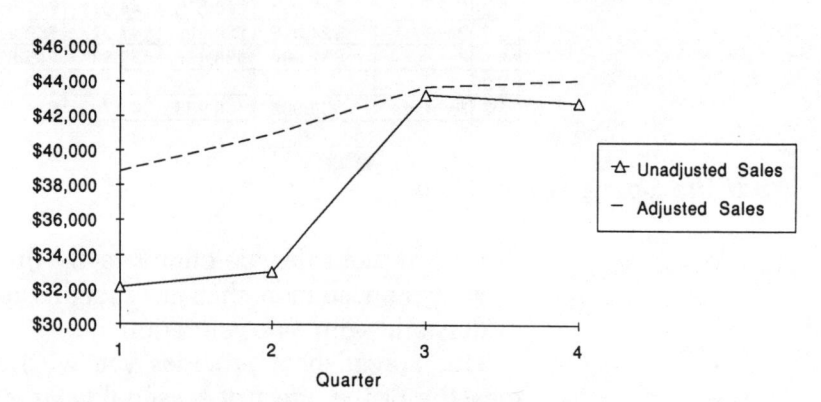

11.9 Adjusted and unadjusted sales trends

The Cell Contents and Formulas

	A	B	C	D	E	F	G
1	COMPUTING A SEASONAL INDEX						
2							
3							
4							
5			Sales/Year			Average	Seasonal
6						Sales	Index
7			1984	1985	1986		
8							
9	Quarter						
10							
11	1	30100	37500	41200	38000	=AVERAGE(B11:E11)	=F11/$F$16
12	2	38000	29000	41000	32000	=AVERAGE(B12:E12)	=F12/$F$16
13	3	26000	31000	49800	53200	40000	=F13/$F$16
14	4	34500	34700	41000	48000	=AVERAGE(B14:E14)	=F14/$F$16
15							
16	Average	=AVERAGE(B11:B14)	=AVERAGE(C11:C14)	=AVERAGE(D11:D14)	=AVERAGE(E11:E14)	=AVERAGE(F11:F14)	
17							
18							
19							
20	Corrected Sales Data						
21							
22							
23			Sales/Year				
24		1983	1984	1985	1986		
25							
26	Quarter						
27							
28	1	=B11/$G$11	=C11/$G$11	=D11/$G$11	=E11/$G$11		
29	2	=B12/$G$12	=C11/$G$12	=D11/$G$12	=E11/$G$12		
30	3	=B13/$G$13	=C13/$G$13	=D13/$G$13	=E13/$G$13		
31	4	=B14/$G$14	=C14/$G$14	=D14/$G$14	=E14/$G$14		
32							
33	Average	=AVERAGE(B28:E31)	=AVERAGE(C28:F31)	=AVERAGE(D28:G31)	=AVERAGE(E28:H31)		

Excel Business Applications

Markup Ratios

	A	B	C	D
1	MARKUP RATIOS			
2				
3	Product: Instalarm			
4				
5	Cost	$32.50	Markdowns	$600
6	Markup	$8.50	Customer Allowances	$200
7	Selling Price	$41.00	Total Sales	$20,000
8			Average Inventory	$2,000
9			Total Costs of Goods	$13,000
10				
11	Ratios			
12				
13	Markup On Selling Price	20.73%		
15	Markup On Cost	26.15%		
17	Markdown	4.00%		
18	Inventory Turnover	7		

What the Spreadsheet Does

In addition to computing markup percentages and the value of a markup (another term for gross margin), retailers use ratios to make sense out of their markup strategies. Here's a spreadsheet that takes information about a specific product and computes a variety of these ratios, including the all-important return on investment.

Working with the Spreadsheet

To work with this spreadsheet, you need to enter the following information.

- **B5** cost of item
- **B6** markup
- **B7** selling price
- **D5** markdowns (reduction in price needed to make up for slow sales)

D6 costs allowances (customer credits, etc., for the product)
D7 total sales
D8 average inventory at cost
D9 total cost of goods

When the spreadsheet is complete, it will provide you with the following information.

B13 markup on selling price (%)
B15 markup on cost (%)
B17 markdown (%)
B18 inventory turnover (per year)

What It Looks Like

The pie chart in Figure 11.10 compares the cost of the product with its markup.

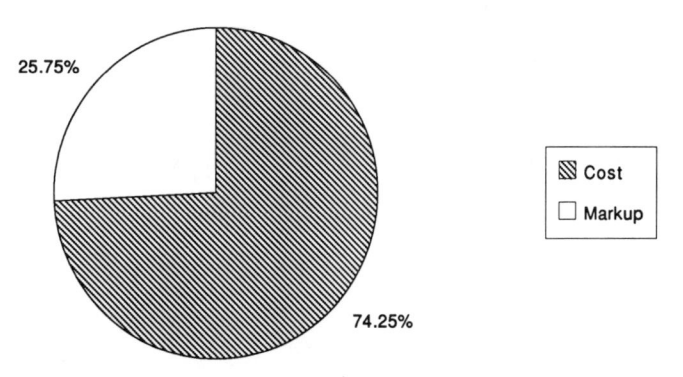

25.75%

74.25%

Cost
Markup

11.10 Product costs and markup

Excel Business Applications

The Cell Contents and Formulas

	A	B	C	D
1	MARKUP RATIOS			
2				
3	Product: Instalarm			
4				
5	Cost	32.5	Markdowns	600
6	Markup	8.5	Customer Allowances	200
7	Selling Price	=B5+B6	Total Sales	20000
8			Average Inventory	2000
9			Total Costs of Goods	13000
10				
11	Ratios			
12				
13	Markup On Selling	=(B6/B7)		
14	Price			
15	Markup On	=(B7-B5)/B5		
16	Cost			
17	Markdown	=(D5+D6)/D7		
18	Inventory	=ROUND(D9/D8,0)		
19	Turnover			

Retail Worksheets

Merchandise Budgeting

	A	B	C	D	E	F	G	H
1	MERCHANDISE BUDGETING							
2								
3			Jan	Feb	March	Summary		
4						Total	Average	
5	Sales							
6		Last Year	$43,567	$51,456	$49,878	$144,901	$48,300	
7		Planned	$41,678	$43,762	$45,950	$131,390	$43,797	
8		Actual	$42,567	$44,564	$47,654	$134,785	$44,928	
9		Difference	$889	$802	$1,704	$3,395	$1,132	
10								
11	Retail Stock							
12		Last Year	$197,456	$185,678	$198,789	$581,923	$193,974	
13		Planned	$156,345	$164,162	$172,370	$492,878	$164,293	
14		Actual	$165,456	$165,453	$176,564	$507,473	$169,158	
15		Difference	$9,111	$1,291	$4,194	$14,595	$4,865	
16								
17	Purchases							
18		Last Year	$35,678	$35,241	$36,567	$107,486	$35,829	
19		Planned	$36,457	$32,154	$34,543	$103,154	$34,385	
20		Actual	$35,467	$32,143	$36,546	$104,156	$34,719	
21		Difference	$990	$11	($2,003)	($1,002)	($334)	
22								
23	Reductions (%)							
24		Last Year	12.00%	11.00%	10.00%			
25		Planned	8.00%	8.00%	8.00%			
26		Actual	8.20%	5.68%	7.80%			
27		Difference	0.20%	-2.32%	-0.20%			
28								
29	Markups (%)							
30		Last Year	53.00%	51.00%	54.00%			
31		Planned	45.00%	42.00%	43.00%			
32		Actual	42.00%	43.70%	49.80%			
33		Difference	-3.00%	1.70%	6.80%			

What the Spreadsheet Does

Businesses need to keep track of the difference between planned and actual expenses.

This spreadsheet provides a three-month budgeting plan based on last year's sales, this month's plan, and actual disbursements. It also computes reductions and markups as a percent.

Excel Business Applications

Working with the Spreadsheet

To work with this spreadsheet, you need to enter the following information.

C6...G6	sales/month
C12...G15	retail stock on hand/month
C18...G21	purchases/month
C24...G27	reductions (%)
C30...E33	markups (%)

When the spreadsheet is complete, it will provide you with the following information.

Col F	total of all values across quarter
Col G	average of all values across quarter
Rows 9,15,21	differences between planned and actual values
Rows 27,33	differences in reduction (%) and markup (%)

The Cell Contents and Formulas

	A	B	C	D	E	F	G
1	MERCHANDISE BUDGET						
2							
3							
4			Jan	Feb	March	Summary	
5	Sales					Total	Average
6		Last Year	43567	51456	49878	=SUM(C6:E6)	=AVERAGE(C6:E6)
7		Planned	41678	=C7*1.05	=D7*1.05	=SUM(C7:E7)	=AVERAGE(C7:E7)
8		Actual	42567	44564	47654	=SUM(C8:E8)	=AVERAGE(C8:E8)
9		Difference	=C8-C7	=D8-D7	=E8-E7	=SUM(C9:E9)	=AVERAGE(C9:E9)
10							
11	Retail Stock						
12		Last Year	197456	185678	198789	=SUM(C12:E12)	=AVERAGE(C12:E12)
13		Planned	156345	=C13*1.05	=D13*1.05	=SUM(C13:E13)	=AVERAGE(C13:E13)
14		Actual	165456	165453	176564	=SUM(C14:E14)	=AVERAGE(C14:E14)
15		Difference	=C14-C13	=D14-D13	=E14-E13	=SUM(C15:E15)	=AVERAGE(C15:E15)
16							
17	Purchases						
18		Last Year	35678	35241	36567	=SUM(C18:E18)	=AVERAGE(C18:E18)
19		Planned	36457	32154	34543	=SUM(C19:E19)	=AVERAGE(C19:E19)
20		Actual	35467	32143	36546	=SUM(C20:E20)	=AVERAGE(C20:E20)
21		Difference	=C19-C20	=D19-D20	=E19-E20	=SUM(C21:E21)	=AVERAGE(C21:E21)
22							
23	Reductions (%)						
24		Last Year	0.12	0.11	0.1		
25		Planned	0.08	0.08	0.08		
26		Actual	0.082	0.0568	0.078		
27		Difference	=C26-C25	=D26-D25	=E26-E25		
28							
29	Markups (%)						
30		Last Year	0.53	0.51	0.54		
31		Planned	0.45	0.42	0.43		
32		Actual	0.42	0.437	0.498		
33		Difference	=C32-C31	=D32-D31	=E32-E31		

Excel Business Applications

Multiple Regression

What the Spreadsheet Does

You can use linear regression to predict one variable based on the performance of another. Multiple regression is a similar technique that uses two or more predictor variables.

This spreadsheet computes the various regression coefficients (one for each independent variable) as well as the regression constant. It then produces the appropriate regression equation for predicting Y from X1 and X2. For example, this regression equation predicts sales from customer base and years of employment. Several of the columns (such as columns E and F) are used for computation purposes only. As you can see, the best individual predictor of sales is customer base, which has a correlation of .87. The spreadsheet also contains the application of the prediction equation used in Figure 11.11.

Working with the Spreadsheet

To work with this spreadsheet, you need to enter the following information. Note that this data has previously been collected and will be used to predict future performance given a knowledge of X1 (customer base) and X2 (years employed).

- **Col A**   employee identification
- **Col B**   sales
- **Col C**   customer base
- **Col D**   years employed

When the spreadsheet is complete, it will provide you with the following information.

- **C26**   samples size
- **C28**   correlation of X1 and Y
- **C29**   correlation of X2 and Y
- **C30**   correlation of X1 and X2
- **C35**   first regression coefficient

MULTIPLE REGRESSION

Employee	Sales (000) Y	Cust Base X1	Years Emp X2	Cross Product X1*Y	Cross Product X2*Y	Cross Product X1*X2	Sales Squared Y	Time Squared X1	Years Squared X2	Pred Y
N	11.20	30	5	336	56	150	125	900	25	4.96
E	12.10	28	10	339	121	280	146	784	100	4.97
A	12.70	31	7	394	89	217	161	961	49	6.98
G	12.70	27	4	343	51	108	161	729	16	1.15
B	13.70	28	15	384	206	420	188	784	225	7.22
C	15.60	35	13	546	203	455	243	1225	169	14.16
O	17.20	49	11	843	189	539	296	2401	121	28.94
L	18.00	43	10	774	180	430	324	1849	100	21.77
J	19.70	42	11	827	217	462	388	1764	121	21.10
I	22.80	39	14	889	319	546	520	1521	196	19.09
H	23.00	50	10	1150	230	500	529	2500	100	29.61
F	23.10	45	15	1040	347	675	534	2025	225	26.26
M	25.00	51	15	1275	375	765	625	2601	225	32.98
D	26.00	49	13	1274	338	637	676	2401	169	29.84
K	27.20	48	14	1306	381	672	740	2304	196	29.17

N	15									
Average	18.67	39.67	11.13	781.23						
Sum	280	595	167	11719	3300	6856	5657	24749	2037	
St Dev	5.54	9.05	3.56	371.45	111.91	197.23	211.01	705.01	71.60	

Pearson r (X1*Y) = 0.87
Pearson r (X2*Y) = 0.66
Pearson r (X1*X2) = 0.51

Regression Coefficients

B1 = 1.12
B2 = 0.45

Constant

a1 = -30.89

Multiple Regression Equation

Predicted Y' = X1+X2+a

Y= 1.12 X1+ 0.45 X2+ -30.89

Excel Business Applications

C36	second regression coefficient
C41	regression constant
Col E	cross products of X1 and Y
Col F	cross products of X2 and Y
Col G	cross products of X1 and X2
Col H	Y squared
Col I	X1 squared
Col J	X2 squared
Col K	predicted Y scores
Row 24	average scores
Row 25	sum of scores
Row 26	standard deviations of scores
Row 47	final regression equation

What It Looks Like

The line chart in Figure 11.11, which plots actual and predicted sales, provides a visual indication of the accuracy of the regression equation for each employee. To produce a line with a clearly positive or negative slope, the records were sorted on the sales (X1) variable.

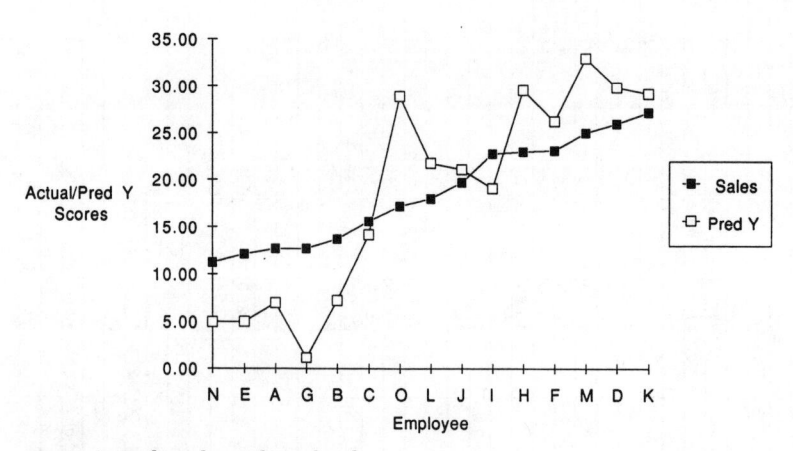

11.11 Actual and predicted sales

The Cell Contents and Formulas

	A	B	C
1	MULTIPLE REGRESSION		
2			
3	Employee	Sales	Cust
4		(000)	Base
5		Y	X1
6			
7	N	11.2	30
8	E	12.1	28
9	A	12.7	31
10	G	12.7	27
11	B	13.7	28
12	C	15.6	35
13	O	17.2	49
14	L	18	43
15	J	19.7	42
16	I	22.8	39
17	H	23	50
18	F	23.1	45
19	M	25	51
20	D	26	49
21	K	27.2	48
22			
23	N	=COUNT(B7:B21)	
24	Average	=AVERAGE(B7:B21)	=AVERAGE(C7:C21)
25	Sum	=SUM(B7:B21)	=SUM(C7:C21)
26	St Dev	=STDEV(B7:B21)	=STDEV(C7:C21)
27			
28	Pearson r (X1*Y) =		=((B23*E25)-(B25*C25))/SQRT(((B23*H25)-(B25^2))*((B23*I25)-(C25^2)))
29	Pearson r (X2*Y) =		=((B23*F25)-(B25*D25))/SQRT(((B23*H25)-(B25^2))*((B23*J25)-(D25^2)))
30	Pearson r (X1*X2) =		=((B23*G25)-(C25*D25))/SQRT(((B23*I25)-(C25^2))*((B23*J25)-(D25^2)))
31			
32			
33	Regression Coefficients		
34			
35	B1 =		=(B26*(C28-C29*C30))/(D26*(1-(C30^2)))
36	B2 =		=(B26*(C29-C28*C30))/(D26*(1-(C30^2)))
37			
38			
39	Constant		
40			
41	a1 =		=B24-(C36*D24)-(C35*C24)
42			
43	Multiple Regression Equation		
44			
45	Predicted Y' = X1+X2+a		
46			
47	Y'=		=C35

The Cell Contents and Formulas (Continued)

	D	E	F	G	H	I	J	K
1								
2								
3	Years	Cross	Cross	Cross	Sales	Time	Years	Pred Y
4	Emp	Product	Product	Product	Squared	Squared	Squared	
5	X2	X1*Y	X2*Y	X1*X2	Y	X1	X2	
6								
7	5	=C7*B7	=B7*D7	=C7*D7	=B7^2	=C7^2	=D7^2	=(C7*1.12)+(D7*0.45)-30.89
8	10	=C8*B8	=B8*D8	=C8*D8	=B8^2	=C8^2	=D8^2	=(C8*1.12)+(D8*0.45)-30.89
9	7	=C9*B9	=B9*D9	=C9*D9	=B9^2	=C9^2	=D9^2	=(C9*1.12)+(D9*0.45)-30.89
10	4	=C10*B10	=B10*D10	=C10*D10	=B10^2	=C10^2	=D10^2	=(C10*1.12)+(D10*0.45)-30.89
11	15	=C11*B11	=B11*D11	=C11*D11	=B11^2	=C11^2	=D11^2	=(C11*1.12)+(D11*0.45)-30.89
12	13	=C12*B12	=B12*D12	=C12*D12	=B12^2	=C12^2	=D12^2	=(C12*1.12)+(D12*0.45)-30.89
13	11	=C13*B13	=B13*D13	=C13*D13	=B13^2	=C13^2	=D13^2	=(C13*1.12)+(D13*0.45)-30.89
14	10	=C14*B14	=B14*D14	=C14*D14	=B14^2	=C14^2	=D14^2	=(C14*1.12)+(D14*0.45)-30.89
15	11	=C15*B15	=B15*D15	=C15*D15	=B15^2	=C15^2	=D15^2	=(C15*1.12)+(D15*0.45)-30.89
16	14	=C16*B16	=B16*D16	=C16*D16	=B16^2	=C16^2	=D16^2	=(C16*1.12)+(D16*0.45)-30.89
17	10	=C17*B17	=B17*D17	=C17*D17	=B17^2	=C17^2	=D17^2	=(C17*1.12)+(D17*0.45)-30.89
18	15	=C18*B18	=B18*D18	=C18*D18	=B18^2	=C18^2	=D18^2	=(C18*1.12)+(D18*0.45)-30.89
19	15	=C19*B19	=B19*D19	=C19*D19	=B19^2	=C19^2	=D19^2	=(C19*1.12)+(D19*0.45)-30.89
20	13	=C20*B20	=B20*D20	=C20*D20	=B20^2	=C20^2	=D20^2	=(C20*1.12)+(D20*0.45)-30.89
21	14	=C21*B21	=B21*D21	=C21*D21	=B21^2	=C21^2	=D21^2	=(C21*1.12)+(D21*0.45)-30.89
22								
23	=AVERAGE(D7:D21)	=AVERAGE(E7:E21)						
24								
25	=SUM(D7:D21)	=SUME7:E21)	=SUM(F7:F21)	=SUM(G7:G21)	=SUM(H7:H21)	=SUM(I7:I21)	=SUM(J7:J21)	
26	=STDEV(D7:D21)	=STDEV(E7:E21)	=STDEV(F7:F21)	=STDEV(G7:G21)	=STDEV(H7:H21)	=STDEV(I7:I21)	=STDEV(J7:J21)	
27								
28								
29								
30								
31								
32								
33								
34								
35								
36								
37								
38								
39								
40								
41								
42								
43								
44								
45								
46								
47	X1+	=C36	X2+	=C41				

Retail Worksheets

Overhead to Sales Ratio

	A	B	C	D	E	F	G	H	I
1	OVERHEAD TO SALES RATIOS								
2									
3				Jan	Feb	March	April	May	June
4									
5	Overhead								
6		Rent		$800	$800	$800	$800	$800	$800
7		Utilities		$375	$345	$387	$345	$365	$367
8		Salaries		$7,809	$7,809	$7,809	$7,809	$7,809	$7,809
9		Insurance		$265	$265	$265	$265	$265	$265
10		Debt		$1,278	$1,278	$1,278	$1,278	$1,278	$1,278
11		Other		$0	$0	$0	$0	$0	$0
12									
13	Total Overhead			$10,527	$10,497	$10,539	$10,497	$10,517	$10,519
14									
15	Product Sales								
16									
17		Dept #1 Sales ($)		$8,234	$7,546	$7,564	$8,312	$6,587	$6,477
18		% Overhead		78.22%	71.89%	71.77%	79.18%	62.63%	61.57%
19									
20		Dept #2 Sales ($)		$923.00	$768.00	$746.00	$879.00	$678.00	$988.00
21		% Overhead		8.77%	7.32%	7.08%	8.37%	6.45%	9.39%
22									
23		Dept #3 Sales ($)		$3,143.00	$3,412.00	$3,241.00	$3,786.00	$4,176.00	$3,912.00
24		% Overhead		29.86%	32.50%	30.75%	36.07%	39.71%	37.19%
25									
26	Total Sales			$12,300.00	$11,726.00	$11,551.00	$12,977.00	$11,441.00	$11,377.00
27	Overhead as a Percent of Sales			116.84%	111.71%	109.60%	123.63%	108.79%	108.16%

	J	K	L	M	N	O	P	Q
1								
2								
3	July	Aug	Sept	Oct	Nov	Dec	Total	
4								
5								
6	$800	$800	$800	$800	$800	$800	$9,600	
7	$356	$389	$356	$377	$365	$377	$4,404	
8	$7,809	$7,809	$7,809	$7,809	$7,809	$7,809	$93,708	
9	$265	$265	$265	$265	$265	$265	$3,180	
10	$1,278	$1,278	$1,278	$1,278	$1,278	$1,278	$15,336	
11	$0	$0	$0	$0	$0	$0	$0	
12								
13	$10,508	$10,541	$10,508	$10,529	$10,517	$10,529	$126,228	
14								
15							Sales	Overhead
16								
17	$7,456	$8,677	$7,891	$5,767	$8,787	$8,871	$92,169	
18	70.96%	82.32%	75.10%	54.77%	83.55%	84.25%		73.02%
19								
20	$768.00	$872.00	$836.00	$1,935.00	$859.00	$867.00	$11,119.00	
21	7.31%	8.27%	7.96%	18.38%	8.17%	8.23%		8.81%
22								
23	$4,111.00	$4,231.00	$2,199.00	$2,980.00	$3,165.00	$4,111.00	$42,467.00	
24	39.12%	40.14%	20.93%	28.30%	30.09%	39.04%		33.64%
25								
26	$12,335.00	$13,780.00	$10,926.00	$10,682.00	$12,811.00	$13,849.00	$145,755.00	
27	117.39%	130.73%	103.98%	101.45%	121.81%	131.53%		115.47%

Excel Business Applications

What the Spreadsheet Does

One indicator of the efficiency of a retail operation is its ratio of overhead to cost.

This spreadsheet measures the amount and percentages of overhead accounted for by different departments. Probably the best indicator of a department's success is the percent of overhead that it accounts for.

Working with the Spreadsheet

To work with this spreadsheet, you need to enter the following information.

D6...O10	overhead by category by month
Row 17	department #1 sales by month
Row 20	department #2 sales by month
Row 23	department #3 sales by month

When the spreadsheet is complete, it will provide you with the following information.

Col P	total sales plus overhead
Col Q	average overhead
Row 13	total overhead by month
Row 26	total sales by month
Row 27	overhead as a percent of sales
Rows 18,21,24	department sales as a percent of overhead

Retail Worksheets

What It Looks Like

Figure 11.12 shows an area chart that illustrates the percent of overhead accounted for by each department. You can see how the total by month for all three items is shown as well by Y axis value corresponding to the top of the area chart.

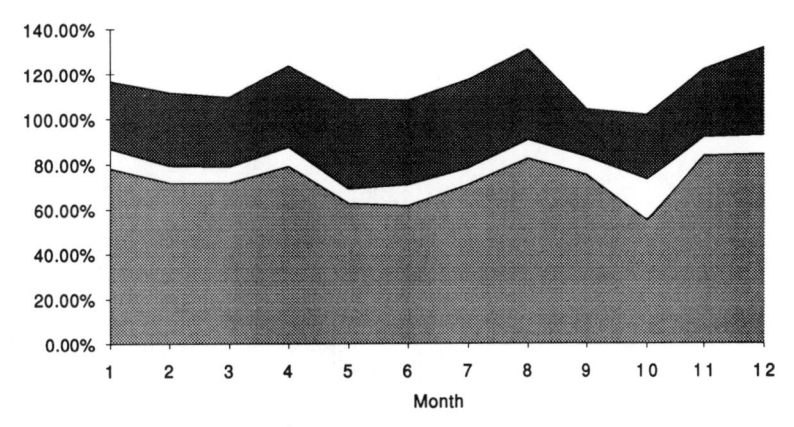

11.12 Percent of overhead by department

The Cell Contents and Formulas

	A	B	C	D	E	F
1	OVERHEAD TO SALES RATIOS					
2						
3				Jan	Feb	March
4						
5	Overhead					
6		Rent		800	800	800
7		Utilities		375	345	387
8		Salaries		7809	7809	7809
9		Insurance		265	265	265
10		Debt		1278	1278	1278
11		Other		0	0	0
12						
13	Total Overhead			=SUM(D6:D10)	=SUM(E6:E10)	=SUM(F6:F10)
14						
15	Product Sales					
16						
17		Dept #1 Sales ($)		8234	7546	7564
18		% Overhead		=D17/D13	=E17/E13	=F17/F13
19						
20		Dept #2 Sales ($)		923	768	746
21		% Overhead		=D20/D13	=E20/E13	=F20/F13
22						
23		Dept #3 Sales ($)		3143	3412	3241
24		% Overhead		=D23/D13	=E23/E13	=F23/F13
25						
26	Total Sales			=D17+D20+D23	=E17+E20+E23	=F17+F20+F23
27	Overhead as a Percent of Sales			=D26/D13	=E26/E13	=F26/F13

	G	H	I	J	K	L
1						
2						
3	April	May	June	July	Aug	Sept
4						
5						
6	800	800	800	800	800	800
7	345	365	367	356	389	356
8	7809	7809	7809	7809	7809	7809
9	265	265	265	265	265	265
10	1278	1278	1278	1278	1278	1278
11	0	0	0	0	0	0
12						
13	=SUM(G6:G10)	=SUM(H6:H10)	=SUM(I6:I10)	=SUM(J6:J10)	=SUM(K6:K10)	=SUM(L6:L10)
14						
15						
16						
17	8312	6587	6477	7456	8677	7891
18	=G17/G13	=H17/H13	=I17/I13	=J17/J13	=K17/K13	=L17/L13
19						
20	879	678	988	768	872	836
21	=G20/G13	=H20/H13	=I20/I13	=J20/J13	=K20/K13	=L20/L13
22						
23	3786	4176	3912	4111	4231	2199
24	=G23/G13	=H23/H13	=I23/I13	=J23/J13	=K23/K13	=L23/L13
25						
26	=G17+G20+G23	=H17+H20+H23	=I17+I20+I23	=J17+J20+J23	=K17+K20+K23	=L17+L20+L23
27	=G26/G13	=H26/H13	=I26/I13	=J26/J13	=K26/K13	=L26/L13

The Cell Contents and Formulas (Continued)

	M	N	O	P	Q
1					
2					
3	Oct	Nov	Dec	Total	
4					
5					
6	800	800	800	=SUM(D6:O6)	
7	377	365	377	=SUM(D7:O7)	
8	7809	7809	7809	=SUM(D8:O8)	
9	265	265	265	=SUM(D9:O9)	
10	1278	1278	1278	=SUM(D10:O10)	
11	0	0	0	0	
12					
13	=SUM(M6:M10)	=SUM(N6:N10)	=SUM(O6:O10)	=SUM(D13:O13)	
14					
15				Sales	Overhead
16					
17	5767	8787	8871	=SUM(D17:O17)	
18	=M17/M13	=N17/N13	=O17/O13		=AVERAGE(D18:O
19					
20	1935	859	867	=SUM(D20:O20)	
21	=M20/M13	=N20/N13	=O20/O13		=AVERAGE(D21:O
22					
23	2980	3165	4111	=SUM(D23:O23)	
24	=M23/M13	=N23/N13	=O23/O13		=AVERAGE(D24:O
25					
26	=M17+M20+M23	=N17+N20+N23	=O17+O20+O23	=SUM(D26:O26)	
27	=M26/M13	=N26/N13	=O26/O13		=AVERAGE(D27:O

Salary and Bonus Summary

	A	C	D	E	F	G	H
1	SALARY AND BONUS						
2							
3	Employee	Years/Service		Salary	Bonus	Total Comp	Bonus as %
4	G.E.	12		$34,123	$2,000	$36,123	5.86%
5	L.T.	5		$23,456	$1,000	$24,456	4.26%
6	R.T.	3		$21,876	$1,200	$23,076	5.49%
7	W.E.	15		$36,546	$1,500	$38,046	4.10%
8	I.T.	7		$26,543	$1,000	$27,543	3.77%
9	Y.R.	3		$22,345	$1,000	$23,345	4.48%
10	W.E.	9		$31,234	$2,300	$33,534	7.36%
11	Y.Y.	11		$33,211	$2,200	$35,411	6.62%
12	Q.I.	1		$21,000	$1,500	$22,500	7.14%
13	A.B.	8		$28,765	$1,600	$30,365	5.56%
14							
15	Average	7.4		$27,910	$1,530	$29,440	5.47%
16							
17	Years of Service		Total Bonus				
18							
19	1 year		0.07				
20	2-5 years		0.14				
21	6-10 years		0.17				
22	11-15 years		0.17				
23							
24	Average Bonus		$1,530				
25							
26	Criteria Table						
27							
28	Years/Service	Years/Service		Years/Service	Years/Service		
29	1	2		6	11		
30		3		7	12		
31		4		8	13		
32		5		9	14		
33				10	15		

What the Spreadsheet Does

This spreadsheet computes individual employees' bonus and salary statistics, taking into account their length of service. It provides such indicators as average per person and bonus as percent of total income and is useful in determining whether bonuses are in line with the past performance of other employees with a similar number of years of service.

Excel Business Applications

Working with the Spreadsheet

To work with this spreadsheet, you need to enter the following information.

Col A	identifying information
Col C	years in service
Col E	current income
Col F	current bonus
A28...F33	criteria table (used with the **=DSUM** and **=DAVG** functions)

When the spreadsheet is complete, it will provide you with the following information.

A19...D22	average bonus by years served
Col G	total compensation
Col H	bonus as a percent of total income
Row 17	average years in service, salary, bonus, total compensation, and percent of bonus

What It Looks Like

Figure 11.13 is an exploded pie chart that compares the total bonus paid out as a function of years in service to the average bonus. One can use it to look for discrepancies given the assumption that the longer the years in service, the higher the average bonus should be.

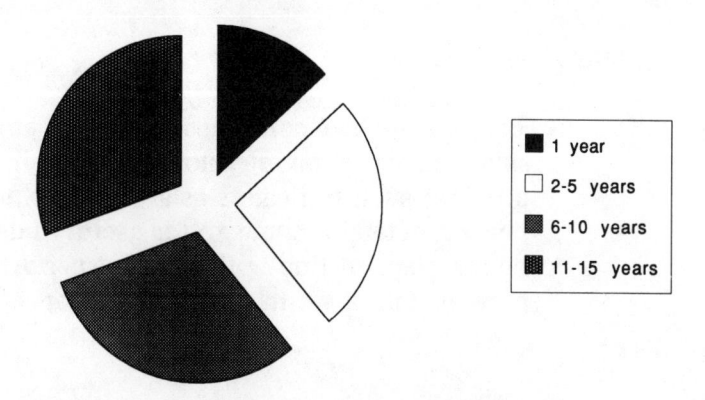

11.13 Total bonus as a function of service

The Cell Contents and Formulas

	A	C	D
1	SALARY AND BONUS		
2			
3	Employee	Years/Service	
4	G.E.	12	
5	L.T	5	
6	R.T.	3	
7	W.E.	15	
8	I.T.	7	
9	Y.R.	3	
10	W.E.	9	
11	Y.Y.	11	
12	Q.I.	1	
13	A.B.	8	
14			
15	Average	=AVERAGE(C4:C13)	
16			
17	Years of Service		Total Bonus
18			
19	1 year		=DSUM(A3:H13,8,A28:A29)
20	2-5 years		=DSUM(A3:H13,8,C28:C32)
21	6-10 years		=DSUM(A3:H13,8,E28:E33)
22	11-15 years		=DSUM(A3:H13,8,F28:F33)
23			
24	Average Bonus		=(F15)
25			
26	Criteria Table		
27			
28	Years/Service	Years/Service	
29	1	2	
30		3	
31		4	
32		5	
33			

Excel Business Applications

The Cell Contents and Formulas (Continued)

	E	F	G	H
1				
2				
3	Salary	Bonus	Total Comp	Bonus as %
4	34123	2000	=E4+F4	=F4/E4
5	23456	1000	=E5+F5	=F5/E5
6	21876	1200	=E6+F6	=F6/E6
7	36546	1500	=E7+F7	=F7/E7
8	26543	1000	=E8+F8	=F8/E8
9	22345	1000	=E9+F9	=F9/E9
10	31234	2300	=E10+F10	=F10/E10
11	33211	2200	=E11+F11	=F11/E11
12	21000	1500	=E12+F12	=F12/E12
13	28765	1600	=E13+F13	=F13/E13
14				
15	=AVERAGE(E4:E13)	=AVERAGE(F4:F13)	=AVERAGE(G4:G13)	=AVERAGE(H4:H13)
16				
17				
18				
19				
20				
21				
22				
23				
24				
25				
26				
27				
28	Years/Service	Years/Service		
29	6	11		
30	7	12		
31	8	13		
32	9	14		
33	10	15		

Salary Versus Commission Comparison

	A	B	C	D	E
1	BREAKEVEN ANALYSIS OF SALARY VERSUS COMMISSION				
2					
3	Commission		7%		
4	Annual Salary		$25,000		
5					
6	Employee	Salary	Annual	Commission	Total
7			Sales		Costs
8					
9	A	$25,000	$100,000	$7,000	$32,000
10	B	$25,000	$200,000	$14,000	$39,000
11	C	$25,000	$300,000	$21,000	$46,000
12	D	$25,000	$400,000	$28,000	$53,000
13	E	$25,000	$500,000	$35,000	$60,000
14	F	$25,000	$600,000	$42,000	$67,000
15	G	$25,000	$700,000	$49,000	$74,000
16	H	$25,000	$800,000	$56,000	$81,000
17	I	$25,000	$900,000	$63,000	$88,000
18	J	$25,000	$1,000,000	$70,000	$95,000
19					
20	Breakeven Point		$357,143		

What the Spreadsheet Does

Many factors contribute to employee compensation, including, of course, sales commission. Several businesses provide their salespeople with a base salary until they develop their customer base and go to a straight commission.

This spreadsheet, which compares the use of salary and commission as compensation tools, allows you to change salary or commission and look at how much sales one needs to exceed straight salary.

Working with the Spreadsheet

To work with this spreadsheet, you need to enter the following information.

    C3   percent of commission
    C4   annual salary

Excel Business Applications

Col A employee identification
Col C sales per person per year

When the spreadsheet is complete, it will provide you with the following information.

C20 breakeven point where commission and salary equal one another
Col D commission
Col E total costs per person

What It Looks Like

Figure 11.14 provides a line chart that shows the breakeven point for the combination of salary and commission.

11.14 The breakeven point

Retail Worksheets

The Cell Contents and Formulas

	A	B	C	D	E
1	BREAKEVEN ANALYSIS				
2					
3	Commission		0.07		
4	Annual Salary		25000		
5					
6	Employee	Salary	Annual	Commission	Total
7			Sales		Costs
8					
9	A	=$C$4	100000	=$C$3*C9	=B9+D9
10	B	=$C$4	=C9+100000	=$C$3*C10	=B10+D10
11	C	=$C$4	=C10+100000	=$C$3*C11	=B11+D11
12	D	=$C$4	=C11+100000	=$C$3*C12	=B12+D12
13	E	=$C$4	=C12+100000	=$C$3*C13	=B13+D13
14	F	=$C$4	=C13+100000	=$C$3*C14	=B14+D14
15	G	=$C$4	=C14+100000	=$C$3*C15	=B15+D15
16	H	=$C$4	=C15+100000	=$C$3*C16	=B16+D16
17	I	=$C$4	=C16+100000	=$C$3*C17	=B17+D17
18	J	=$C$4	=C17+100000	=$C$3*C18	=B18+D18
19					
20	Breakeven Point		=IF($D$18>$C$4,($B$18/$D		

Excel Business Applications

Sales Pricing and Discounts

	A	B	C	D	E	F	G
1	SALES PRICING AND DISCOUNTS						
2							
3	Discount Values						
4							
5	Quantity		Discount				
6							
7	0-10		0.00				
8	11-50		0.03				
9	51-100		0.05				
10	Over 100		0.10				
11							
12							
13							
14	Item	Item	Quantity	Regular	Total		
15	Number	Price	Ordered	Price	Price		
16							
17	1232	$0.87	10	$8.70	$8.70		
18	3423	$3.65	100	$365.00	$346.75		
19	2154	$0.43	45	$19.35	$18.77		
20	4345	$6.59	49	$322.91	$313.22		
21	6565	$0.88	10	$8.80	$8.80		
22	4365	$0.03	60	$1.80	$1.71		
23	7678	$5.40	10	$54.00	$54.00		
24	6544	$0.33	150	$49.50	$44.55		
25	3432	$0.67	100	$67.00	$63.65		
26	3435	$1.23	1	$1.23	$1.23		
27							
28			TOTAL COST		$861.38		
29							
30							
31							
32							
33							

Retail Worksheets

What the Spreadsheet Does

Many producers are willing to give discounts on large orders since the larger the number of products sold, the less it costs to manufacture each one. It's also an added incentive to the buyer to purchase in large lots. This spreadsheet calculates the discounted price based on orders of different sizes.

The main thing you need to enter is discount rates (as a percent) for the various range of quantities. If you want to change the range of quantities, you will have to adjust the formulas.

Working with the Spreadsheet

To work with this spreadsheet, you need to enter the following information.

Col A item number
Col B item price
Col C quantity ordered

When the spreadsheet is complete, it will provide you with the following information.

C8   discount rate for more than 10
C9   discount rate for more than 50
C10 discount rate for more than 100
Col D regular selling price
Col E total including discount
E28 total cost of order

Excel Business Applications

The Cell Contents and Formulas

	A	B	C	D
1	SALES PRICING AND DISCOUNTS			
2				
3	Discount Values			
4				
5	Quantity		Discount (%)	
6				
7	0-10		0	
8	11-50		0.03	
9	51-100		0.05	
10	Over 100		0.1	
11				
12				
13				
14	Item	Item	Quantity	Regular
15	Number	Price	Ordered	Price
16				
17	1232	0.87	10	=C17*B17
18	3423	3.65	100	=C18*B18
19	2154	0.43	45	=C19*B19
20	4345	6.59	49	=C20*B20
21	6565	0.88	10	=C21*B21
22	4365	0.03	60	=C22*B22
23	7678	5.4	10	=C23*B23
24	6544	0.33	150	=C24*B24
25	3432	0.67	100	=C25*B25
26	3435	1.23	1	=C26*B26
27				
28			TOTAL COST	
29				
30				
31				
32				
33				

Retail Worksheets

	E
1	
2	
3	
4	
5	
6	
7	
8	
9	
10	
11	
12	
13	
14	Total
15	Price
16	
17	=IF(C17>100,D17*(1-$C$10),IF(C17>50,D17*(1-$C$9),IF(C17>10,D17*(1-$C$8),D17)))
18	=IF(C18>100,D18*(1-$C$10),IF(C18>50,D18*(1-$C$9),IF(C18>10,D18*(1-$C$8),D18)))
19	=IF(C19>100,D19*(1-$C$10),IF(C19>50,D19*(1-$C$9),IF(C19>10,D19*(1-$C$8),D19)))
20	=IF(C20>100,D20*(1-$C$10),IF(C20>50,D20*(1-$C$9),IF(C20>10,D20*(1-$C$8),D20)))
21	=IF(C21>100,D21*(1-$C$10),IF(C21>50,D21*(1-$C$9),IF(C21>10,D21*(1-$C$8),D21)))
22	=IF(C22>100,D22*(1-$C$10),IF(C22>50,D22*(1-$C$9),IF(C22>10,D22*(1-$C$8),D22)))
23	=IF(C23>100,D23*(1-$C$10),IF(C23>50,D23*(1-$C$9),IF(C23>10,D23*(1-$C$8),D23)))
24	=IF(C24>100,D24*(1-$C$10),IF(C24>50,D24*(1-$C$9),IF(C24>10,D24*(1-$C$8),D24)))
25	=IF(C25>100,D25*(1-$C$10),IF(C25>50,D25*(1-$C$9),IF(C25>10,D25*(1-$C$8),D25)))
26	=IF(C26>100,D26*(1-$C$10),IF(C26>50,D26*(1-$C$9),IF(C26>10,D26*(1-$C$8),D26)))
27	
28	=SUM(E17:E26)
29	
30	
31	
32	
33	

Sales per Square Foot

	A	B	C	D	E	F	G
1	SALES PER SQUARE FOOT						
2							
3	Sales for the month of July, 1987						
4							
5	Product		Code	Square	Sales	Sales/Square	
6				Footage	($)/Month	Foot	
7							
8	machines/prof		A	300	$6,576.89	21.92	
9	machines/home		B	300	$4,561.89	15.21	
10	models		G	150	$546.87	3.65	
11	cotton fabric		D	500	$1,265.78	2.53	
12	wool		C	750	$1,876.98	2.50	
13	patterns		F	250	$546.87	2.19	
14	pins		J	50	$89.35	1.79	
15	rayon fabric		E	500	$673.89	1.35	
16	thread		H	212	$245.76	1.16	
17	interfacing		I	200	$211.78	1.06	
18							
19		Total		3212	$16,596.06		
20							
21		Average sales per square foot				$5.17	

What the Spreadsheet Does

Perhaps the most useful indicator of the success of a particular retail outlet is the amount of sales it generates per square foot of space. This spreadsheet computes the sales per square foot for each of ten products or more if you choose to extend the size of the spreadsheet.

After entering labels and values, you can play with sales and square footage to see the effect of sales per square foot and to determine what products should be allotted the same amount of space they are currently using.

Working with the Spreadsheet

To work with this spreadsheet, you need to enter the following information.

Retail Worksheets

Row A product description
Row C product code (for charting)
Row D square footage used by the product
Row E sales for that product

When the spreadsheet is complete, it will provide you with the following information.

D19 total square footage available
E19 total sales per month
F21 average sales per month per square foot
Row F sales per square foot for the product

What It Looks Like

Figure 11.15 shows a bar chart comparing sales and available space after the sales/month figure was used to sort the records. The pattern of the bars was changed using the **Pattern** option on the Format menu.

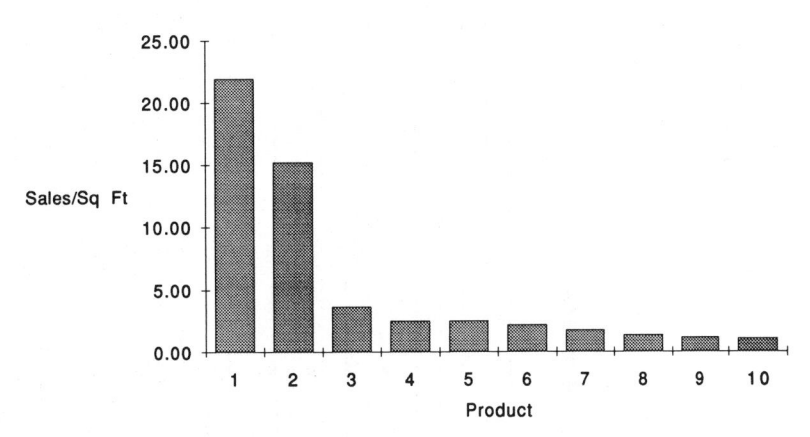

11.15 Available space and sales

The Cell Contents and Formulas

	A	B	C	D	E	F	G
1	SALES PER SQUARE						
2							
3	Sales for the month						
4							
5	Product		Code	Square	Sales	Sales/Square	
6				Footage	($)/Month	Foot	
7							
8	machines/prof		A	300	6576.89	=E8/D8	
9	machines/home		B	300	4561.89	=E9/D9	
10	models		G	150	546.87	=E10/D10	
11	cotton fabric		D	500	1265.78	=E11/D11	
12	wool		C	750	1876.98	=E12/D12	
13	patterns		F	250	546.87	=E13/D13	
14	pins		J	50	89.35	=E14/D14	
15	rayon fabric		E	500	673.89	=E15/D15	
16	thread		H	212	245.76	=E16/D16	
17	interfacing		I	200	211.78	=E17/D17	
18							
19		Total		=SUM(D8:D17)	=SUM(E8:E17)		
20		Average sale					
21						=E19/D19	

Retail Worksheets

Salesperson Analysis

	A	B	C	D	E	F	G	H	I
1	SALESPERSON ANALYSIS								
2									
3	Name	Sales/	Salary	Bonus	Fringes	Total	Expenses	Expenses/	
4		1988				Comp		% Comp	
5									
6	Joe	$198,900	$22,345	$2,567	$6,704	$31,616	$755	2.39%	
7	Bill	$176,567	$21,789	$1,023	$6,537	$29,349	$923	3.14%	
8	Susan	$185,345	$23,154	$3,153	$6,946	$33,253	$778	2.34%	
9	Mike	$200,786	$29,876	$2,243	$8,963	$41,082	$877	2.13%	
10	Catherine	$176,876	$27,657	$2,877	$8,297	$38,831	$586	1.51%	
11	Jay W	$213,432	$29,878	$2,314	$8,963	$41,155	$768	1.87%	
12	Jay R	$176,987	$35,142	$2,511	$10,543	$48,196	$879	1.82%	
13	Kim	$156,455	$28,978	$2,867	$8,693	$40,538	$903	2.23%	
14	Andrea	$132,433	$34,567	$5,400	$10,370	$50,337	$876	1.74%	
15	Allison	$231,432	$34,123	$3,745	$10,237	$48,105	$967	2.01%	
16									
17	Totals	$1,849,213	$287,509	$28,700	$86,253	$402,462	$8,312		
18	Average	$184,921	$28,751	$2,870	$8,625	$40,246	$831	2.12%	

What the Spreadsheet Does

This spreadsheet computes the total compensation for salespersons and provides you with information to judge total productivity as a ratio to total costs.

It assumes that the average fringe benefit is 30% of base salary and that total compensation consists of salary, bonuses, and fringe benefits. Bonuses are assigned based on an arbitrary set of rules, and the amount is not a function of any formula in the spreadsheet.

Working with the Spreadsheet

To work with this spreadsheet, you need to enter the following information.

Col A name
Col B sales total ($)
Col C salary
Col D bonus
Col G expenses

Excel Business Applications

When the spreadsheet is complete, it will provide you with the following information.

Col E	fringe benefits
Col F	total compensation
Col H	expenses as a percent of total compensation
Row 17	column totals
Row 18	column averages

What It Looks Like

Figure 11.16 shows a line chart that compares salary with total compensation for each of the salespersons in the spreadsheet.

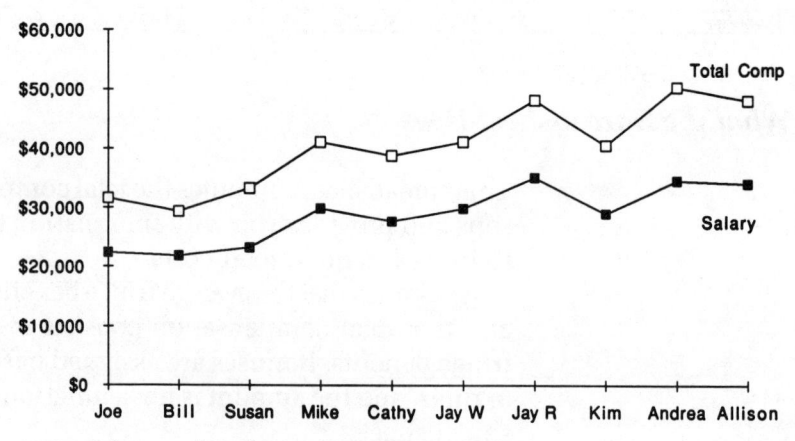

11.16 Salary and total compensation

Retail Worksheets

The Cell Contents and Formulas

	A	B	C
1	SALESPERSON ANALYSIS		
2			
3	Name	Sales/	Salary
4		1988	
5			
6	Joe	198900	22345
7	Bill	176567	21789
8	Susan	185345	23154
9	Mike	200786	29876
10	Catherine	176876	27657
11	Jay W	213432	29878
12	Jay R	176987	35142
13	Kim	156455	28978
14	Andrea	132433	34567
15	Allison	231432	34123
16			
17	Totals	=SUM(B6:B15)	=SUM(C6:C15)
18	Average	=AVERAGE(B6:B15)	=AVERAGE(C6:C15)

	D	E	F	G	H
1					
2					
3	Bonus	Fringes	Total	Expenses	Expenses/
4			Comp		% Comp
5					
6	2567	=C6*0.3	=SUM(C6:E6)	755	=G6/F6
7	1023	=C7*0.3	=SUM(C7:E7)	923	=G7/F7
8	3153	=C8*0.3	=SUM(C8:E8)	778	=G8/F8
9	2243	=C9*0.3	=SUM(C9:E9)	877	=G9/F9
10	2877	=C10*0.3	=SUM(C10:E10)	586	=G10/F10
11	2314	=C11*0.3	=SUM(C11:E11)	768	=G11/F11
12	2511	=C12*0.3	=SUM(C12:E12)	879	=G12/F12
13	2867	=C13*0.3	=SUM(C13:E13)	903	=G13/F13
14	5400	=C14*0.3	=SUM(C14:E14)	876	=G14/F14
15	3745	=C15*0.3	=SUM(C15:E15)	967	=G15/F15
16					
17	=SUM(D6:D15)	=SUM(E6:E15)	=SUM(F6:F15)	=SUM(G6:G15)	
18	=AVERAGE(D6:D15)	=AVERAGE(E6:E15)	=AVERAGE(F6:F15)	=AVERAGE(G6:G15)	=AVERAGE(H6:H15)

12

Statistical Worksheets

Item Analysis

	A	B	C	D	E	F	G	H	I
1	ITEM ANALYSIS								
2									
3									
4	Item #13								
5									
6		Item Description:	Which of the following business analysis can						
7			be used to predict outcomes?						
8									
9			*a. regression						
10			b. factor analysis						
11			c. Chi-square						
12			d. analysis of variance						
13			e. t-test between correlated means						
14									
15									
16			Alternative	A	B	C	D	E	Total
17									
18			Upper 30%	30	15	56	22	18	141
19									
20			Lower 30%	24	17	9	44	35	129
21									
22			Total	54	32	65	66	53	270
23									
24		Difficulty Level =		20%					
25		Discrimination Level =		0.25					

Statistical Worksheets

What the Spreadsheet Does

To accurately evaluate a company's employees, it is important to use different types of testing instruments. Often when employers need to determine their workers' level of knowledge about a particular topic, they administer multiple choice exams. Item analysis is a technique that tells you which questions, or items, in a multiple choice test are doing a good job of predicting employee performance.

This spreadsheet computes the difficulty level and the discrimination level of one item. The difficulty level is based on the number of people who responded correctly to the item, and the discrimination level is the ratio of people in the top 30% of the group who responded correctly compared with the number of people in the lower 30% who responded correctly. The most valuable items discriminate between those in the upper and lower groups (100% discrimination, or a value of 1.0) and have about a 50% difficulty level. In order to use this spreadsheet you must rearrange the data so that the data for the correct response is under choice A.

Working with the Spreadsheet

To work with this spreadsheet, you need to enter the following information.

A4	item number
A6	item description
Row 18 and Row 20	item responses for the top 30% and the bottom 30%

When the spreadsheet is complete, it will provide you with the following information.

E24	difficulty level
E25	discrimination level
Row 22	total responses
Row 24	percent responses

Excel Business Applications

The Cell Contents and Formulas

	A	B	C
1	ITEM ANALYSIS		
2			
3			
4	Item #13		
5			
6	Item Description:		Which of the following business analysis can
7			be used to predict outcomes?
8			
9			*a. regression
10			b. factor analysis
11			c. Chi-square
12			d. analysis of variance
13			e. t-test between correlated means
14			
15			
16			Alternative
17			
18			Upper 30%
19			
20			Lower 30%
21			
22			Total
23			
24		Difficulty Level =	
25		Discrimination Level	

	D	E	F	G	H	I
1						
2						
3						
4						
5						
6						
7						
8						
9						
10						
11						
12						
13						
14						
15						
16	A	B	C	D	E	Total
17						
18	30	15	56	22	18	=SUM(A18:H18)
19						
20	24	17	9	44	35	=SUM(A20:H20)
21						
22	=SUM(D18:D20)	=SUM(E18:E20)	=SUM(F18:F20)	=SUM(G18:G20)	=SUM(H18:H20)	=SUM(I18:I20)
23						
24	=D22/I22					
25	=(D18-D20)/D20					

Statistical Worksheets

Pearson Correlation between Two Variables

	A	B	C	D	E	F
1	PEARSON PRODUCT MOMENT CORRELATION						
2						
3			Time Out			
4	Employee	Sales	Of Office	Cross	Sales	Time
5		(000's)	(hours)	Product	(Squared)	(Squared)
6						
7	F	65	5.50	357.50	4225	30.25
8	G	61	5.60	341.60	3721	31.36
9	B	58	4.50	261.00	3364	20.25
10	E	57	4.80	273.60	3249	23.04
11	K	56	3.90	218.40	3136	15.21
12	L	53	3.70	196.10	2809	13.69
13	O	50	3.30	165.00	2500	10.89
14	M	47	2.80	131.60	2209	7.84
15	D	44	2.90	127.60	1936	8.41
16	C	41	3.00	123.00	1681	9.00
17	N	40	2.20	88.00	1600	4.84
18	A	40	2.00	80.00	1600	4.00
19	J	39	2.10	81.90	1521	4.41
20	I	38	1.35	51.30	1444	1.82
21	H	37	1.10	40.70	1369	1.21
22						
23	N	15				
24	Average	48.40	3.25			
25	Sum	726	48.75	2537.30	36364	186.22
26						
27	Pearson R =		0.96			
28	R Squared =		0.93			

What the Spreadsheet Does

Correlation is a statistical technique used to generate a numerical index that reflects the degree of association between two variables.

This spreadsheet computes the zero order correlation coefficient between two variables: sales and number of hours out of office. The squared correlation coefficient measures the amount of variance in one variable caused by another. In this case, about 60% of the variance in sales can be explained by the amount of time people spend out of their office, presumably making sales calls.

Excel Business Applications

Working with the Spreadsheet

To work with this spreadsheet, you need to enter the following information.

> **Col A** employee identification
> **Col B** amount of monthly sales for 15 employees (variable x)
> **Col C** amount of time out of office in hours per week (variable y)

When the spreadsheet is complete, it will provide you with the following information.

> **B24** sample size
> **B25** average sales
> **D27** Pearson product moment correlation coefficient
> **D28** squared correlation coefficient
> **Rows D,E,F** computed for Pearson formula

What It Looks Like

The positive slope of the line in Figure 12.1, a scatter chart without grids, reflects the direct relationship between the two variables. To complete this chart, you need to use the **Paste** special option on the Edit menu.

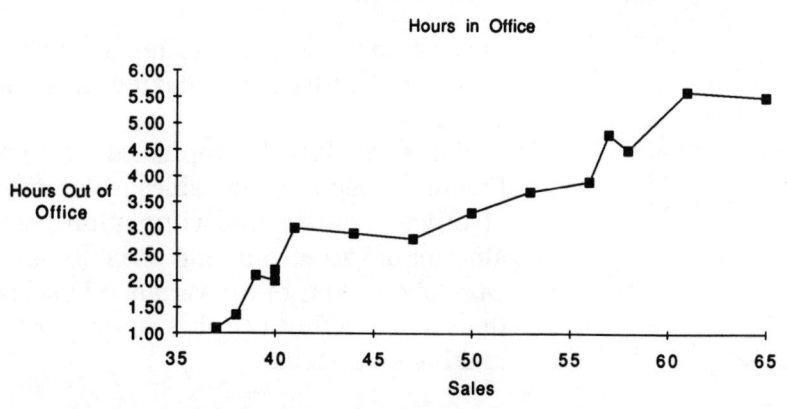

12.1 Scatter plots that examine relationships

Statistical Worksheets

The Cell Contents and Formulas

	A	B	C
1	PEARSON PRODUCT		
2			
3			Time Out
4	Employee	Sales	Of Office
5		(000's)	(hours)
6			
7	H	37	1.1
8	I	38	1.35
9	J	39	2.1
10	N	40	2.2
11	A	40	2
12	C	41	3
13	D	44	2.9
14	M	47	2.8
15	O	50	3.3
16	L	53	3.7
17	K	56	3.9
18	E	57	4.8
19	B	58	4.5
20	G	61	5.6
21	F	65	5.5
22			
23	N	=COUNT(B7:B21)	
24	Average	=AVERAGE(B7:B21)	=AVERAGE(C7:C21)
25	Sum	=SUM(B7:B21)	=SUM(C7:C21)
26			
27	Pearson R =		=((B23*D25)-(B25*C25))/SQRT(((B23*E25)-(B25^2))*((B23*F25)-(C25^2)))
28	R Squared =		=C27^2

	D	E	F
1			
2			
3			
4	Cross	Sales	Time
5	Product	(Squared)	(Squared)
6			
7	=C7*B7	=B7^2	=C7^2
8	=C8*B8	=B8^2	=C8^2
9	=C9*B9	=B9^2	=C9^2
10	=C10*B10	=B10^2	=C10^2
11	=C11*B11	=B11^2	=C11^2
12	=C12*B12	=B12^2	=C12^2
13	=C13*B13	=B13^2	=C13^2
14	=C14*B14	=B14^2	=C14^2
15	=C15*B15	=B15^2	=C15^2
16	=C16*B16	=B16^2	=C16^2
17	=C17*B17	=B17^2	=C17^2
18	=C18*B18	=B18^2	=C18^2
19	=C19*B19	=B19^2	=C19^2
20	=C20*B20	=B20^2	=C20^2
21	=C21*B21	=B21^2	=C21^2
22			
23			
24			
25	=SUM(D7:D21)	=SUM(E7:E21)	=SUM(F7:F21)
26			
27			
28			

Significance of the Difference between Correlated Proportions

	A	B	C	D
1	Significance of the Difference between			
2	Two Correlated Proportions			
3				
4		Item #1		
5		Pass	Fail	Total
6	Item #2			
7	Pass	10	50	60
8	Fail	110	30	140
9	Total	120	80	200
10				
11	sp1-p2	0.03		
12				
13	z value	3.16		

What the Spreadsheet Does

This spreadsheet computes the z value, which measures the significance between two proportions.

Working with the Spreadsheet

To work with this spreadsheet, you need to enter the following information.

  B7...C9 pass and fail frequencies for items 1 and 2

When the spreadsheet is complete, it will provide you with the following information.

  B11   the standard error of the pooled proportions
  B13   the z value
  B9, C9, D7, D8, and
   D9   row and column totals

The Cell Contents and Formulas

	A	B	C	D
1	Significance of the Differe			
2	Two Correlated Proportio			
3				
4		Item #1		
5		Pass	Fail	Total
6	Item #2			
7	Pass	10	50	=B7+C7
8	Fail	110	30	=B8+C8
9	Total	=B7+B8	=C7+C8	=B9+C9
10				
11	sp1-p2	=SQRT(((B7/D9)+(C8/D9))/D9)		
12				
13	z value	=((C9/D9)-(D7/D9))/B11		

Excel Business Applications

Spearman Rank Order Correlation

	A	B	C	D	E	F
1	SPEARMAN RANK ORDER CORRELATION					
2						
3	Employee	Sales	Competitor		D	
4		Rank	Assessment	D	Squared	
5						
6	L	15	2	13	169	
7	K	14	3	11	121	
8	J	13	1	12	144	
9	H	12	4	8	64	
10	F	11	5	6	36	
11	D	10	9	1	1	
12	B	9	7	2	4	
13	O	7	11	-4	16	
14	N	7	6	1	1	
15	I	6	10	-4	16	
16	C	5	8	-3	9	
17	E	4	15	-11	121	
18	M	3	13	-10	100	
19	G	2	14	-12	144	
20	A	1	12	-11	121	
21						
22						
23	N =	15				
24	Sum				1067	
25						
26	Rho =	-0.90				

What the Spreadsheet Does

Often you will want to measure the relationship between two sets of ranked items. In such cases, you should use the Spearman Rho correlation coefficient, which provides a numerical index of the relationship between two ranked variables, such as sales rank and employer assessment.

This spreadsheet computes the Spearman Rho value for two ranked variables: sales ranking from highest (1) to lowest (15) and competitor's assessment. The strong negative correlation between the variables indicates that they are inversely, though not causally, related; thus, the higher the sales, the lower the competitor's assessment.

Statistical Worksheets

Working with the Spreadsheet

To work with this spreadsheet, you need to enter the following information.

Col A   employee identification
Col B   sales rank
Col C   competitor's assessment

When the spreadsheet is complete, it will provide you with the following information.

A23   sample size
A26   value of Rho coefficient
E24   sum of differences squared
Cols D,E used in computation

What It Looks Like

The scatter chart in Figure 12.2 shows a negative correlation between the two variables, illustrating that the paired rankings tend to move in opposite directions.

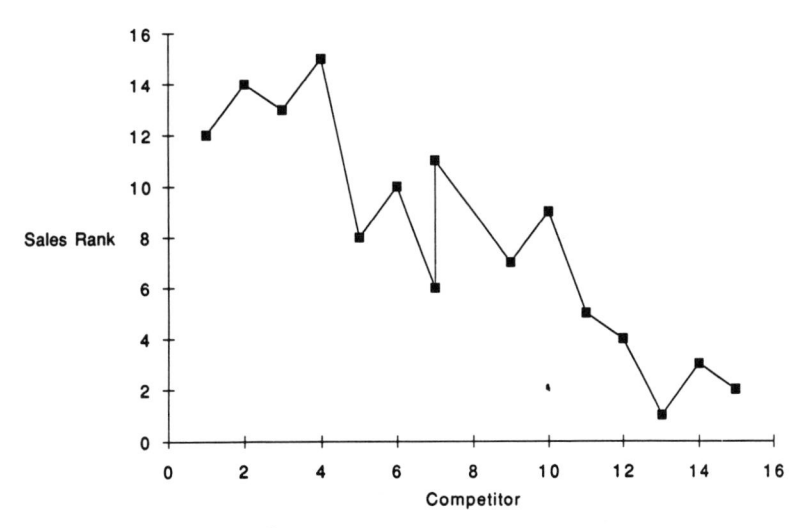

12.2 A negative correlation

Excel Business Applications

The Cell Contents and Formulas

	A	B	C	D	E
1	SPEARMAN RANK OF				
2					
3	Employee	Sales	Competitor		D
4		Rank	Assessment	D	Squared
5					
6	L	15	2	=B6-C6	=D6^2
7	K	14	3	=B7-C7	=D7^2
8	J	13	1	=B8-C8	=D8^2
9	H	12	4	=B9-C9	=D9^2
10	F	11	5	=B10-C10	=D10^2
11	D	10	9	=B11-C11	=D11^2
12	B	9	7	=B12-C12	=D12^2
13	O	7	11	=B13-C13	=D13^2
14	N	7	6	=B14-C14	=D14^2
15	I	6	10	=B15-C15	=D15^2
16	C	5	8	=B16-C16	=D16^2
17	E	4	15	=B17-C17	=D17^2
18	M	3	13	=B18-C18	=D18^2
19	G	2	14	=B19-C19	=D19^2
20	A	1	12	=B20-C20	=D20^2
21					
22					
23	N =	=COUNTA(B1:B20)			
24	Sum				=SUM(E6:E20)
25					
26	Rho =	=1-((6*E24)/(B23*(B23^2)-1))			

290

Significance of the Difference between Correlation Coefficients

	A	B	C	D
1	Significance of the Difference			
2	between Correlation Coefficients (r12/r13)			
3				
4	r12	0.60		
5	r13	0.50		
6	r23	0.50		
7				
8	n	100		
9				
10	t value	1.29		

What the Spreadsheet Does

This spreadsheet produces a t value, which measures the difference between two simple zero order correlations.

Working with the Spreadsheet

To work with this spreadsheet, you need to enter the following information.

Col B the values of r12, r13, and r23

When the spreadsheet is complete, it will provide you with the following information.

B10 the t value

The Cell Contents and Formulas

	A	B
1	Significance of the Difference	
2	between Correlation Coefficients (r12/r1	
3		
4	r12	0.6
5	r13	0.5
6	r23	0.5
7		
8	n	100
9		
10	t value	=(B4-B5)*(SQRT((B8-3)*(1+B6)))/SQ

Excel Business Applications

Survey Analysis

	A	B	C	D	E	F	G	H	I
1	SURVEY ANALYSIS								
2									
3	Item : 27								
4	Item Description: How important is it to you that you have a choice								
5				in retirement plans?					
6									
7					Very			Somewhat	Very
8					Important	Important	Undecided	Important	Important
9					(1)	(2)	(3)	(4)	(5)
10									
11	Subject	Age	Sex						
12	Number								
13									
14	1	22	1		1	0	0	0	0
15	2	23	2		0	1	0	0	0
16	3	21	2		0	1	0	0	0
17	4	35	2		0	0	1	0	0
18	5	32	2		0	0	0	1	0
19	6	21	1		0	0	0	1	0
20	7	43	2		0	0	1	0	0
21	8	32	1		0	1	0	0	0
22	9	44	2		0	0	1	0	0
23	10	22	2		0	0	0	0	1
24									
25	Average	29.5		Total					
26				Responses	1	4	3	2	1
27									
28				Percent	10%	40%	30%	20%	10%
29									
30									
31									
32	Chi-Square Analysis								
33				Observed	1	4	3	2	1
34				Value					
35				Expected					
36				Value	2	2	2	2	2
37									
38				(O-E)^2/E2	0.5	2	0.5	0	0.5
39									
40				Chi-Square	3.5				

Statistical Worksheets

What the Spreadsheet Does

This spreadsheet allows you to enter data for ten subjects that has been collected using a Likert five-point response scale for one question on a survey or questionnaire and to analyze the results using a chi-square test for goodness of fit. It allows you to judge whether the number of responses within each category is due to chance or some other factor, which in this case would be preference for changes in retirement plans. The expected value in the summary table is the values you would expect by chance for each response category. The more the observed responses vary from the expected values, the greater the likelihood that the differences are due to something other than chance.

You will need a separate spreadsheet for each of the questions.

Working with the Spreadsheet

To work with this spreadsheet, you need to enter the following information.

A3	number of question
A4	question description
E14...I23	item responses
Col A	subject number
Col B	age
Col C	sex

When the spreadsheet is complete, it will provide you with the following information.

B25	average age
E33...I26	chi-square summary table
E40	chi-square value
R26	total response
R28	percent response

Excel Business Applications

The Cell Contents and Formulas

	A	B	C
1	SURVEY ANALYSIS		
2			
3	Item : 27		
4	Item Description: How important is it to you that you have a cho		
5			in retirement plans?
6			
7			
8			
9			
10			
11	Subject	Age	Sex
12	Number		
13			
14	1	22	1
15	2	23	2
16	3	21	2
17	4	35	2
18	5	32	2
19	6	21	1
20	7	43	2
21	8	32	1
22	9	44	2
23	10	22	2
24			
25	Average	=AVERAGE(B14:B23)	
26			
27			
28			
29			
30			
31			
32	Chi-Square Analysis		
33			
34			
35			
36			
37			
38			
39			
40			

Statistical Worksheets

	D	E
1		
2		
3		
4		
5		
6		
7		Very
8		Important
9		(1)
10		
11		
12		
13		
14		1
15		0
16		0
17		0
18		0
19		0
20		0
21		0
22		0
23		0
24		
25	Total	
26	Responses	1
27		
28	Percent	=E26/COUNTA(E14:E23)
29		
30		
31		
32		
33	Observed	=(E26)
34	Value	
35	Expected	
36	Value	=COUNTA($E$14:$E$23)/COUNTA($E$28:$I$28)
37		
38	(O-E)^2/E2	=(E33-E36)^2/E36
39		
40	Chi-Square Value =	=SUM(E38:I38)

295

Excel Business Applications

The Cell Contents and Formulas (Continued)

	F	G
1		
2		
3		
4		
5		
6		
7		
8	Important	Undecided
9	(2)	(3)
10		
11		
12		
13		
14	0	0
15	1	0
16	1	0
17	0	1
18	0	0
19	0	0
20	0	1
21	1	0
22	0	1
23	0	0
24		
25		
26	4	=SUM(G14:G23)
27		
28	=F26/COUNTA(F14:F23)	=G26/COUNTA(G14:G23)
29		
30		
31		
32		
33	=(F26)	=(G26)
34		
35		
36	=COUNTA($E$14:$E$23)/COUNTA($E$28:$I$28)	=COUNTA($E$14:$E$23)/COUNTA($E$28:$I$28)
37		
38	=(F33-F36)^2/F36	=(G33-G36)^2/G36
39		
40		

	H	I
1		
2		
3		
4		
5		
6		
7	Somewhat	Very
8	Important	Important
9	(4)	(5)
10		
11		
12		
13		
14	0	0
15	0	0
16	0	0
17	0	0
18	1	0
19	1	0
20	0	0
21	0	0
22	0	0
23	0	1
24		
25		
26	=SUM(H14:H23)	=SUM(I14:I23)
27		
28	=H26/COUNTA(H14:H23)	=I26/COUNTA(I14:I23)
29		
30		
31		
32		
33	2	=(I26)
34		
35		
36	=COUNTA($E$14:$E$23)/COUNTA($E$28:$I$28)	=COUNTA($E$14:$E$23)/COUNTA($E$28:$I$28)
37		
38	=(H33-H36)^2/H36	=(I33-I36)^2/I36
39		
40		

Excel Business Applications

t-Test for Dependent Means

	A	B	C	D	E	F
1	t test (dependent means)					
2						
3		Employee	Score 1	Score 2	D	D Squared
4		1	12	18	-6	36
5		2	14	17	-3	9
6		3	21	16	5	25
7		4	22	18	4	16
8		5	16	17	-1	1
9		6	17	15	2	4
10		7	15	16	-1	1
11		8	24	18	6	36
12		9	10	17	-7	49
13		10	9	12	-3	9
14						
15	n	10		Average	-0.4	
16				SD	4.53	
17	t value	-0.28				

What the Spreadsheet Does

This spreadsheet measures the significance in the difference between two dependent or correlated means, such as when one group of individuals is tested twice.

Working with the Spreadsheet

To work with this spreadsheet, you need to enter the following information.

    Col B employee identification
    Col C score 1
    Col D score 2

When the spreadsheet is complete, it will provide you with the following information.

    B15 sample size
    B17 t value
    E15 average score
    E16 sample standard deviation

The Cell Contents and Formulas

	A	B	C
1	t test (dependent means)		
2			
3		Employee	Score 1
4		1	12
5		2	14
6		3	21
7		4	22
8		5	16
9		6	17
10		7	15
11		8	24
12		9	10
13		10	9
14			
15	n	=COUNT(B4:B13)	
16			
17	t value	=E15/(E16/SQRT(B15))	

	D	E	F
1			
2			
3	Score 2	D	D Squared
4	18	=C4-D4	=E4^2
5	17	=C5-D5	=E5^2
6	16	=C6-D6	=E6^2
7	18	=C7-D7	=E7^2
8	17	=C8-D8	=E8^2
9	15	=C9-D9	=E9^2
10	16	=C10-D10	=E10^2
11	18	=C11-D11	=E11^2
12	17	=C12-D12	=E12^2
13	12	=C13-D13	=E13^2
14			
15	Average	=AVERAGE(E4:E13)	
16	SD	=STDEV(E4:E13)	
17			

Excel Business Applications

t-Test between Independent Means

	A	B	C
1	t-test (independent means)		
2			
3		Group 1 Scores	Group 2 Scores
4		76	68
5		87	76
6		99	55
7		67	67
8		87	89
9		69	87
10		80	99
11		73	85
12		85	
13		88	
14			
15	N	10	8
16	Average	81.10	78.25
17	SD	9.95	14.37
18			
19	t value	0.48	

What the Spreadsheet Does

This spreadsheet measures the significance in the difference between two independent or uncorrelated means, such as when one group of individuals is tested twice.

Working with the Spreadsheet

To work with this spreadsheet, you need to enter the following information.

Col B group 1 scores
Col C group 2 scores

When the spreadsheet is complete, it will provide you with the following information.

B15 and C15 sample sizes
B16 and C16 averages
B17 and C17 sample standard deviation
B19 t value

300

The Cell Contents and Formulas

	A	B	C
1	t-test (independent means)		
2			
3		Group 1 Scores	Group 2 Scores
4		76	68
5		87	76
6		99	55
7		67	67
8		87	89
9		69	87
10		80	99
11		73	85
12		85	
13		88	
14			
15	N	=COUNT(B4:B13)	=COUNT(C4:C13)
16	Average	=AVERAGE(B4:B13)	=AVERAGE(C4:C13)
17	SD	=STDEV(B4:B13)	=STDEV(C4:C13)
18			
19	t value	=(B16-C16)/SQRT((B17^2/B15)+(C17^2/C15))	

Part III
The Excel Financial Functions

By now you've discovered that Excel functions are both valuable and convenient. For the business person, Excel offers a specialized set of these functions, some of which were used to create the worksheets in Part II. These as well as other functions are presented in this section so you can see how each one is applied in its own specialized way.

Remember, all of these functions return a specific value to the cell in which the function is located.

The Excel Financial Functions

Depreciation of an Asset (DDB)

	A	B	C	D	E
1	Depreciation				
2					
3	Cost	Value	Useful Life	Period of Use	Depreciated Cost
4					
5	$7,500	$2,500	10	1	$1,500
6	$7,500	$2,500	10	2	$1,200
7	$7,500	$2,500	10	3	$960
8	$7,500	$2,500	10	4	$768
9	$7,500	$2,500	10	5	$572
10	$7,500	$2,500	10	6	$0
11	$7,500	$2,500	10	7	$0
12	$7,500	$2,500	10	8	$0
13	$7,500	$2,500	10	9	$0
14	$7,500	$2,500	10	10	$0

What the Function Does

The **DDB** function returns the depreciation of an asset for a specific period of time. The function uses the double-declining balance method, which assumes that depreciation takes place at a faster rate earlier in the life of the product.

For example, you may want to compute the amount of depreciation of a $7,500 item with a current value of $2,500 and a useful life of 10 years over a period of 20 years.

As you can see in the worksheet presented here, you can claim the largest depreciation ($1,500) during the first year.

Working with the Worksheet

To work with this worksheet, you need to enter the following information.

Col A the initial cost of the item
Col B the salvage value of the item
Col C the useful life of the item
Col D the length of time the item will be used

The Excel Financial Functions

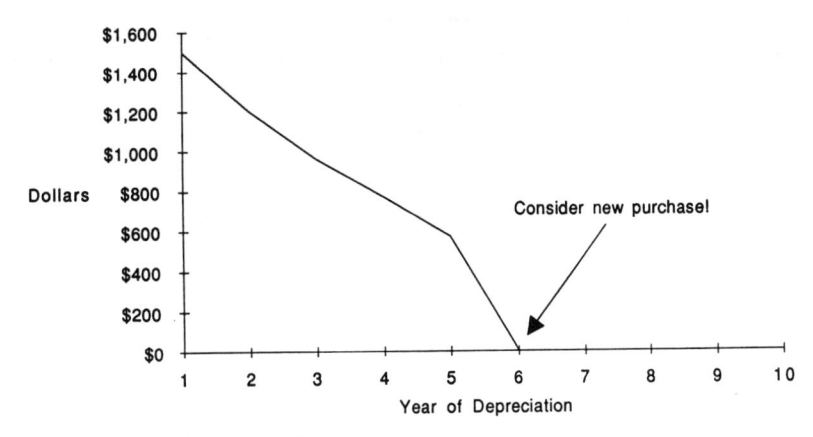

13.1 Depreciation in dollars

When the worksheet is complete, it will provide you with the following information.

Col E the depreciated costs of the item given varying times of use

What It Looks Like

Figure 13.1 shows a line chart in which depreciation in dollars is presented as a function of years 1 through 10.

The Cell Contents and Formulas

	A	B	C	D	E
1	Depreciation				
2					
3	Cost	Value	Useful Life	Period of Us	Depreciated Cost
4					
5	7500	2500	10	1	=DDB(A5,B5,C5,D5)
6	7500	2500	10	2	=DDB(A6,B6,C6,D6)
7	7500	2500	10	3	=DDB(A7,B7,C7,D7)
8	7500	2500	10	4	=DDB(A8,B8,C8,D8)
9	7500	2500	10	5	=DDB(A9,B9,C9,D9)
10	7500	2500	10	6	=DDB(A10,B10,C10,D10)
11	7500	2500	10	7	=DDB(A11,B11,C11,D11)
12	7500	2500	10	8	=DDB(A12,B12,C12,D12)
13	7500	2500	10	9	=DDB(A13,B13,C13,D13)
14	7500	2500	10	10	=DDB(A14,B14,C14,D14)

The Excel Financial Functions

Future Value of an Investment (FV)

	A	B	C	D	E	F
1	Future Value					
2						
3	Interest Rate	Period	Payment	Present Value	Type	Future Value
4	10.00%	20	($200.00)	($100.00)	1	$13,273.25
5	10.25%	20	($200.00)	($100.00)	1	$13,697.34
6	10.50%	20	($200.00)	($100.00)	1	$14,136.03
7	10.75%	20	($200.00)	($100.00)	1	$14,589.83
8	11.00%	20	($200.00)	($100.00)	1	$15,059.26
9	11.25%	20	($200.00)	($100.00)	1	$15,544.86
10	11.50%	20	($200.00)	($100.00)	1	$16,047.19
11	11.75%	20	($200.00)	($100.00)	1	$16,566.83
12	12.00%	20	($200.00)	($100.00)	1	$17,104.38

What the Function Does

The **FV** function returns the value of an investment given the interest rate, the amount of time, and the size of the payment. This is the tool to use if you need to know the future value of an investment given additional payments into the investment.

For example, if you add $200 each period to your base of $100, after 20 years your investment will have increased to $13,273.25 at 10% interest or to $17,104.38 at 12% interest.

Working with the Worksheet

To work with this worksheet, you need to enter the following information.

  Col A the interest rate
  Col B the period of investment
  Col C the payment (notice that it is a negative value)
  Col D the present value of the investment
  Col E the type of investment

When the worksheet is complete, it will provide you with the following information.

  Col F the future value of the investment

The Excel Financial Functions

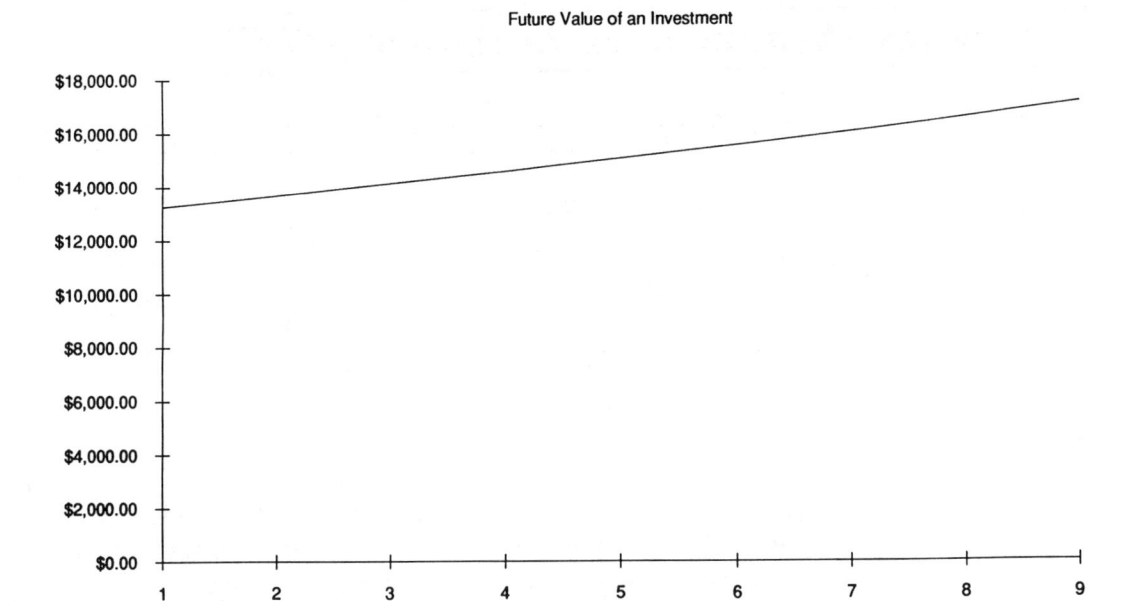

Future Value of an Investment

14.1 Value of investment

What It Looks Like

Figure 14.1 shows a line chart that illustrates how the value of the investment increases as a function of increasing interest rates.

The Cell Contents and Formulas

	A	B	C	D	E	F
1	Future Value					
2						
3	Interest Rate	Period	Payment	Present Value	Type	Future Value
4	0.1	20	-200	-100	1	=FV(A4,B4,C4,D4,E4)
5	0.1025	20	-200	-100	1	=FV(A5,B5,C5,D5,E5)
6	0.105	20	-200	-100	1	=FV(A6,B6,C6,D6,E6)
7	0.1075	20	-200	-100	1	=FV(A7,B7,C7,D7,E7)
8	0.11	20	-200	-100	1	=FV(A8,B8,C8,D8,E8)
9	0.1125	20	-200	-100	1	=FV(A9,B9,C9,D9,E9)
10	0.115	20	-200	-100	1	=FV(A10,B10,C10,D10,E10)
11	0.1175	20	-200	-100	1	=FV(A11,B11,C11,D11,E11)
12	0.12	20	-200	-100	1	=FV(A12,B12,C12,D12,E12)

The Interest Payment on an Investment (IPMT)

	A	B	C	D	E
1	Interest Payment				
2					
3	Rate	Period	Number of Periods	Present Value	Interest Payment
5	12.00%	1	360	$72,000	($720)
6	13.00%	1	360	$72,000	($780)
7	14.00%	1	360	$72,000	($840)
8	15.00%	1	360	$72,000	($900)

What the Function Does

The **IPMT** function computes the interest payment for a given investment based on a certain period of time and interest rates. In the principal and interest equation, this is the part of the payment that is the interest.

For example, a $72,000 loan at 12% over 360 periods would have an interest payment of $720. At 15% the same loan would have a $900 payment attached.

Working with the Worksheet

To work with this worksheet, you need to enter the following information.

Col A the interest rate
Col B the period
Col C the number of periods
Col D the present value of the loan

When the worksheet is complete, it will provide you with the following information.

Col E the interest payment

The Excel Financial Functions

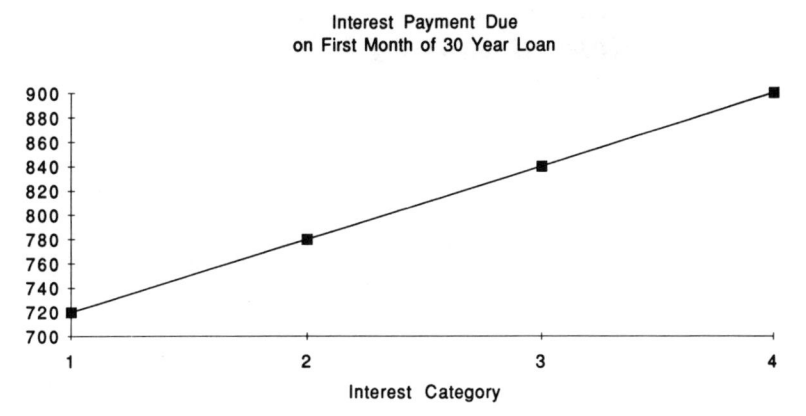

Interest Payment Due on First Month of 30 Year Loan

15.1 Interest payment due

What It Looks Like

Figure 15.1 shows the interest payment due on the first month of a 30-year (360-month) loan at a variety of interest rates. The plot area was selected and screened using the **Patterns** option on the Format menu.

The Cell Contents and Formulas

	A	B	C	D	E
1	Interest Paymen				
2					
3	Rate		Period	Number o	Present	Interest
4				Periods	Value	Payment
5	0.12	1	360	72000	=IPMT(A5/12,B5,C5,D5)
6	0.13	1	360	72000	=IPMT(A6/12,B6,C6,D6)
7	0.14	1	360	72000	=IPMT(A7/12,B7,C7,D7)
8	0.15	1	360	72000	=IPMT(A8/12,B8,C8,D8)

The Excel Financial Functions

Internal Rate of Return (IRR)

	A	B	C	D
1	Internal Rate of Return			
2				
3	Initial Cost	($25,000)	Time	IRR
4	Income Yr1	$20,000	5 Years	77%
5	Income Yr2	$20,400	4 Years	72%
6	Income Yr3	$20,808	3 Years	62%
7	Income Yr4	$21,224	2 Years	39%
8	Income Yr5	$21,649	1 Years	-20%

What the Function Does

The **IRR** function computes the internal rate of return of an investment, or the percent of return that is expected if the present value of the investment is equal to zero.

Working with the Worksheet

To work with this worksheet, you need to enter the following information.

    B3   the initial cost of the investment
    B4 through B8 income generated

When the worksheet is complete, it will provide you with the following information.

    Col D the rate of return on the investment

The Excel Financial Functions

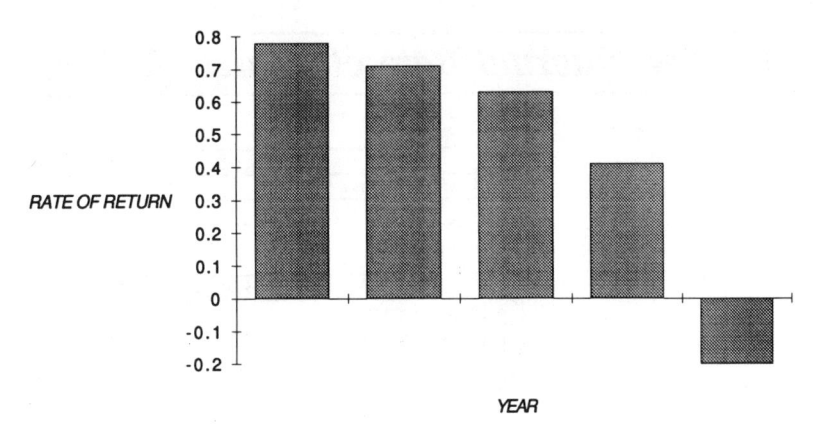

16.1 Rate of return

What It Looks Like

The column chart in Figure 16.1 shows the rate of return as a function of income over a five-year period, with a negative rate of return during (after) the fifth year.

The Cell Contents and Formulas

	A	B	C	D
1	Internal Rate of Return			
2				
3	Initial Cost	-25000	Time	IRR
4	Income Yr1	20000	5 Years	=IRR($B$3:B8)
5	Income Yr2	=B4*1.02	4 Years	=IRR($B$3:B7)
6	Income Yr3	=B5*1.02	3 Years	=IRR($B$3:B6)
7	Income Yr4	=B6*1.02	2 Years	=IRR($B$3:B5)
8	Income Yr5	=B7*1.02	1 Years	=IRR($B$3:B4)

The Excel Financial Functions

Modified Internal Rate of Return (MIRR)

	A	B	C	D
1	Modified Internal			
2	Rate of Return			
3				
4	Cost of			
5	Ice Cream Machines	($50,000)	MIRR After	MIRR
6	Year 1 Income	$12,546	1 Year	-74.91%
7	Year 2 Income	$21,678	2 Years	-15.47%
8	Year 3 Income	$17,564	3 Years	4.82%
9	Year 4 Income	$22,134	4 Years	14.73%
10	Year 5 Income	$19,675	5 Years	18.47%

What the Function Does

The **MIRR** function computes a rate of return that can be modified to fit a series of payments and the interest rate associated with them.

For example, the modified rate of return on a $50,000 investment after the first year is 74.91% given a 10% interest rate on the purchase of the equipment and a 12% rate paid on investments.

Working with the Worksheet

To work with this worksheet, you need to enter the following information.

Cell B5   the initial cost of the investment
Cells B6 through B10   income generated

When the worksheet is complete, it will provide you with the following information.

Col D   the modified rate of return

The Excel Financial Functions

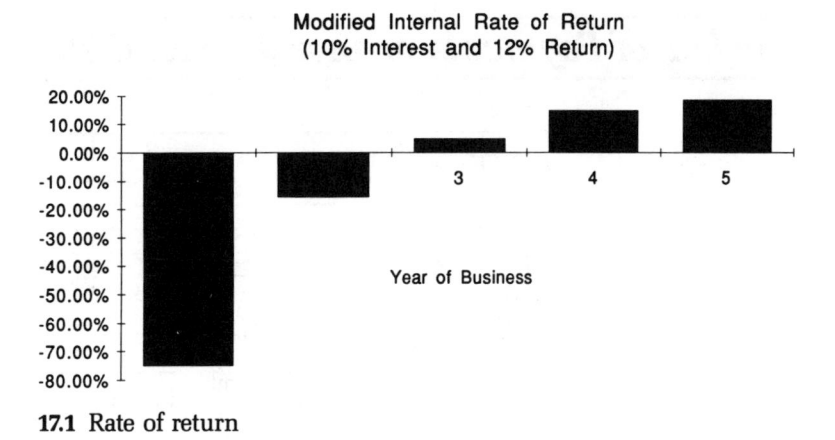

Modified Internal Rate of Return
(10% Interest and 12% Return)

17.1 Rate of return

What It Looks Like

Figure 17.1, a column chart, shows a negative rate of return for the first two years.

The Cell Contents and Formulas

	A	B	C	D
1	Modified Internal			
2	Rate of Return			
3				
4	Cost of			
5	Ice Cream Machines	-50000	MIRR After	MIRR
6	Year 1 Income	12546	1 Year	=MIRR($B$5:B6,10%,12%)
7	Year 2 Income	21678	2 Years	=MIRR($B$5:B7,10%,12%)
8	Year 3 Income	17564	3 Years	=MIRR($B$5:B8,10%,12%)
9	Year 4 Income	22134	4 Years	=MIRR($B$5:B9,10%,12%)
10	Year 5 Income	19675	5 Years	=MIRR($B$5:B10,10%,12%)

The Excel Financial Functions

Number of Payments of Investments (NPER)

	A	B	C	D	E
1	Number of Periods				
2	for Loan Amortization				
3					
4					
5	Interest Rate	Payment	Present Value	Payoff Period (months)	
6	10.00%	($1,300)	$72,000	75	
7	10.50%	($1,300)	$72,000	76	
8	11.00%	($1,300)	$72,000	78	
9	11.50%	($1,300)	$72,000	79	
10	12.00%	($1,300)	$72,000	81	
11	12.50%	($1,300)	$72,000	83	
12	13.00%	($1,300)	$72,000	85	
13	13.50%	($1,300)	$72,000	87	
14	14.00%	($1,300)	$72,000	90	
15	14.50%	($1,300)	$72,000	92	
16	15.00%	($1,300)	$72,000	95	
17	15.50%	($1,300)	$72,000	98	
18	16.00%	($1,300)	$72,000	101	
19	16.50%	($1,300)	$72,000	105	
20	17.00%	($1,300)	$72,000	109	
21	17.50%	($1,300)	$72,000	114	
22	18.00%	($1,300)	$72,000	119	
23	18.50%	($1,300)	$72,000	126	
24	19.00%	($1,300)	$72,000	133	
25	19.50%	($1,300)	$72,000	143	
26	20.00%	($1,300)	$72,000	155	

What the Function Does

The **NPER** function tells you the number of periods it will take to pay off a certain amount.

For example, a loan of $72,000 borrowed at an interest rate of 12% with payments of $1,300 will take 81 months to pay off.

Working with the Spreadsheet

To work with this spreadsheet, you need to enter the following information.

Col A interest rate
Col B payment
Col C value of the loan

The Excel Financial Functions

When the spreadsheet is complete, it will provide you with the following information.

Col D the number of periods until payoff

What It Looks Like

Figure 18.1 shows how the number of months until payoff changes with varying interest rates given a fixed payment. The column chart's series pattern was obtained with the **Patterns** option on the Format menu.

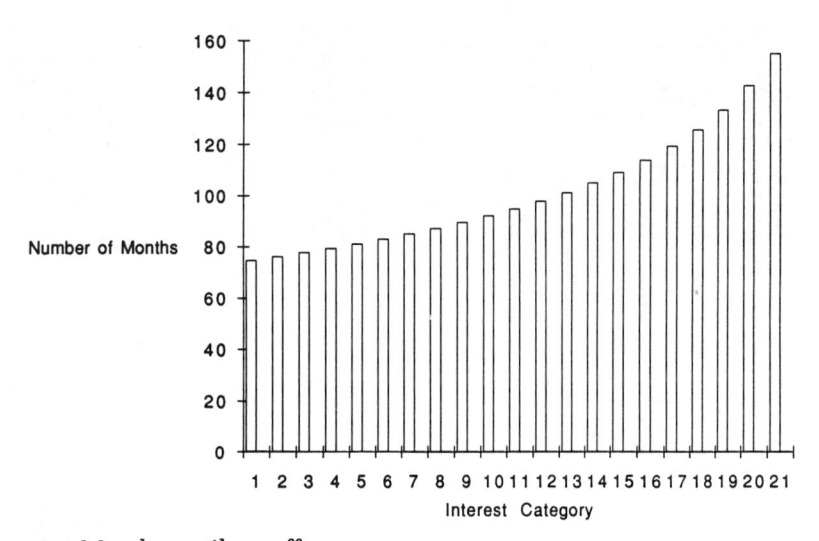

18.1 Months until payoff

The Excel Financial Functions

The Cell Contents and Formulas

	A	B	C	D
1	Number of Periods			
2	for Loan Amortizatio			
3				
4				
5	Interest Rate	Payment	Present Value	Payoff Period (months)
6	0.1	-1300	72000	=NPER(A6/12,B6,C6)
7	=A6+0.005	-1300	72000	=NPER(A7/12,B7,C7)
8	=A7+0.005	-1300	72000	=NPER(A8/12,B8,C8)
9	=A8+0.005	-1300	72000	=NPER(A9/12,B9,C9)
10	=A9+0.005	-1300	72000	=NPER(A10/12,B10,C10)
11	=A10+0.005	-1300	72000	=NPER(A11/12,B11,C11)
12	=A11+0.005	-1300	72000	=NPER(A12/12,B12,C12)
13	=A12+0.005	-1300	72000	=NPER(A13/12,B13,C13)
14	=A13+0.005	-1300	72000	=NPER(A14/12,B14,C14)
15	=A14+0.005	-1300	72000	=NPER(A15/12,B15,C15)
16	=A15+0.005	-1300	72000	=NPER(A16/12,B16,C16)
17	=A16+0.005	-1300	72000	=NPER(A17/12,B17,C17)
18	=A17+0.005	-1300	72000	=NPER(A18/12,B18,C18)
19	=A18+0.005	-1300	72000	=NPER(A19/12,B19,C19)
20	=A19+0.005	-1300	72000	=NPER(A20/12,B20,C20)
21	=A20+0.005	-1300	72000	=NPER(A21/12,B21,C21)
22	=A21+0.005	-1300	72000	=NPER(A22/12,B22,C22)
23	=A22+0.005	-1300	72000	=NPER(A23/12,B23,C23)
24	=A23+0.005	-1300	72000	=NPER(A24/12,B24,C24)
25	=A24+0.005	-1300	72000	=NPER(A25/12,B25,C25)
26	=A25+0.005	-1300	72000	=NPER(A26/12,B26,C26)

Net Present Value (NPV)

	A	B	C	D	E	F
1	Net Present Value					
2						
3	Interest Rate	Value	Return Y1	Return Y2	Return Y3	Present Value
4	10%	($40,000)	$25,000	$35,000	$40,000	$37,914
5	10%	($44,000)	$25,000	$35,000	$40,000	$34,278
6	10%	($48,400)	$25,000	$35,000	$40,000	$30,278
7	10%	($53,240)	$25,000	$35,000	$40,000	$25,878
8	10%	($58,564)	$25,000	$35,000	$40,000	$21,038
9	10%	($64,420)	$25,000	$35,000	$40,000	$15,714
10	10%	($70,862)	$25,000	$35,000	$40,000	$9,857
11	10%	($77,949)	$25,000	$35,000	$40,000	$3,415
12	10%	($85,744)	$25,000	$35,000	$40,000	($3,671)

What the Function Does

The **NPV** function returns the present value of an investment based on periodic cash payments, which need not be constant as with the **PV** function.

For example, a $40,000 investment at 10% will yield a net present value of $37,914 with yearly returns of $25,000, $35,000, and $40,000.

Working with the Spreadsheet

To work with this spreadsheet, you need to enter the following information.

Col A interest rate
Col B varying value of the investment (increasing by 10% [cell contents *1.11])
Cols C, D, and E amount of income

When the spreadsheet is complete, it will provide you with the following information.

Col F the present value of the investment

The Excel Financial Functions

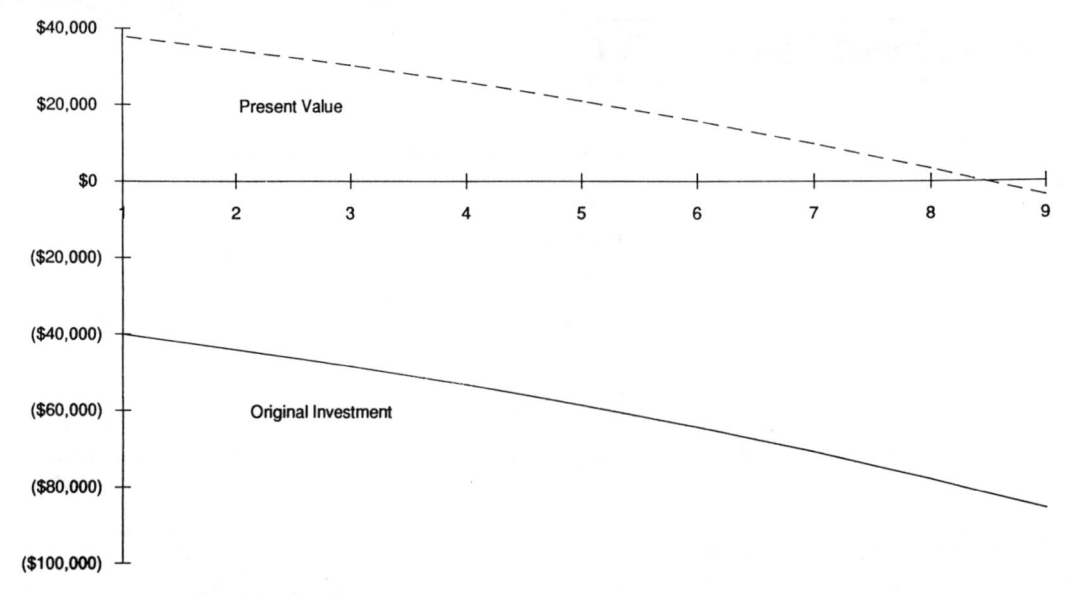

19.1 Present and original value

What It Looks Like

Figure 19.1 contrasts the original and present value of the investment. When the original investment exceeds $85,000, the value reaches zero.

The Cell Contents and Formulas

	A	B	C	D	E	F
1	Net Present Value					
2						
3	Interest Rate	Value	Return Y1	Return Y2	Return Y3	Present Value
4	0.1	-40000	25000	35000	40000	=NPV(A4,B4,C4,D4,E4)
5	0.1	=B4*1.1	25000	35000	40000	=NPV(A5,B5,C5,D5,E5)
6	0.1	=B5*1.1	25000	35000	40000	=NPV(A6,B6,C6,D6,E6)
7	0.1	=B6*1.1	25000	35000	40000	=NPV(A7,B7,C7,D7,E7)
8	0.1	=B7*1.1	25000	35000	40000	=NPV(A8,B8,C8,D8,E8)
9	0.1	=B8*1.1	25000	35000	40000	=NPV(A9,B9,C9,D9,E9)
10	0.1	=B9*1.1	25000	35000	40000	=NPV(A10,B10,C10,D10,E10)
11	0.1	=B10*1.1	25000	35000	40000	=NPV(A11,B11,C11,D11,E11)
12	0.1	=B11*1.1	25000	35000	40000	=NPV(A12,B12,C12,D12,E12)

Periodic Payment on an Investment (PMT)

	A	B	C	D
1	Payment on Investment			
2				
3	Interest Rate	Period	Value	Payment
4	12%	360	$72,000	($741)
5	12%	300	$72,000	($758)
6	12%	240	$72,000	($793)
7	12%	180	$72,000	($864)
8	12%	120	$72,000	($1,033)
9				
10	11%	360	$72,000	($686)
11	11%	300	$72,000	($706)
12	11%	240	$72,000	($743)
13	11%	180	$72,000	($818)
14	11%	120	$72,000	($992)
15				
16	10%	360	$72,000	($632)
17	10%	300	$72,000	($654)
18	10%	240	$72,000	($695)
19	10%	180	$72,000	($774)
20	10%	120	$72,000	($951)

What the Function Does

The **PMT** function returns the payment due on an investment given the interest rate, the number of periods for the payoff, and the value of the loan.

For example, at a 12% rate, the payment on $72,000 over 360 months will be $741. Over 240 months (or 20 years) the payments would be $793.

Working with the Spreadsheet

To work with this spreadsheet, you need to enter the following information.

    Col A varying interest rates
    Col B varying numbers of periods
    Col C amount of the loan

The Excel Financial Functions

When the spreadsheet is complete, it will provide you with the following information.

Col D payment amount

What It Looks Like

Figure 20.1 shows a line graph representing each of the interest rates over the five time periods that were selected in the worksheet.

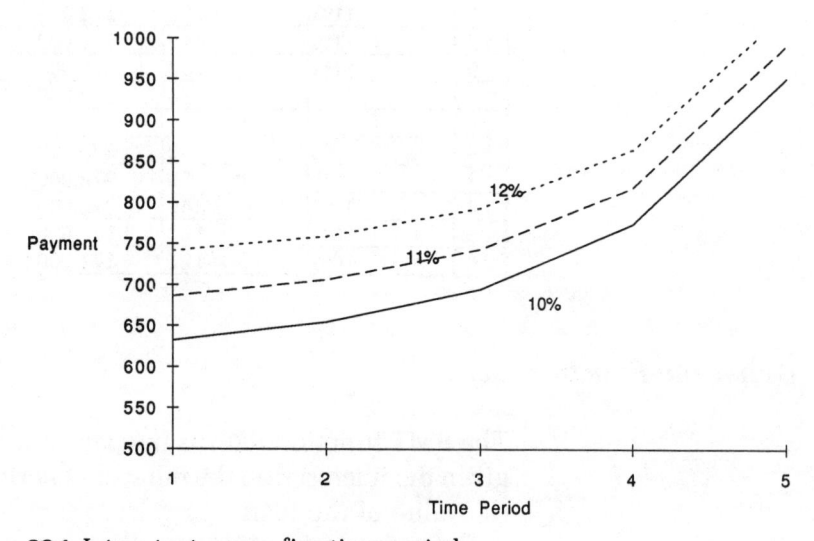

20.1 Interest rates over five time periods

The Cell Contents and Formulas

	A	B	C	D
1	Payment on Investme			
2				
3	Interest Rate	Period	Value	Payment
4	0.12	360	72000	=PMT(A4/12,B4,C4)
5	0.12	300	72000	=PMT(A5/12,B5,C5)
6	0.12	240	72000	=PMT(A6/12,B6,C6)
7	0.12	180	72000	=PMT(A7/12,B7,C7)
8	0.12	120	72000	=PMT(A8/12,B8,C8)
9				
10	0.11	360	72000	=PMT(A10/12,B10,C10)
11	0.11	300	72000	=PMT(A11/12,B11,C11)
12	0.11	240	72000	=PMT(A12/12,B12,C12)
13	0.11	180	72000	=PMT(A13/12,B13,C13)
14	0.11	120	72000	=PMT(A14/12,B14,C14)
15				
16	0.1	360	72000	=PMT(A16/12,B16,C16)
17	0.1	300	72000	=PMT(A17/12,B17,C17)
18	0.1	240	72000	=PMT(A18/12,B18,C18)
19	0.1	180	72000	=PMT(A19/12,B19,C19)
20	0.1	120	72000	=PMT(A20/12,B20,C20)

The Excel Financial Functions

Payment on the Principal of an Investment (PPMT)

	A	B	C	D	E
1	Principal Payment				
2					
3	Interest	Period	Number of	Value	Payment
4			Periods		
5	10%	1	360	$12,000	($5.31)
6	10%	1	359	$12,000	($5.36)
7	10%	1	358	$12,000	($5.40)
8	10%	1	357	$12,000	($5.45)
9	10%	1	356	$12,000	($5.50)
10	10%	1	355	$12,000	($5.55)
11	10%	1	354	$12,000	($5.59)
12	10%	1	353	$12,000	($5.64)
13	10%	1	352	$12,000	($5.69)
14	10%	1	351	$12,000	($5.74)
15	10%	1	350	$12,000	($5.79)
16	10%	1	349	$12,000	($5.85)
17	10%	1	348	$12,000	($5.90)
18					
19	10%	1	12	$12,000	($954.99)
20	10%	1	11	$12,000	($1,046.21)
21	10%	1	10	$12,000	($1,155.68)
22	10%	1	9	$12,000	($1,289.50)
23	10%	1	8	$12,000	($1,456.79)
24	10%	1	7	$12,000	($1,671.90)
25	10%	1	6	$12,000	($1,958.74)
26	10%	1	5	$12,000	($2,360.33)
27	10%	1	4	$12,000	($2,962.76)
28	10%	1	3	$12,000	($3,966.85)
29	10%	1	2	$12,000	($5,975.10)
30	10%	1	1	$12,000	($12,000.00)

What the Function Does

The **PPMT** function returns the principal part of a principal and interest payment.

For example, on a $12,000 loan at 10%, the principal due during the first of 360 periods is $5.31; the principal due during the first of 12 periods is $954.99.

Working with the Spreadsheet

To work with this spreadsheet, you need to enter the following information.

The Excel Financial Functions

Col A the interest
Col B period of payment
Col C number of periods
Col D value of the loan

When the spreadsheet is complete, it will provide you with the following information.

Col E the principal component of the loan

The Cell Contents and Formulas

	A	B	C	D	E
1	Principal Paymen				
2					
3	Interest	Period	Number of Periods	Value	Payment
4					
5	0.1	1	360	12000	=PPMT(A5/12,B5,C5,D5)
6	0.1	1	=C5-1	12000	=PPMT(A6/12,B6,C6,D6)
7	0.1	1	=C6-1	12000	=PPMT(A7/12,B7,C7,D7)
8	0.1	1	=C7-1	12000	=PPMT(A8/12,B8,C8,D8)
9	0.1	1	=C8-1	12000	=PPMT(A9/12,B9,C9,D9)
10	0.1	1	=C9-1	12000	=PPMT(A10/12,B10,C10,D10)
11	0.1	1	=C10-1	12000	=PPMT(A11/12,B11,C11,D11)
12	0.1	1	=C11-1	12000	=PPMT(A12/12,B12,C12,D12)
13	0.1	1	=C12-1	12000	=PPMT(A13/12,B13,C13,D13)
14	0.1	1	=C13-1	12000	=PPMT(A14/12,B14,C14,D14)
15	0.1	1	=C14-1	12000	=PPMT(A15/12,B15,C15,D15)
16	0.1	1	=C15-1	12000	=PPMT(A16/12,B16,C16,D16)
17	0.1	1	348	12000	=PPMT(A17/12,B17,C17,D17)
18					
19	0.1	1	12	12000	=PPMT(A19/12,B19,C19,D19)
20	0.1	1	=C19-1	12000	=PPMT(A20/12,B20,C20,D20)
21	0.1	1	=C20-1	12000	=PPMT(A21/12,B21,C21,D21)
22	0.1	1	=C21-1	12000	=PPMT(A22/12,B22,C22,D22)
23	0.1	1	=C22-1	12000	=PPMT(A23/12,B23,C23,D23)
24	0.1	1	=C23-1	12000	=PPMT(A24/12,B24,C24,D24)
25	0.1	1	=C24-1	12000	=PPMT(A25/12,B25,C25,D25)
26	0.1	1	=C25-1	12000	=PPMT(A26/12,B26,C26,D26)
27	0.1	1	=C26-1	12000	=PPMT(A27/12,B27,C27,D27)
28	0.1	1	=C27-1	12000	=PPMT(A28/12,B28,C28,D28)
29	0.1	1	=C28-1	12000	=PPMT(A29/12,B29,C29,D29)
30	0.1	1	=C29-1	12000	=PPMT(A30/12,B30,C30,D30)

The Excel Financial Functions

Present Value of an Investment (PV)

	A	B	C	D
1	Present Value			
2				
3	Interest Rate	Period	Return	Present Value
4	6.00%	20	$1,000	($11,469.92)
5	6.50%	20	$1,000	($11,018.51)
6	7.00%	20	$1,000	($10,594.01)
7	7.50%	20	$1,000	($10,194.49)
8	8.00%	20	$1,000	($9,818.15)
9	8.50%	20	$1,000	($9,463.34)
10	9.00%	20	$1,000	($9,128.55)
11	9.50%	20	$1,000	($8,812.38)
12	10.00%	20	$1,000	($8,513.56)

What the Function Does

The **PV** function applies to annuities and returns the amount of money that must be invested to secure a specific return.

For example, you must invest $11,469.92 at a rate of 6% to get a return of $1,000 over 20 years. At 10%, only $8,513.56 must be invested.

Working with the Spreadsheet

To work with this spreadsheet, you need to enter the following information.

    Col A interest rate
    Col B period of time
    Col C anticipated return

When the spreadsheet is complete, it will provide you with the following information.

    Col D present value

The Excel Financial Functions

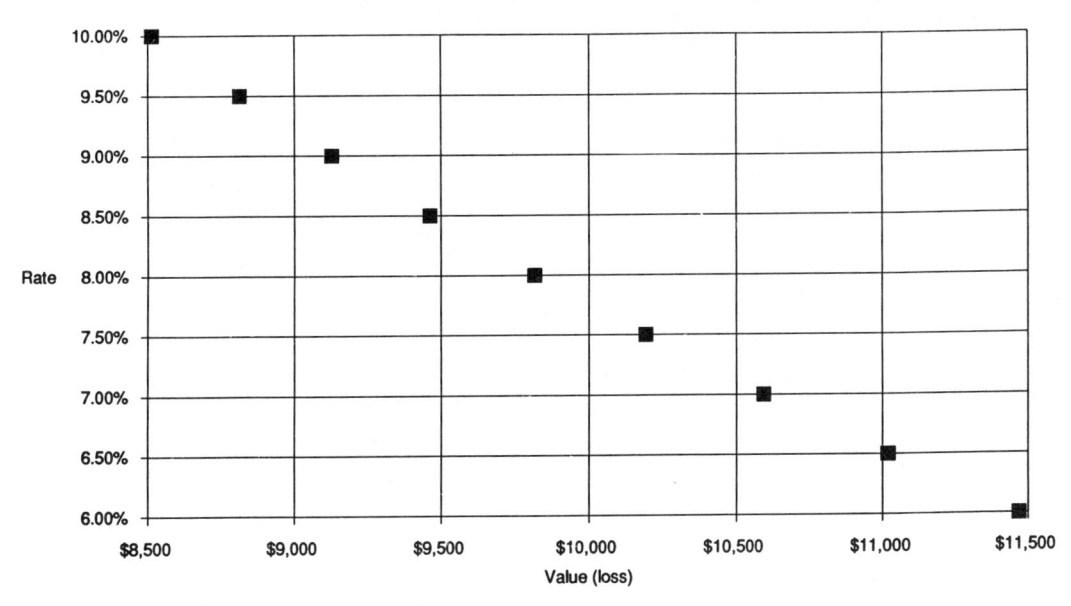

Present Value of $1,000 at Different Interest Rates

21.1 Rate of investment and value of investment

What It Looks Like

Figure 21.1, a scatter chart with grids, shows present value as a function of rate and investments made.

The Cell Contents and Formulas

	A	B	C	D
1	Present Value			
2				
3	Interest Rate	Period	Return	Present Value
4	0.06	20	1000	=PV(A4,B4,C4)
5	0.065	20	1000	=PV(A5,B5,C5)
6	0.07	20	1000	=PV(A6,B6,C6)
7	0.075	20	1000	=PV(A7,B7,C7)
8	0.08	20	1000	=PV(A8,B8,C8)
9	0.085	20	1000	=PV(A9,B9,C9)
10	0.09	20	1000	=PV(A10,B10,C10)
11	0.095	20	1000	=PV(A11,B11,C11)
12	0.1	20	1000	=PV(A12,B12,C12)

The Excel Financial Functions

Rate of Return on an Investment (RATE)

	A	B	C	D
1	Rate of Interest			
2				
3				
4	Period	Payment	Value	Rate
5	240	($1,500)	$100,000	17%
6	240	($1,400)	$100,000	16%
7	240	($1,300)	$100,000	15%
8	240	($1,200)	$100,000	13%
9	240	($1,100)	$100,000	12%
10	240	($1,000)	$100,000	11%
11	240	($900)	$100,000	9%
12	240	($800)	$100,000	7%
13	240	($700)	$100,000	6%
14	240	($600)	$100,000	4%

What the Function Does

The **RATE** function returns the interest rate for an annuity.

For example, the rate of return for a $100,000 loan with payments of $1,500 over 240 periods is 17%. If the payment is lowered to $900, the rate of return changes to 9%.

Working with the Spreadsheet

To work with this spreadsheet, you need to enter the following information.

Col A period
Col B payment
Col C value of loan

When the spreadsheet is complete, it will provide you with the following information.

Col D rate of return

The Excel Financial Functions

Monthly Payment and Interest Rate

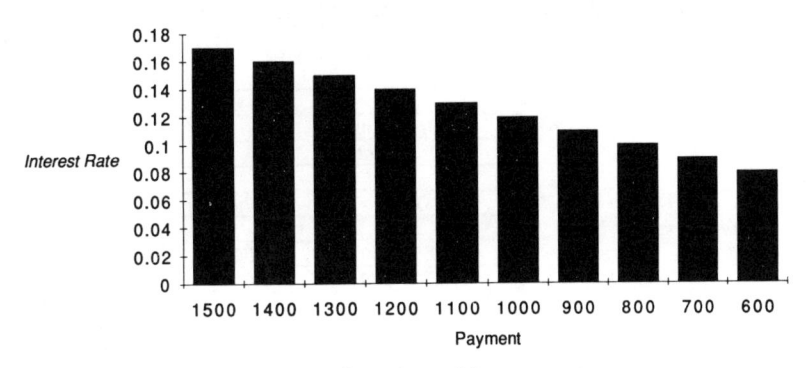

[Column chart: Interest Rate (y-axis, 0 to 0.18) vs Payment (x-axis: 1500, 1400, 1300, 1200, 1100, 1000, 900, 800, 700, 600)]

22.1 Monthly payment as a function of interest rate

What It Looks Like

Figure 22.1 shows a column chart with monthly payment as a function of interest rate.

The Cell Contents and Formulas

	A	B	C	D
1	Rate of Intere			
2				
3				
4	Period	Payment	Value	Rate
5	240	-1500	100000	=RATE(A5,B5,C5)*12
6	240	=B5+100	100000	=RATE(A6,B6,C6)*12
7	240	=B6+100	100000	=RATE(A7,B7,C7)*12
8	240	=B7+100	100000	=RATE(A8,B8,C8)*12
9	240	=B8+100	100000	=RATE(A9,B9,C9)*12
10	240	=B9+100	100000	=RATE(A10,B10,C10)*12
11	240	=B10+100	100000	=RATE(A11,B11,C11)*12
12	240	=B11+100	100000	=RATE(A12,B12,C12)*12
13	240	=B12+100	100000	=RATE(A13,B13,C13)*12
14	240	=B13+100	100000	=RATE(A14,B14,C14)*12

The Excel Financial Functions

Straight-Line Depreciation (SLN)

	A	B	C	D
1	Straight Line			
2	Depreciation			
3				
4	Cost	Salvage Value	Life	Depreciation
5				Allowance
6	$500,000	$75,000	20	$21,250
7	$500,000	$75,000	19	$22,368
8	$500,000	$75,000	18	$23,611
9	$500,000	$75,000	17	$25,000
10	$500,000	$75,000	16	$26,563
11	$500,000	$75,000	15	$28,333
12	$500,000	$75,000	14	$30,357
13	$500,000	$75,000	13	$32,692
14	$500,000	$75,000	12	$35,417
15	$500,000	$75,000	11	$38,636
16	$500,000	$75,000	10	$42,500
17	$500,000	$75,000	9	$47,222
18	$500,000	$75,000	8	$53,125
19	$500,000	$75,000	7	$60,714
20	$500,000	$75,000	6	$70,833
21	$500,000	$75,000	5	$85,000
22	$500,000	$75,000	4	$106,250
23	$500,000	$75,000	3	$141,667
24	$500,000	$75,000	2	$212,500
25	$500,000	$75,000	1	$425,000

What the Function Does

The **SLN** function returns the depreciated value of an asset for a single period using the straight-line method, which assumes that depreciation is a linear function of time.

For example, the depreciation allowed for an item that costs $500,000 and has a salvage value of $75,000 and a life of 20 years is $21,250 during the first year and $425,000 during the twentieth year.

The Excel Financial Functions

Working with the Spreadsheet

To work with this spreadsheet, you need to enter the following information.

Col A original cost
Col B salvage value
Col C life of the item

When the spreadsheet is complete, it will provide you with the following information.

Col D amount of allowed depreciation

What It Looks Like

Figure 23.1 shows the depreciated value as a function of age of the item.

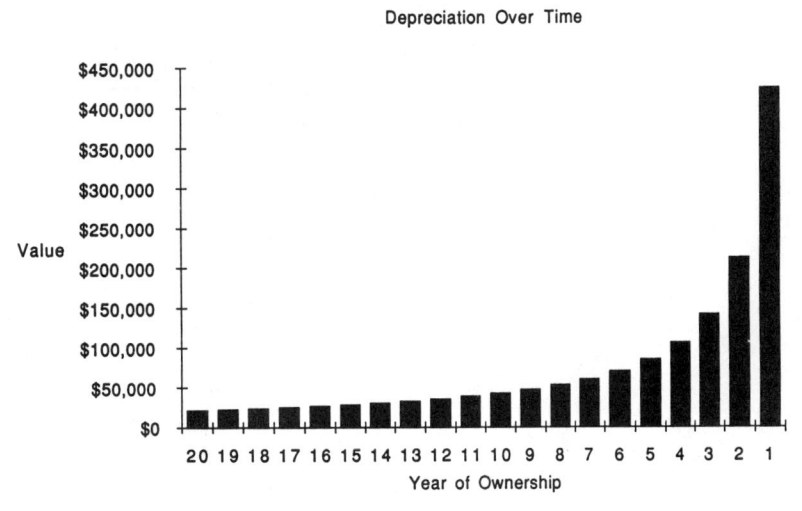

23.1 Depreciated value

The Excel Financial Functions

The Cell Contents and Formulas

	A	B	C	D
1	Straight Line			
2	Depreciation			
3				
4	Cost	Salvage Value	Life	Depreciation
5				Allowance
6	500000	75000	20	=SLN(A6,B6,C6)
7	500000	75000	=C6-1	=SLN(A7,B7,C7)
8	500000	75000	=C7-1	=SLN(A8,B8,C8)
9	500000	75000	=C8-1	=SLN(A9,B9,C9)
10	500000	75000	=C9-1	=SLN(A10,B10,C10)
11	500000	75000	=C10-1	=SLN(A11,B11,C11)
12	500000	75000	=C11-1	=SLN(A12,B12,C12)
13	500000	75000	=C12-1	=SLN(A13,B13,C13)
14	500000	75000	=C13-1	=SLN(A14,B14,C14)
15	500000	75000	=C14-1	=SLN(A15,B15,C15)
16	500000	75000	=C15-1	=SLN(A16,B16,C16)
17	500000	75000	=C16-1	=SLN(A17,B17,C17)
18	500000	75000	=C17-1	=SLN(A18,B18,C18)
19	500000	75000	=C18-1	=SLN(A19,B19,C19)
20	500000	75000	=C19-1	=SLN(A20,B20,C20)
21	500000	75000	=C20-1	=SLN(A21,B21,C21)
22	500000	75000	=C21-1	=SLN(A22,B22,C22)
23	500000	75000	=C22-1	=SLN(A23,B23,C23)
24	500000	75000	=C23-1	=SLN(A24,B24,C24)
25	500000	75000	=C24-1	=SLN(A25,B25,C25)

Sum-of-Year Depreciation (SYD)

	A	B	C	D	E
1	Sum Of Year				
2	Depreciation				
3					
4	Cost	Salvage Value	Life	Period	Depreciation
5					Allowance
6	$500,000	$75,000	20	1	$40,476
7	$500,000	$75,000	19	1	$42,500
8	$500,000	$75,000	18	1	$44,737
9	$500,000	$75,000	17	1	$47,222
10	$500,000	$75,000	16	1	$50,000
11	$500,000	$75,000	15	1	$53,125
12	$500,000	$75,000	14	1	$56,667
13	$500,000	$75,000	13	1	$60,714
14	$500,000	$75,000	12	1	$65,385
15	$500,000	$75,000	11	1	$70,833
16	$500,000	$75,000	10	1	$77,273
17	$500,000	$75,000	9	1	$85,000
18	$500,000	$75,000	8	1	$94,444
19	$500,000	$75,000	7	1	$106,250
20	$500,000	$75,000	6	1	$121,429
21	$500,000	$75,000	5	1	$141,667
22	$500,000	$75,000	4	1	$170,000
23	$500,000	$75,000	3	1	$212,500
24	$500,000	$75,000	2	1	$283,333
25	$500,000	$75,000	1	1	$425,000

What the Function Does

The **SYD** function computes depreciation value as a function of the cost of the item minus its salvage value.

For example, the depreciation allowance for a $500,000 piece of equipment with a salvage value of $75,000 and a life of 20 years is $40,476 during its first year. During its last year, it is $425,000.

Working with the Spreadsheet

To work with this spreadsheet, you need to enter the following information.

The Excel Financial Functions

Col A original cost
Col B salvage value
Col C item life
Col D period

When the spreadsheet is complete, it will provide you with the following information.

Col E depreciation allowance

What It Looks Like

Figure 24.1 shows the depreciated value as a function of the age of the item.

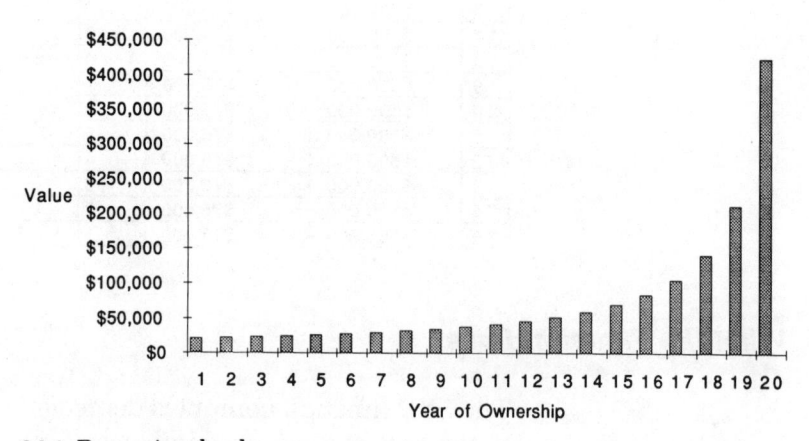

24.1 Depreciated value

The Excel Financial Functions

The Cell Contents and Formulas

	A	B	C	D	E
1	Sum Of Year				
2	Depreciation				
3					
4	Cost	Salvage Value	Life	Period	Depreciation
5					Allowance
6	500000	75000	20	1	=SYD(A6,B6,C6,D6)
7	500000	75000	=C6-1	1	=SYD(A7,B7,C7,D7)
8	500000	75000	=C7-1	1	=SYD(A8,B8,C8,D8)
9	500000	75000	=C8-1	1	=SYD(A9,B9,C9,D9)
10	500000	75000	=C9-1	1	=SYD(A10,B10,C10,D10)
11	500000	75000	=C10-1	1	=SYD(A11,B11,C11,D11)
12	500000	75000	=C11-1	1	=SYD(A12,B12,C12,D12)
13	500000	75000	=C12-1	1	=SYD(A13,B13,C13,D13)
14	500000	75000	=C13-1	1	=SYD(A14,B14,C14,D14)
15	500000	75000	=C14-1	1	=SYD(A15,B15,C15,D15)
16	500000	75000	=C15-1	1	=SYD(A16,B16,C16,D16)
17	500000	75000	=C16-1	1	=SYD(A17,B17,C17,D17)
18	500000	75000	=C17-1	1	=SYD(A18,B18,C18,D18)
19	500000	75000	=C18-1	1	=SYD(A19,B19,C19,D19)
20	500000	75000	=C19-1	1	=SYD(A20,B20,C20,D20)
21	500000	75000	=C20-1	1	=SYD(A21,B21,C21,D21)
22	500000	75000	=C21-1	1	=SYD(A22,B22,C22,D22)
23	500000	75000	=C22-1	1	=SYD(A23,B23,C23,D23)
24	500000	75000	=C23-1	1	=SYD(A24,B24,C24,D24)
25	500000	75000	=C24-1	1	=SYD(A25,B25,C25,D25)

APPENDIX
List of Worksheets by Area

Accounting
Accounts Receivable 75
Accounts Payable 79
Balance Sheet and Ratio
   Analysis 82
Consolidated Income 86
Fixed Assets Management 89
Inventory Count, Location, and
   Control 93
Net Worth 97
Promissory Note/Loan
   Application 100
Royalty Computation 104
A Simple Invoice 106

Forecasting
Charting Market Trends 109
Exponential Smoothing and Sales
   Prediction 113
Forecasting Sales/Linear
   Regression 118
Moving Averages Forecasting
   Accuracy 123

Investment
Amortization Schedule 128
Computing the Interest Rate 132
Future Value of an Annuity 136
Internal Rate of Return 139
Stock Portfolio 142

Management
Analysis of Personnel
   Referrals 146
Bidding on a Project 150
Breakeven Analysis 154
Hourly Work Sheet 158
Payroll Ledger 165

Appendix

Property Management 170
Tracking Utility Expenses 174
Weighted Employee
  Comparison 177

Personal

Comparing Job
  Opportunities 183
Conversion of Foreign
  Currency 188
Conversion of Measurement
  Units 192
Personal/Family Budget 196
Personal Asset Inventory 202
Personal Finances 208
Starting a Business 213

Retail

Advertisement Analysis 216
Analysis of
  Productivity—Products 220
Analysis of
  Productivity—Sales 222
Cash Flow Analysis 226
Determining Markup Based on
  Retail 231
Determining a Retail Price Based
  on Markup 233
Estimating Size of Salesforce 235
Keeping Track of Auto
  Expenses 238
Making Seasonal
  Adjustments 243
Markup Ratios 246
Merchandise Budgeting 249
Multiple Regression 252
Overhead to Sales Ratio 257

Salary and Bonus Summary 263
Salary Versus Commission 267
Sales Pricing and Discounts 270
Sales per Square Foot 274
Salesperson Analysis 277

Statistical

Item Analysis 280
Pearson Correlation 283
Significance of the Difference
  between Proportions 286
Spearman Rank Order
  Correlation 288
Survey Analysis 292
t-Test for Dependent Means 298
t-Test for Independent
  Means 300

Financial Functions

DDB (Depreciation) 304
FV (Future Value) 306
IPMT (Interest Payment) 308
IRR (Internal Rate of Return) 310
MIRR (Modified Internal Rate of
  Return) 312
NPER (Number of Periods for
  Loan Amortization) 314
NPV (Net Present Value) 317
PMT (Payment on Interest) 319
PPMT (Principal Payment) 322
PV (Present Value) 324
RATE (Rate of Interest) 326
SLD (Straight-Line
  Depreciation) 328
SYD (Sum-of-Year
  Depreciation) 331

Index

@DDB, 304
@FV, 306
@IMPT, 308
@IRR, 310
@MIRR, 312
@NPER, 314
@NPV, 317
@PMT, 319
@PPMT, 322
@PV, 324
@RATE, 326
@SLN, 328
@SYD, 331

A

Accounts payable, 79
Accounts receivable, 75
Advertisement analysis, 216
Aligning labels, center, 35
Aligning labels, left, 35
Aligning labels, right, 36
Amortization schedule, 128
Analysis of personnel referrals, 146
Analysis of productivity, products, 220
Analysis of productivity, sales, 222
Arrow, adding, 63

B

Balance sheet and ratio analyses, 82
Bidding on a project, 150
Breakeven analysis, 154

C

Cash flow analysis, 226
Cell entries, editing, 27
Chart, creating, 55
Chart elements, 57
Chart, formatting, 59
Chart gallery, 57
Charting market trends as a moving average, 109
Comparing job opportunities, 183
Computing the interest rate, 132
Consolidated income, 86
Conversion of foreign currency, 188
Conversion of measurement units, 192
Criteria range, creation, 50

Index

D

Data entering, 25
Data forms, creation, 52
Data menu, 21
Database, creating, 46
Database, searching, 49
Database, sorting, 47
Depreciation of an asset, 304
Determining a markup based on retail, 231
Determining a retail price based on markup, 233

E

Editing cell entries, 28
Edit menu, 21
Entering data, 27
Estimating size of salesforce, 235
Exponential smoothing and sales prediction, 113
Extracting records, 51

F

File menu, 21
Finding database records, 51
Fixed assets management, 89
Forecasting sales using linear regression, 118
Format menu, 21
Formatting worksheets, 32
Formulas, using, 37
Functions, 40
Future value of an annuity, 136
Future value of an investment, 304

H

Hardware, necessary to use Excel, 7

Help, 22
Hourly work sheet, 158

I

Installing Excel, 11
Interest payment on an investment, 308
Internal rate of return, 139, 310
Inventory count, location and control, 93
Item analysis, 286

K

Keeping track of auto expenses, 238
Keyboard versus mouse, 16

L

Legend, adding, 58

M

Macro library, building, 71
Macro menu, 21
Macro sheet, 68
Macros, creating, 67
Macros, definition, 66
Macros, executing, 69
Macros, naming, 67
Macros, placing and location of, 66
Making seasonal adjustments, 243
Markup ratios, 246
Menus, Excel, 20
Merchandise budgeting, 249
Modified internal rate of return, 312
Mouse, using, 16

Moving averages forecasting accuracy, 123
Multiple regression, 252

N

Net present value, 317
Net worth, 97
Number of payments of investments, 314
Numbers, entering, 29

O

Opening screen, 12
Options menu, 21
Overhead to sales ratio, 257

P

Password, using, 31
Paste function, 40
Payment on the principal of an investment, 323
Payroll ledger, 165
Pearson correlation between two variables, 283
Periodic payment of an investment, 319
Personal asset inventory, 202
Personal/family budget, 196
Personal finances, 208
Pointing, formula creation, 39
Present value of an investment, 324
Preview, screen, 42
Printing, 43
Promissory note/loan application worksheet, 100
Property management, 170

R

Rate of return on an investment, 326

Retrieving a spreadsheet, 30
Royalty compensation, 104

S

Salary and bonus summary, 263
Salary versus commission comparison, 267
Salesperson analysis, 277
Sales per square foot, 274
Sales pricing and discounts, 270
Selecting ranges and cells, 33
Significance of the difference between correlated proportions, 286
Significance of the difference between correlation coefficients, 291
Simple invoice, 106
Spearman rank order correlation, 288
Starting a business, 213
Starting Excel, 9
Stock portfolio, 142
Straight line depreciation, 328
Sum of year depreciation, 331
Survey analysis, 292

T

Text, attached, 60
Text, entering, 27
Text, unattached, 60
Tracking utility expenses, 174
t-Test for dependent means, 298
t-Test for independent means, 300

W

Weighted employee comparison, 177
Window menu, 21
Windows, working with, 177

Disk Offer

If you would like the Excel applications in this book on disk, please provide the information and include a check or money order for $20.00. If you would like overnight delivery, please add an additional $20.00.

Mail a copy of this coupon to

Delphi Associates
POB 1465
Lawrence, KS 66044

Name _____

Address _____

City/State/Zip _____

Please check one:

__ IBM Excel 5.25"   __ IBM Excel 3.5"   __ Mac Excel 3.5"